BITTERSWEET SURRENDER

*The Journey of Faith Through Grief
and the COVID Pandemic*

LISA FULSOM

I dedicate this book, first and foremost, to my late husband, Todd Fulsom. Todd, you loved me so well for nearly 30 years. I am a better woman because of you, and I eagerly await the day we reunite in eternity.

And to our children, Jacob Fulsom and Anna Fulsom McCollum—I am profoundly blessed that God chose me to be your mother. Through the depths of grief, you have stood by me, encouraging me to put these words onto the page and protecting me with unwavering strength. You are the most beautiful souls, and I am forever grateful for you.

AUTHOR'S NOTE

When the person you love dies, the life you've known, the future you envisioned, shatters into a million pieces. The fragments are so jagged, so scattered, that imagining life ever feeling normal again seems impossible.

Our culture makes space for life before loss, but it often fails to acknowledge the life that comes after; the painful process of picking up the pieces and learning to move forward.

As you journey through the pages of this book, you will come to see the young woman I was and the mature woman I am still striving to become, through the rawness of loss and the absolute redemption found in God's plans.

In this memoir, I share the journey of love and loss, the depths of grief, and the strength it takes to rebuild. But above all, this is God's story. Because without His grace and guidance, I don't believe I would be here. Every moment of healing, every glimpse of hope, every ounce of strength—it has been His doing. And I give Him all the glory.

My hope is that as you read it, you feel seen, supported, and loved—that you find solace in knowing you are not alone in processing the death of someone so dear.

In grief and in faith,
Lisa

CONTENTS

Author's Note v

Chapter 1: Our Love Story 1

Chapter 2: Journey to Rebaptism 11

Chapter 3: Child of God 27

Chapter 4: His Illness 33

Chapter 5: Our Longest Separation (Or So I Thought) 43

Chapter 6: Intubation 55

Chapter 7: ICU Experience 61

Chapter 8: Making Progress 73

Chapter 9: Life in the ICU..79

Chapter 10: Todd's Passing...97

Chapter 11: Telling the Kids..109

Chapter 12: Coming Home 123

Chapter 13: Preparation 133

Chapter 14: Saying Our Goodbyes....................................149

Chapter 15: The Funeral..157

Chapter 16: Grief is Not My Friend 169

Chapter 17: The Monthly Journals 183

Chapter 18: Back to Work 195

Chapter 19: The Holidays are Upon Us 203

Chapter 20: The Air of December 211

Chapter 21: Honoring His Legacy 219

Chapter 22: Bringing in the New Year 227

Chapter 23: What is Heaven Like? 239

Chapter 24: Belongings and Bills 247

Chapter 25: The Clouds are Breaking 255

Chapter 26: Lisa, Party of One 267

Chapter 27: Medical File Nightmare 279

Chapter 28: Do Hard Things 301

Chapter 29: Crooked Roads 311

Chapter 30: Warm Weather Feels Like Hope 319

Chapter 31: No More Saying "Months" 327

Chapter 32: Remembrance Day has Come 335

Chapter 33: A Fondness 345

Chapter One

OUR LOVE STORY

Todd and I were like peas and carrots—a phrase we took from a quote from one of our favorite movies, *Forrest Gump*. We had a perfect match of friendship and love, like the pairing of peas and carrots in a dish.

Saying goodbye to Todd was the hardest thing I ever had to do in this lifetime.

We were the quintessential high school sweethearts. From the moment we began dating, Todd and I were inseparable. Todd and I shared thirty-two years of love, laughter, and togetherness, with moments of sadness and struggle sprinkled throughout.

We attended the same high school, and Todd and I had never officially met until later in school. Although, he caught my eye first. A friend and I stayed after school one afternoon to watch the boys' soccer game during freshman year. That was the moment I first noticed him, a tall, blonde, handsome boy on the field. I was quiet, shy, and never saw myself as particularly pretty, certainly not compared to the other girls at school. I convinced myself I didn't stand a chance with the athletic boy running across the field past me, even as I was starstruck at the moment.

I contented myself with watching him from the stands during his games, never letting on that I wanted to strike up a conversation with him, or wanting to get to know him. I caught glimpses of him on the occasion of passing him in the hallways between classes, but over time, my crush on Todd faded. As I joked with him in later years, I felt he was out of my league!

My next encounter with Todd was on the first day of our sophomore year. That day, another friend and I found ourselves in a class together before lunch period. When the bell rang to dismiss us, we headed towards the cafeteria to grab some lunch and enjoy some social time.

During the lunch period on the first day of each school year, it was customary for all of the student body to scramble to find a table, knowing it would be our permanent spot for the rest of the school year. The tables filled up fast, and she and I found ourselves scanning the room, holding our trays of food. She spotted two empty chairs at a boys' table. I could see only the back of the heads of these boys, so I wasn't sure who was sitting there.

I panicked!

Oh, no! I am not going to sit at a table full of boys. No way! No how!

Growing up with three brothers, I longed for female friendships. I was shy around boys, so sitting with them at a lunch table took me completely out of my comfort zone. I'm sure I audibly voiced my apprehension, but knowing my friend's bubbly, outgoing nature, she likely reassured me that everything would be fine. With effortless confidence, she weaved through the tables toward two empty seats, and I followed close behind.

As I set my tray down, a meal consisting of the unhealthiest daily choice of chocolate donuts and a chocolate shake, I glanced up and froze. Todd was sitting directly across from me. Like a deer caught in headlights, I was utterly and completely unprepared for this! The boy I had secretly admired was right there, within arm's reach. Summoning as much composure as any 15-year-old girl could manage, I sat down, steadied my thoughts, and introduced myself.

After thirty years of thinking back to this moment at the lunch table, I can't recall any of the conversations we all had, but I do remember this: Todd and I began to build a friendship that day.

Our friendship carried us into our junior year of high school. As I spent more time getting to know Todd, I discovered his sweet demeanor and quick wit. That year, we ended up in Driver's Education together. The seating was arranged alphabetically, so with his last name starting with a "F" and mine with an "S," we were separated—seated across the room but parallel to each other near the back. Over the course of the class, I often found myself glancing his way, only for him to catch my eye and make a funny face. His antics never failed to make me laugh, though they frequently earned me a reprimand from the teacher.

Our friendship was easy and natural, flowing effortlessly. Todd and I never rode together during the driving portion of the class, but I would tease him that he should drive me around since he always made "4s," while I scored mostly "3s and 2s." It was the beginning of my love for the idea of being a passenger princess, especially with Todd at the wheel.

Toward the end of the school day, we attended classes in neighboring rooms. Mine was Child Development, which included the infamous two-week egg project. Each student had to care for their egg as if it were a baby, carrying it at all times and ensuring it survived the duration of the assignment. Determined to get a good grade, I constructed a small basket lined with shredded paper to cushion my "baby" against cracks and breaks.

After class, Todd would always be waiting for me so we could walk to our lockers together. As we strolled down the hallway, he would ask, "How's my boy?" referring to the egg. I would always answer, "Good," then embellish our "baby's" imaginary antics. We named the egg Corey.

I took meticulous care of Corey, making sure he survived. When the project ended, I jokingly told Todd that our egg no longer tied us together, so he didn't need to check on me after class anymore. He ignored the remark entirely, continuing to wait for me at the door each day so we could walk together, laughing and talking about life. It was a rhythm I grew to cherish. Our time was filled with banter, familiarity, and the kind of effortless companionship that made school feel lighter.

THE FALL MONTHS BLENDED INTO the winter months. After we returned from winter break, our school hosted an annual candy-gram during Valentine's Day to raise money for some cause at school. Candy-grams were paper Valentines that had a sucker attached to it, and were delivered to the recipient of your choosing. With a little trepidation, yet wanting Todd to receive a candy-gram from yours truly, I bought one and sent it to him anonymously.

You see, I had realized over the last few months that as I had gotten to know Todd better as a friend, I was beginning to again have feelings for him. I wanted nothing more than to be his girlfriend, but worried it would ruin the friendship we had built.

I never asked Todd if he had received a candy-gram. But decades later, as we sifted through memory boxes in our new home, he found it. He had forgotten he had saved it, always wondering who had sent it. I finally revealed that it was me.

Todd was my friend, a close school friend, but we didn't spend time together outside of school. We lived in separate cities, and in a time before cell phones, it was common not to see friends until the next school year. Both of us worked, and on weekends, we spent time with our own friend groups who lived nearby.

Though we had been friends for a couple of years, Todd and I had never exchanged phone numbers. Instead, we simply enjoyed each other's company in the moments we shared walking the high school halls. He had his circle of friends, and I had mine.

During that time, I went on a few dates with young men, and I'm sure Todd did the same with young women. In fact, I knew he had, because over the years, I had heard plenty of stories about his dates! Our junior year ended with a casual "see you next year" as we each set off to enjoy our summers.

THE FIRST DAY OF SENIOR year arrived with excitement and anticipation; it was finally our last year of high school. When I spotted Todd in the hallway, I remember being struck by how much he had changed over the summer. Oh, the kind of change that made my heart flutter. Maybe it was his sun-kissed skin, or perhaps the bleach-blonde mullet that was all the rage in the '80s. Whatever it was, my long-buried crush on him came rushing back in, full force.

I ran up to Todd, hugged him, and asked about his summer. He asked about mine, and I told him it had been pretty good, although due to some bad choices I had made, I was grounded. Starting my senior year without the freedom to hang out with friends was frustrating, but I knew I had to face the consequences, even if I didn't want to.

When we compared schedules, Todd and I discovered we had both signed up for COE—Cooperative Education. If a senior had fulfilled most of their class credits, they could use the last half of the school day to work, earning credit toward graduation. There were two COE classes, and we were in the same one—together, in our first-hour class. I was thrilled to have a class with him.

So, together, we walked down the hallway to begin our first day of senior year. I found an empty desk and sat down, and he chose the one right beside me. Every morning before class started, Todd would ask, "Are you ungrounded yet?"

"Nope," I'd reply, usually with a sigh trailing behind my answer. He'd sigh in response, not in impatience, but in quiet understanding that I was still stuck under the rules of my parents. At the time, I thought he was teasing me. Now, I realize, it was because he was waiting for me.

Soon, we realized that our schedules aligned so that neither of us had to report to work for about an hour after classes ended. One day, Todd asked if I wanted to go to a park for lunch. Of course, I agreed, excited to finally spend time with him outside of school.

We drove separately to a nearby park and ate lunch at a picnic table. Afterward, we hopped onto the merry-go-round, spinning and laughing hysterically as I tried to hold onto the metal bars without losing my sandwich I had just eaten or flying off and making a fool of myself.

Before we left, we sat on the edge of the equipment, catching our breath. And then Todd asked again, "Are you ungrounded yet?"

I was starting to notice just how persistent he was with that question.

"No," I replied.

"Do you think you will be ungrounded by homecoming?" My heart fluttered.

"I hope so," was my response.

"Would you go to homecoming with me, if you're ungrounded?" he asked.

"Yes, I would love to," I replied.

Back then, there were no elaborate homecoming proposals, no grand gestures drawing attention to the question. Just the two of us, sitting on a merry-go-round—simple and pure.

The following weekend, I finally regained my teenage freedom, released on "good behavior." On Monday morning, I ran up to Todd, bursting with excitement, and told him the news: I was officially ungrounded, and we were going to homecoming together.

With a few weeks to prepare, we started planning our outfits—matching colors, of course, since tradition dictated that a boy's tie should complement his date's dress. We finally exchanged phone numbers, making it easier to coordinate. And with that, I set off to find the perfect dress.

UNBEKNOWNST TO ME, TODD HAD felt the same way about me long before he asked me to be his date for homecoming. I only learned this after his passing, during a dinner with one of his closest high school friends, Scott. As Scott and I reminisced about the past, he revealed something I had never known.

"You may not realize this," Scott said, "but the first time Todd wanted to ask you on a date, he was so nervous. He would pick up the receiver of the phone, dial the number, and then hang up before you answered."

Todd had my number before I had ever given it to him; he must have asked one of my friends for it.

"Really?!?" I gasped. After all these years, there I was, deep in the grief of missing him, suddenly learning how vulnerable he had been, stepping so hesitantly out of his comfort zone just to call me.

A FEW DAYS AFTER HIS homecoming invitation, Todd called me and stayed on the phone long enough for me to answer and for him to ask me out on a date. Our first date was planned for the following Friday, and he wanted to take me to the movies. I accepted.

On Friday evening he was to pick me up. I was in my bedroom doing my makeup and hair in preparation for our date. As the clock ticked closer to his arrival time, my excitement grew. I was still in my room when my mom asked, "Does Todd have blonde hair?"

He's here, I thought. "Yes," I called out from my bedroom.

"Looong blonde hair?" she asked in a concerning tone.

"Yes," I replied.

"He's here," she said, with the undertone of discontentment in her voice.

Over the summer, Todd had grown out his hair, and with his bleach-blonde mullet, he bore a striking resemblance to tennis star Andre Agassi in the '80s. I loved it. My mother, however, did not.

After the introductions and small talk with my parents, Todd and I said our goodbyes and headed to the car. As we walked, he admitted that he had borrowed his mother's car for our date. He owned an old Ford Torino, an unsightly shade of yellow, that he and his friend had affectionately nicknamed the Mustard Monster.

There was no way he was taking me out in that vehicle, he explained. He had bought it for $400, complete with a hole in the trunk so large that, as he joked, a case of beer could fall right through. I knew he knew that from experience, but I wasn't about to say a word about it!

Todd walked me to the passenger side door, opened it, and waited for me to settle in before shutting it and heading to his own seat. *What a gentleman.* I wasn't used to this kind of chivalry. Truthfully, I hadn't been on many dates, and the last boy I had gone out with had complained about me leaving fingerprints on his freshly waxed car while trying to open my own door. Todd was decidedly different.

Me accompanying Todd to his senior homecoming dance

Dating someone who had been my friend for years was both comforting and nerve-wracking. We had taken classes together, joked about an egg-turned-imaginary-baby, and ate lunch side by side. It felt right.

We had a wonderful evening, and when Todd took me home, I surprised him by asking if I could take him to dinner the next day. He accepted. After that dinner came another invitation, this time from him—to celebrate his 17th birthday with his family. Of course, I accepted.

After his birthday dinner, we sat in the front room, chatting about the upcoming homecoming dance and our weekend plans. As we talked, he leaned in. His eyes met mine, as if to ask, "Can I kiss you?" I looked down with a faint smile spreading across my face, then looked back at him and nodded. In a nanosecond, thoughts flooded my mind, with one being, *Please don't make a joke that may send me into a fit of laughter.* He had a tendency to do that with his quick wit and one-liners. *Was he as nervous as I was?* He had this light-heartedness about life about him. I didn't want my actions to ruin the significance of this occasion.

His lips touched mine, and my heart immediately melted. Todd was so tender in kissing me, and any thought of worry or anticipation that crossed my mind in the moments before quickly evaporated.

It was as if the world stopped.

In the drive to take me home, we held hands and sat in silence, both of us taking in what transpired that night. The silence was soothing, almost as if we knew confidently what this first kiss meant for both of us. We moved beyond the friendship phase. He walked me to my front door, and we kissed again before I walked into the house. I felt like I was floating on a cloud.

We returned to school on Monday, eager to see each other again after a weekend spent together. He walked me to my classes whenever his schedule allowed, and if we had time, my friend

Kelly and I would meet him at a nearby fast-food restaurant before heading to work for the afternoon.

By Wednesday, as we left school, Todd walked me to my car and stood there, watching me.

"What?" I asked, puzzled by the look on his face.

"Will you go with me?" he asked.

"Go where?" I replied, looking confused.

He glanced down, then said, "No, not *where*. Go steady with me. Will you?"

I laughed, trying to hide my embarrassment in not understanding what he was asking me. I felt bad adding this bit of awkwardness to the moment, but recovered quickly.

"Yes," I said, confidently.

I had never been officially asked to become someone's girlfriend. I was elated. From all the other girls that may have crossed his path in the halls of our high school, he chose me. And I, him. We were officially boyfriend and girlfriend.

From then on, our love never wavered; we were inseparable. Until now.

Chapter Two

JOURNEY TO REBAPTISM

After three years of dating, Todd proposed to me at one of our favorite restaurants. It was the same place we had gone after formal high school dances and anniversaries. I suspected the proposal was coming, considering he had given me a promise ring on our last anniversary, and we had already discussed spending our future together.

My suspicions were confirmed when he asked numerous times if I needed to use the restroom. He told me later that he was trying to give the ring inconspicuously to the waiter, as they had planned in a call he made to the restaurant earlier in the day. Todd wanted to deliver the ring to me as part of my dessert at the end of the meal, but he wasn't prepared for my having no reason to leave the table! His nervousness grew, and then I knew. Todd was going to propose to me tonight. I thought it was a perfect backdrop for it. The restaurant became an important fixture for all of our celebrations thus far, so why not this one?

I sat through dinner holding my breath, wondering when he was going to pop the question. After our dinner plates were cleared from the table, Todd looked at me and stood up as if getting ready to leave.

Instead, Todd dropped to one knee in front of everyone in the restaurant, and asked for my hand in marriage.

It felt surreal, as if time stood still. He slipped the most beautiful engagement ring on my finger. I looked down at the ring, with its dazzling marquis diamond at its center with square cut diamond lining the band on each side of it. It was absolutely breathtaking. I looked up from the ring and at Todd, trying to take in the moment as I felt all eyes in the restaurant on us.

"Yes, I will," I said.

Other than a burst of applause coming from fellow patrons in the restaurant, there was no fanfare; just two twenty-year-olds ready to take the next step. The idea of building a life with someone who sees you, chooses you, and wants to walk beside you forever is exhilarating.

We booked his family's church for our wedding on October 2 of the following year. As a requirement for getting married in Todd's church, I had to attend new member classes. Intimidated by the thought of attending alone, I asked Todd to join me, and he gladly did. Having attended the church since childhood, he felt at ease moving through the building and conversing with familiar parishioners.

DURING OUR YEARS OF DATING, I had attended Sunday services with Todd and his family occasionally, but going to a structured religious education class was unfamiliar to me. My family never belonged to a church, and I had no idea what faith we practiced. Religion simply wasn't discussed. I knew the familiar Bible stories—Adam and Eve, Moses parting the Red Sea, Noah and the Ark—but the pastor's sermons, filled with parables and deeper teachings, felt foreign. In one of the first new member sessions, the instructor looked at me and asked, "Were you baptized?"

Until that moment, baptism had never crossed my mind. At twenty years old, I had no idea whether I had been baptized. And suddenly, I found myself wondering if that meant I wouldn't go to Heaven. No one had ever asked me that question, nor had anyone ever told me the story of my own baptism.

Though I hadn't grown up in a Christian household, I always believed in a higher power. I knew there was a God, and I understood the concepts of Heaven and hell. But our Christmases had been about Santa, and our Easters about Peter Cottontail, not about Jesus' birth or resurrection. Faith had never been a topic of conversation in my family, leaving me completely unaware of my baptismal status.

Sitting in that class, my ignorance weighed heavily on me. Shame crept in, followed by a deep concern for my salvation. After class, the weight of that uncertainty consumed me so much that the next day, I picked up the phone and called my dad, the one person I knew would tell me the truth.

"Well, I *think* you were," he said. "You were born so early, and they were afraid you wouldn't survive, so I'm sure they did it at the hospital."

His explanation made sense. I had been born a month premature and rushed to the neonatal ICU. Could they have baptized me without my parents present? I wanted to believe so. And with my dad's answer, I decided to accept that I had been baptized.

That's a relief. With that assumption, I felt justified, even without paperwork or proof. Todd and I completed our premarital and new member classes, and the wedding proceeded as planned.

ON A BEAUTIFUL AUTUMN DAY in October, Todd and I exchanged our marriage vows. Leading up to the ceremony, I was so nervous. The anticipation to marry him was building at the hours ticked by until the start of the wedding, which was set to begin at 4 o'clock in the afternoon.

When the wedding started and the processional music began playing to prompt me to walk down the aisle, I locked eyes with

Todd. He smiled. He looked so handsome in his black tuxedo, the hunter green satin cummerbund catching the light just enough to make my heart skip. To this day, I still love the color green. As I made my way down the aisle accompanied by my father, I kept my eyes on Todd. At that moment, he wasn't just my date, he was my forever, and I couldn't wait to be his wife.

And life continued.

Church remained an occasional event, something we attended sporadically with his parents.

Back then, I believed in God, and I loved Him. That, I thought, was enough.

Now, I realize how easy it is to justify lukewarm faith when one's heart is focused on earthly things—how effortlessly one can settle into believing without truly pursuing a relationship with God.

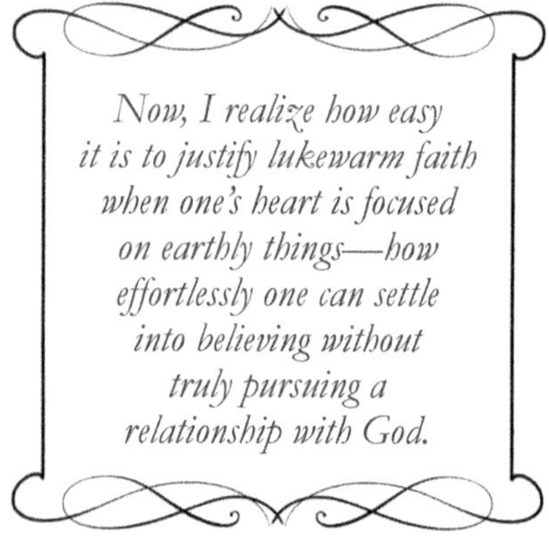

Over the years of being married and raising our children, the word baptism stayed in the back of my mind. I never had the paperwork to prove I had been, and there was that little pinch of a thought of "what if I hadn't been" poking me in my brain. I considered being baptized so I could finally be at peace with it.

I wanted to be baptized for so many years, but I was holding myself back. One question kept me from moving forward with baptism; one I considered to be the most important. Was I worthy enough?

I knew I was a good person, one who had always lived life as someone never desiring attention, and always feeling like an outsider, even within my own family at times. Never feeling I belonged. Throughout childhood, I was a wallflower and late bloomer, striving for perfection because I didn't want others to see

Our first dance as husband and wife

my faults or shortcomings. All these things, I realized, were holding me back from taking the step of baptism.

And then, my worst fear was standing in front of a bunch of strangers. To me, baptism was too precious and private of an act to do in front of others. I knew I would be more worried about everyone watching me and feeling judged, that I wouldn't follow through. *Why didn't she do this sooner? How can she raise her children and come to church and wait so long to do this?*

I knew I would feel I was being placed on the chopping block. I was scared. Scared I would not be accepted as a member of the church or Heaven.

Subsequently, other internal questions would begin to fill my head. *Did this mean I wasn't going to Heaven if I died? How could I not know this information?*

I know now that all these thoughts were not logical and wrapped tightly around my insecurities. But those thoughts were not enough for me to follow through with being baptized, so I went about with life. Better to avoid it than face it, or so I thought.

AND THEN TWO YEARS LATER, when I was twenty-three years old, my mom died of a sudden heart attack, due to years of drug and alcohol abuse. She was 48 years old. She and my father divorced when I was 6 or 7, and Dad was granted custody of us, so I only visited her on mandated weekends when she chose to pick us up. I don't have many memories of her prior to age 6, so I didn't have a close relationship with her due to her living situation. I loved her, yet was ashamed of her.

I carried this undeserved, complex emotion throughout most of my childhood. It was a shame that was not mine to own, but how do you tell your peers you are a child of a mother who lived a life of addiction and one who decided to live free from the responsibility of her children?

I didn't understand why she lived the way she did. And I was too young to be able to put it into words to ask anyone. I remember spending many hours sitting on a large rock in the front yard waiting for her to come pick us up, only for my dad or stepmom to come outside to tell me she wasn't coming and to go play.

On the day my mom died, I had just settled into my cubicle at work when the call came through from my brother telling me that she had passed away that morning on the way to the hospital. I thought he was joking. I wasn't prepared to receive such news.

Although I did not have a close relationship with her, she was still my mom. I had just talked to her a few weeks prior. She called to say she wasn't feeling well, and I urged her to go to the doctor. I was frustrated with her for not taking care of her health, and she knew I was annoyed by her many excuses as to why she couldn't go. She finished the phone call with an "I love you," as she always did, but in this call I didn't return the sentiment. After we hung up, I remember picking up the receiver to dial her phone number so I could tell her I loved her, but instead I placed the receiver back on the phone base and walked out of the kitchen.

That was the last time I spoke to her.

Later that day, my stepmom accompanied my brothers and me that afternoon to make the necessary arrangements for her funeral. We, her children, were responsible for paying for the expenses incurred, which was a lot of money for us. With the options offered to us by the funeral home, we decided to go with cremation.

And then the internal battle of questions began in my head. *Was I being respectful to my mom and her wishes?* As her daughter, it was important to me that I respect her wishes in death, regardless of her transgressions in life. I realized how much I did not know about her. I knew my mom was of Catholic faith, so I questioned, *are we making the right choice for her? Was she baptized?* I did not know. Ultimately, we chose to have a small service so her friends could come and pay their respects.

At the funeral, the mother of her long-term partner, whom she had lived with for more than fifteen years, gave the eulogy. I sat in the front row and listened as my mother was portrayed as a loving woman who always helped her with their family's birthday parties. If there was any moment ever that I wanted to stand up and walk out of a room, it was then. *Why didn't she do that for my brothers and me? Did she not care about us?*

I sat there, not wanting to make a scene, and stared at her as years of hurt bubbled to the surface. I felt so betrayed. The one person who should love and protect you at all costs didn't—and nothing would ever be made right.

Ironically, it was the first and last time I ever met my maternal grandmother and uncle, too. My mother had been placed in foster care as an adolescent, and I never knew much about her side of the family. I don't know why they chose to attend her visitation, or how they even found out about it. But to then disappear into the sunset of life, never reaching out to me again left me bewildered. It felt surreal. Her past felt like a locked room I had no key to, and the day of her visitation only deepened the mystery.

After the funeral, one of the family members handed me one of my mother's favorite gardening books for me to keep. To this day, I still have it. It's a quiet reminder of the parts of her I did know, and the ones I never will.

Her passing left behind more than grief, it unraveled a trail of confusion and unanswered questions about her life, pieces I knew I'd never be able to gather. But it also stirred something deeper. In the silence that followed, I found myself facing not only the mystery of her past, but the uncertainty of my own faith. Her death brought questions I wasn't prepared to answer—about God's law, about salvation, about what it truly meant to trust Him. I realized how little I knew. And how much I longed to understand.

Weeks later, when the time came to pick up my mom's remains from the crematorium, my brothers and I decided that we would spread them in a nearby park. Regardless of how she lived her life, I felt we needed to do something to honor her as we spread her remains onto the earth with a prayer. At that moment, I realized I knew none, except The Lord's Prayer. I had heard it many times, said it at church, and saw it printed on the bulletin when we attended, but I could not recite it verbatim. So, with embarrassment in my heart, and tears of shame in my eyes, I asked my husband, "Can you teach me how to say The Lord's Prayer?" And he did.

I spent every morning, while getting ready for work, practicing, so when the time came to spread her ashes, the prayer could be said. To this day I know The Lord's Prayer by heart because of Todd.

Our Father, who art in Heaven
Hallowed it be thy name
Thy Kingdom come
Thy will be done

On Earth as it is in Heaven
Give us this day our daily bread
And forgive us our trespasses
And we forgive those who trespass against us
And deliver us from evil
For thine is the kingdom
And the power
And the glory
Forever and ever. Amen.

But, I still went about with life.

A FEW YEARS LATER, TODD and I were blessed with beautiful babies: our sweet baby boy, Jacob, was born in May of 1999, and his beautiful baby sister, Anna, following in May of 2001. And knowing I never wanted them to question their baptism, I made sure both were baptized within weeks of their births. They were

Todd with Jake and baby Anna

baptized at the same church Todd and I were married in. I felt it was my obligation to my children to make sure they knew God. And again, I was reminded of my own insecurities in reaching out my hand to do the same; I felt so unequipped as a parent to talk to them about it as they grew up.

Although I had knowledge of many stories of the Bible, I didn't feel I knew enough to share any more than that, and my fear crept in again; I was afraid to tell them incorrectly, and mostly afraid they would ask questions that I would not have an answer for. So, in trying to do my best with the knowledge I knew, I sent them to vacation bible school during the summers, bought them books, and gave them Veggie Tales videos to watch. When someone was sick or hurt, we would say a little prayer for healing. When someone was going through something difficult, we would pray for peace and strength.

And I went about my life.

When it came time for Jacob and Anna to go through confirmation classes, I immediately signed them up. They were not going to be like me. I thought the confirmation process would at least "make us" go to church, because part of their work was attending church services and answering questions pertaining to the sermon given. I was so proud of them in how they were learning the Word of God. And I stood back and felt shame in not knowing more than I did.

And still, I went about with life.

Being a Christian for me was Christianity being "part" of my life, but not my "full" life. I thought I was doing what I needed to get to Heaven. I was morally upstanding. I made good choices for myself and my family and was raising my children to be good citizens with the same moral responsibility. I felt justified by my own actions. I showed gratefulness to Him when good things happened to us. We would say grace at holiday dinners. When there was a good Bible verse on social media that spoke to me, I shared it. I felt I had it covered.

My favorite mantra was "Let go and let God," especially during our son's reconstruction surgeries, after a bite to his face from a family friend's dog. I knew in my heart that God was protecting him and guiding the surgeon's skilled hands in repairing the damage done to Jacob's face.

I felt I was doing everything "right," but the thought of my baptism still lingered in my head after all those years.

And then, everything changed.

I realized that God was slowly preparing me for a true and deep relationship with Him, not the lukewarm version I had settled for. He worked in small, deliberate ways, knowing me better than I knew myself. He understood that I was never going to jump in feet first. I've always been the type to dip my toe in, test the waters, and slowly ease in.

But God knew what was coming. He was preparing me with the faith I would need to cling to Him through the hardest and darkest journey of my life. His plan was strategic.

The first step came in the form of a young man who entered my teenage daughter's life. This was a boy so unapologetic in his love for the Lord that it left in awe. In a world where so many young people test the boundaries of rules, Jake stood firm in his beliefs, walking with unwavering confidence in his faith; something I rarely saw even in adults. And he did it with such ease.

For one of his first dates with Anna, Jake invited her to a Fellowship of Christian Athletes (FCA) chili dinner. Jake simply lived as an example of unwavering faith, treating our daughter with unconditional love, care, and respect. A few months into their relationship, I told his mother, "It's almost as if God walked in with this one." And I truly believed He did.

Shortly after Jake came into our lives, so did a book. One night, Anna, Jake, and I were discussing the struggles families face when drugs and alcohol are involved, and how deeply it affects their loved ones.

As I shared my past, Jake mentioned a book he had read—*Fearless* by Eric Blehm. The next day, he brought it to our house.

And once I started reading, I couldn't put it down. I finished the nearly 300-page book in a single day.

While reading the biography of a young man battling drug addiction, one thought stayed with me: after years of struggle and turmoil, he found God, overcame his addiction, and became a Navy SEAL. And his parents, witnessing his journey, gave their lives to Jesus as well.

That realization pushed me farther.

I can do this.

I could no longer justify simply going through the motions. I had to become an active participant in my relationship with God.

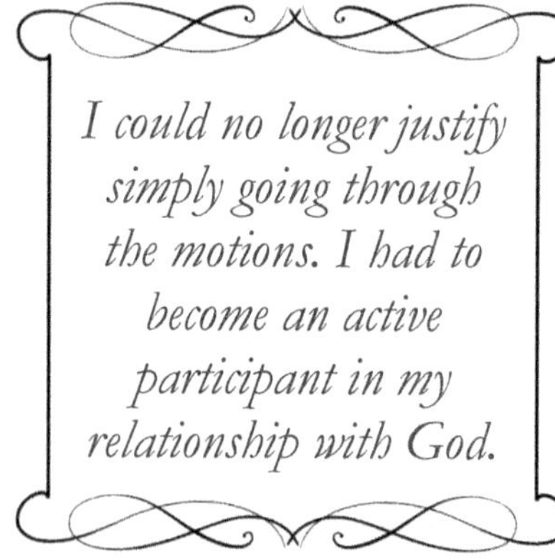

Shortly after, I asked Todd if we could go back to saying grace before our meals every evening. I did not know why we stopped. Maybe it was because of the hectic schedules of our children that had put many meals on hold, or placed in shifts, with "grab and go" as our meal of choice. It happens to all families, but I would no longer accept this as an excuse to forgo thankfulness to our Lord for our food He provides us.

Then, I announced that I wanted to begin going back to church. Attending church and hearing God's Word became important to me. I felt I needed to be surrounded with people doing the same. I felt humbled because there was so much I felt I needed to know while sitting in church listening to the sermons and taking notes. I felt I was playing decades of catch-up in biblical knowledge. On many occasions, as we would be driving home after the service, I would start to cry. Todd would motion the kids to go on into the house, as he and I would sit in the car while my tears flowed.

"I feel so stupid," I would say.

There was just too much information, and I felt I needed to know it all to be worthy of being re-baptized. Was I worthy? In his loving way, Todd would console me and explain I was probably doing more than most people sitting in a pew on Sunday, in living my life as a Christian, and told me how proud he was of me. With a hug and a wiping of my tears, he would remind me that I was my own worst critic. Todd was right about that.

Then, one weekend, Todd went out of town on a fishing trip, and my anxiety set in. I wanted to attend church but dreaded going alone. Insecurities crept in—the fear of introducing myself to unfamiliar faces, the worry of sitting alone in the pew. But I went anyway. My courage was building. As I stepped through the doors and found an empty spot, I felt proud of myself for pushing past my doubts. I had no idea even then, God was preparing me.

By this time, the holidays were approaching, and I wanted to be fully present—mindful of *why* we celebrate the season. Todd and I decided to scale back on gifts, focusing instead on reflection and gratitude. Each evening, I spent time recognizing the true significance of the holiday beyond simply acknowledging Jesus' birth.

And that's when I finally opened my Bible.

I had owned one for years. It was a graduation gift from a kind-hearted school secretary, given to me during my high school co-operative education program. She had even taken the time to have it inscribed with my name. At the time, I had thanked her sincerely, but truthfully I had no idea what to do with it. The thought of reading the Bible intimidated me. So, I placed it on a shelf in my bedroom, where it remained, traveling with me through three moves. Now, as I began building my relationship with God, I understood why I had kept it all these years.

The old me would have justified leaving it unopened. After all, wasn't attending church each week enough? But not anymore. On

December 1, 2019, I finally cracked its spine and began reading the Book of Luke, underlining and highlighting as I went.

Around this time, I began thinking about my baptism again. The idea of *thinking* I was baptized was no longer enough. Whenever I sifted through family paperwork, the truth stared back at me. There was no record of my baptism. My family's certificates sat neatly in place, yet mine was absent. It weighed on me.

In my usual fashion of handling emotional subjects, I chose to write rather than speak. On my Christmas list to Todd, I wrote one simple request: *I want to be baptized again, and I need your help because I don't know how to go about it by myself.*

The shame returned. I couldn't bring myself to pick up the phone and ask because I knew I would cry. So, I sent Todd on the mission. Bless his heart, he tried his best to help, but his timing was...less than ideal. As we walked into church one Sunday, just minutes before the service began, he nearly approached the pastor to ask. Panicked, I grabbed his arm. *Not like this. Not in front of all these people.* That day wasn't the right time. We eventually decided that making such a request during the busiest season at church wasn't wise. I continued my nightly readings, attending services as usual—all while baptism lingered in the back of my mind.

Then came Christmas Day. Todd gifted me a diamond-studded cross. I started to cry. It was one of the most meaningful gifts he had ever given me. He understood my journey and my struggles, and it was his quiet way to show his love and support.

A funny thing happened once I started wearing that necklace. When I needed comfort, I would hold onto it and say a prayer. Countless times, while out shopping or running errands, strangers would approach me, sharing stories about sermons they had heard or prayers they had offered for loved ones. It allowed me to speak openly about my faith in return. It was as if the cross signaled to others that I was a safe place for those conversations—a willing listener, a fellow believer.

Just like my promise ring and wedding band on my fingers, the necklace became a permanent fixture around my neck.

God was placing people and situations in my life, slowly leading me to step out of my comfort zone and fully into my faith. Christian music, books, invitations to faith-based events—they surrounded me, making it easier to embrace my journey.

I finally voiced my desire for baptism to a coworker, though I admitted my reservations; I was nervous about having it performed in front of the congregation.

His response? "Why? It's an amazing experience, and they would be nothing but happy for you."

He was right.

Now, I had no more excuses.

Chapter Three

CHILD OF GOD

And then—COVID hit. The COVID restrictions affected our world in a way none of us had ever experienced, and the stress level hit our household at an all-time high. Government restrictions placed on the public and businesses required social distancing and the closure of some businesses, while others remained open for essential use only. The company Todd and I worked at was a company that specialized in underground utilities, so it was considered essential; he was the vice-president and operations manager, and I worked in the office part-time processing payroll. The stay-in-place order placed by our county's executive kept me at home, working remotely, which also included attending church online. I knew I would have to wait for my request to be baptized, but I had a goal in mind.

As the weeks went by and the shelter-at-home order was lifted, we were invited to a wedding ceremony of our boss at his home. It just so happened to be officiated by our pastor. The wedding was beautiful, the dinner was delicious, and we had a lovely conversation with our pastor and his wife and others at our table. As our pastor stated that it was time for them to leave, I felt God fully open the door, push me through it, and say, "Now is your chance. You need to do this." I looked at our pastor and simply asked, "Do you mind if I speak to you for a moment?" There was no hesitation. It was now or never. I was confident in my relationship with God, even if I was still learning. I needed to let go of my control and let Him lead me. I fully trusted Him.

Our pastor, his wife, and I stood amongst the trees away from the wedding guests, and I said quietly, almost in a whisper, "I want to be rebaptized." I began to cry and stumbled through my words as to why I needed to be baptized. I shared my reservations of being baptized in front of the congregation because I was such an introverted person at heart. I didn't want attention placed on myself.

His reaction was one of extreme excitement. He happily said, "Absolutely, we can. This is amazing."

He began to ask me questions such as how much I knew about the stories in the Bible. I explained I knew the well-known stories, but I felt so inadequate in the knowledge of many of the other ones. He calmed my fears by explaining that it was okay, and many times there were elders still teaching him information, which was so reassuring to me. He said he would be happy to perform the baptism with only my family in attendance. His wife asked if I had been to any Bible study classes. I explained that I had not because it was just too intimidating for me. Again, I felt I needed to have enough knowledge going into the classes so I could be engaged in the discussions, so I avoided it instead.

As we were driving home, I was overcome with emotion again. I had the courage to FINALLY step out of the proverbial boat!

Now it was time to tell the family. I did not need a lot of fanfare. I wanted my husband, son, daughter, and her boyfriend, Jake, in attendance. It was such a private, intimate moment in my life, and I wanted them to share it with me. I requested them to come sit in the sunroom because I had something to tell them, and I wanted to tell them together. My son didn't understand why I couldn't just tell him as we waited for the others to come into the room, and I said, "Because I don't want to cry twice." He knew I wore my heart on my sleeve, so he waited patiently for the others to come into the room.

Once we were all settled in our chairs and their eyes were on me. I began to speak, but no words came out—only tears. I looked at my husband, my rock. I think they thought I had bad news to share, but Todd explained what was beginning to transpire and that I wanted all of us to be present for my baptismal experience.

I made the necessary arrangement with the church and the date was set for the following week. The necessary paperwork was sent to me, I filled it out, and then I proudly wrote the date on my calendar—July 8, 2020. I could not believe it. For an entire week, I would look at the ink with the word "baptism" written in the box on a typical Wednesday, and it made me smile.

THE EVENING BEFORE MY BAPTISM, I sat down at the patio table, and wrote letters to each of the attendees of my upcoming baptism, thanking them for supporting me and telling them how much of an impact they had in my life.

The day arrived on the calendar, and it began like any other. But I knew by the end of the day, my life would be forever changed. I made sure I applied waterproof mascara; it was a must on a day like this. I went on to work, sent a reminder text to my family about when we needed to be at the church, and went about my day. When I came home from work, Anna announced that she wanted to give me a gift that I could wear for my baptism. It was a beaded charm bracelet. I placed it proudly on my wrist.

We had a couple hours before the baptism and the kids and I were in the kitchen when Jake asked, "What does John 3:16 say?" I froze like a deer in headlights. I knew if he said the first couple words in the verse, I would have been able to finish it. He meant no harm whatsoever, but I felt put on the spot, and then had to play it off as being nervous. After a couple minutes of attempting to keep my composure, I excused myself to my bedroom, sat on the floor and began to sob. "How can I be worthy of this act taking place in a couple of hours when I can't even recite a Bible verse?" I thought to myself. It was all too much. And how can others in the world take their baptisms for granted when I felt that I was taking the most important test of my life? I wanted to make God proud of me.

After I calmed myself down and took a deep breath, I reminded myself that again God was in control, and I needed to trust Him. I did not need to know all the answers. He would provide them for me. He loves me. I realized that my faith had been building in my heart since I was a child, and my baptism will be the grace given to me after all these years of thinking I was not worthy of such sacrament. *I was not perfect, but I was worthy.* I picked myself off the floor, wiped my tears from my face, and went back downstairs.

WE ARRIVED AT CHURCH. The same church where I walked down the aisle to marry the love of my life, the church where I handed both babies over to be baptized, and the church that we had attended since we were married. I was taking it all in; it was now my turn. I was calm, and I was ready.

Our pastor was standing at the altar and welcomed us in.

"You ready?" he asked with a smile.

"I am," I said.

Everything was ready for the baptism. He directed us over to the baptismal font, and we started the service by saying The Lord's Prayer. The pastor began to ask me questions about God and accepting Him as my Lord and Savior, and with each question I answered, "Yes" or "I will." It was such an odd feeling knowing my family was standing behind me and I could not see them out of my peripheral vision. I was in full focus and awareness of what was happening. The pastor asked me to approach the font and bow my head. I was baptized in the name of the Father, the Son, and the Holy Spirit, as water was poured over my forehead.

My baptism

The feeling at that moment was indescribable. As I was dabbing my head with the cross embossed napkin given to me, I became overwhelmed with emotion again.

I had firmly stepped into my faith.

I am strong…
I am worthy…
I am loved…
I am a child of God.

I made a realization after years of struggling with my faith. With everything in life, there must be consistency. If we want health, we need to feed our bodies with healthy food and vegetables each day; if we want strong bodies, we need to work them physically daily. If we want a strong relationship, just texting back and forth isn't going to work. We need to be present in one another's lives.

It is the same with our relationship with God. It will not grow strong with periodic check-ins. As in other things in life, it needs to be a daily encounter with Him. This was when I knew I had a relationship with HIM and was ready to move forward, being bold with my action in now being baptized.

Chapter Four

HIS ILLNESS

After my baptism, I felt a sense of renewed purpose and clarity. Life went forward—as normally as one could say when a pandemic is going on in our world. But still, I had felt a deeper, more settled feeling, even amongst the uncertainty and fear. We heard news of people becoming severely ill, but knew of no one personally who needed to be hospitalized or died, only hearing stories about them on the evening news.

Weeks ahead of his hospitalization, Todd texted me as he normally would throughout the day, and when he would be leaving from work to head home. We worked together, and after almost 30 years of marriage, he still felt the need to stay connected with me and made sure that I was a priority to him. For that I was thankful. He would text me throughout the day, and again as he was leaving work.

One day, Todd texted me as usual—or so I thought.

"Heading home," his text said.

"Migraine?" I asked.

"No, I think fever," he responded.

"Uh-oh," I commented.

In the year of the pandemic, that was not a statement one wants to hear. And if this symptom was spoken out loud, everyone would be on high alert. That was just the state of our world. Earlier that day, he complained of having a headache. Todd was prone to migraines, so neither of us thought it was anything but that. I knew he was under intense pressure at work, and he never slept well, only getting about four hours of sleep each night, with those four hours interrupted by his snoring. For years, I encouraged him to go get a sleep apnea test, but to no avail. Todd worked so many hours, and I believed his stress was contributing to some health issues I witnessed in him recently.

Todd had a lot of responsibility on his shoulders due to his title and dedication to making sure he gave the best service to customers through running his crews on job sites in a professional manner, and had handled the constantly changing mandates as best he could, while still making sure his crew worked, so they could put food on their table for their families. But the pandemic, with all that it entailed, was beginning to take a toll on him. The mask mandates and social distancing had subsided, thankfully, but Todd's stress level did not, especially with the uptick of mandates for the pandemic's newest precaution placed on its citizens—COVID vaccinations. These new vaccination requirements added to Todd's stress.

The media was full of fear and propaganda by this time, and the suppression of remedies opposite of the government protocol was rampant. Everyone seemed to have an opinion about it, too. It was clear society was divided on the issue. Now that the vaccine was rolled out and promised to protect one against the virus, pressure was being placed on every citizen to get vaccinated due to the FDA approving it for EUA (emergency use authorization). Incentives such as free donuts were offered, and then threats came down from government officials, requiring vaccine passports to be shown in order to enter a place of business, work, or attend school. I felt our world had gone mad.

Todd wanted to respect the employees' individual freedoms to choose if they wanted to get the vaccine or not. He struggled in knowing how to proceed with the current jobs, knowing the customers he worked with had a different opinion on the matter. He understood their stance, but he also wanted them to understand his, especially since our daughter had not handled other vaccines well. In Todd's opinion, it was obscene for hospitals and the government to make a blanket statement, mandating everyone to be vaccinated—including his men, who worked outside, no less—on contracted property. He felt there was not enough data at the time to prove the vaccine prevented transmission of the virus.

ADDING TO OUR CONCERN OF Todd's fever, our son recently recovered from COVID, the Delta variant, with nothing more than an aggravating sore throat, and the comment, "I've had colds worse than this." Jacob isolated himself in his room, and I was the only source of contact with his bedroom door separating us for the exchange of food and supplements. I was his nursemaid, and made sure he was supporting his immune system, resting, staying hydrated, and checking to make sure his oxygen levels stayed high. We didn't want a trip to the urgent care. Or worse, a trip to the emergency room. We knew what that would bring. But after a couple days of rest and extra loving care, Jacob felt back to his old self again.

Upon hearing the news of Todd's fever, I mentally prepared myself to nurse him back to health as I did when our son was sick, figuratively placing my nursemaid's hat back on my head. I packed up items in my office to sustain myself in working from home over the course of separation to prepare to isolate ourselves from our co-workers for the allotted ten days, and I headed for home. In witnessing my son's reaction to the virus, I was expecting the remainder of our quarantine to be able to just hang out at the house together, with the thought that this was God's way of forcing him to take a break from work. He was the hardest working man I knew, aside from my father.

I was quite excited to be able to spend these days with Todd. Most of our marriage was spent with him working twelve-to-fourteen-hour days. He rarely took a vacation and would lose his three-weeks' worth of allotted vacation hours every time the calendar flipped to a new year, by his own choosing. He worked his way up from being a part-time welder in the shop, to shop manager, to eventually vice-president and operations manager, a position he humbly held for fifteen years. Todd prided himself on making sure the employees in the company were taken care of, before himself. He multitasked like no one's business, and a lot of people depended on him with their requests, because a lot of behind-the-scenes activity happened when running a job as an underground utilities' contractor. Being a co-worker myself, I would joke with him that he needed a number ticker hung outside his office door, when I needed to "wait in line" because other employees needed his assistance before I did. I always waited patiently for my turn.

But for the next ten days, he was all mine! I welcomed it and was grateful for this time home with him and I being quarantined together. What a mini-vacation this would be, I thought. I quietly thanked God for giving us this moment to reconnect. Something we both needed now that our lives were winding down into the life of empty nesters. Our years past were filled with work, activities, and caring for our children, so I was looking forward to this new chapter in our lives.

Driving home, I began to make my plan of action. I already had all the remedies at hand, along with the oximeter to measure his oxygen levels, and plotted to get the house cleaned, yard work done, and all my household duties complete while he spent the first few days in bed getting over what I had begun to call "a pesky virus," looking forward to being able to enjoy the rest of the week catching up in time spent with one another hanging out in our backyard. Neither of us was worried.

We spent the day moving Jacob into his college house

Upon arriving home, I told our son, Jacob, that he needed to head back to school a couple of days early. Since he had already had the virus, he no longer needed to quarantine, and with his senior year of mechanical engineering beginning on Monday, Todd and I both knew he needed to focus on his coursework. His semester would be rigorous, and he was on track to graduate in December 2022.

Thankfully, Jacob was already living in a house with four of his buddies, so moving him back to school wasn't an issue. All he needed to do was pack up his clothes and electronics and make the hour-and-a-half drive back to the home he shared with his roommates off campus.

On Friday morning, Jacob packed up his car ready to head back to school. Today was not only our son's first day back to school, but it was also Todd and my official day back to empty nesting.

When Jacob tested positive a few weeks back, our daughter, Anna, decided it was best for her to head back to college early, so she could avoid possible exposure. With this newfound empty nesting, Todd and I were excited that the kids were spreading their wings and beginning to live life not attached to us. And this day was supposed to be a sendoff to Jacob with dinner at his favorite restaurant, with Todd and I planning a weekend getaway for our 28th wedding anniversary that was coming up in less than two months. But now that Todd was sick, all of that would have to wait.

Todd helping Anna move into her college rental home

"Bye, Buddy," I said as we stepped out onto the front porch. Buddy was one of the many nicknames we had for our son, Jacob.

"Bye, I am sure I will be back soon," he said. "In a week or so, I will have lunch with my boss. I'll let you know."

Since Jacob finished out his internship while being quarantined and working remotely, he did not have a moment to finish his final interview with his boss. They decided to meet for lunch in the upcoming week or so. Todd and I both gave him a hug, and he headed to his car.

"Alright, drive safely, honey," I said.

"See ya!" he said, waving.

"Alright, love you Buddy," Todd said.

"Love you, too," Jacob replied.

As Todd and I stood on the porch, waiting for Jacob to drive away, Todd commented, "Man, I have a bad headache today. It kind of went away yesterday, but…," his voice trailing off.

Only now, in hindsight, do I realize that this was Todd's last physical interaction with our son in this earthly realm.

And I was able to capture it on video; a video of Todd telling his son that he loved him. Those final words, spoken as Jacob left for college, are something I will always hold dear to my heart.

AFTER WE WATCHED HIS CAR drive down the street he had driven down hundreds of times, we made our way back inside. Todd headed to the couch to lay down and attempt to keep his headache from turning into a migraine.

He would get migraines quite frequently, experiencing pain so bad that it would make him vomit. Again, I was thankful this headache wasn't as bad as his previous ones, and the fever he had for a couple of days was low grade. Nothing too concerning. But he was tired. As I went about cleaning the house, he signed into his laptop provided to him to work remotely, so he could respond to emails and plan out the next week's crew list. But by mid-morning, Todd's fever had returned. He laid on the couch and napped while

I spent time mowing the grass, determined to get all my household chores done for the day, when I received a text from him.

"I need you to come inside," he said

I shut off the lawn mower and made my way inside to check on him. One look at his face told me he wasn't doing too well.

"You, okay?" I asked.

"I took my temperature and it's 103.8. Are you almost finished?" He asked.

That's really high.

"I would feel better if you stayed in the house with me, just in case," he said. I could hear the concern in his voice. I was a bit alarmed, too, but didn't lead on. This was not his usual behavior, and I tried not to show my nervousness in noticing it.

"Okay. What can I do to help you bring your fever down? Are you drinking enough water? I don't want you to become dehydrated." He had placed a cold rag across his forehead to cool it, randomly spinning it in the air like a helicopter to cool it off. He had taken some over the counter medications to reduce his fever, but nothing seemed to work at this point.

"I am almost done doing the yard work. Can I finish it? It shouldn't take too long. But call me if you need me. I will come right in," I assured him. He nodded.

I refilled Todd's water jug with ice and fresh water, then stepped back outside into the August heat, restarting the lawn mower to finish cutting the grass as quickly as possible. Within half an hour, I was done. The rest of the day was spent sitting beside him, ensuring I was there for anything he needed. His fever wouldn't break, and soon, the coughing spells began.

Later that night, as his coughing grew more persistent and his fever remained elevated, Todd asked if I would sleep in the family room with him to keep an eye on him. He lay on one couch, while I settled into the loveseat, periodically checking his oxygen levels with an oximeter. His readings remained in the mid-to-low 90s, not dangerously low, I thought, but still concerning.

Before we went to sleep, we discussed a plan of action in case his condition worsened. We talked about reaching out to an online community of doctors known for prioritizing their patients over pandemic politics—ones willing to prescribe ivermectin. But the response time was 48 hours, and we didn't have that kind of time.

"Can you call your doctor tomorrow to see if she has suggestions for what I can do?" he asked.

"She won't be able to give you medical advice since you are not her patient. If you are not feeling relief by the morning, let's take you to urgent care and go from there."

He was one that never went to the doctor, so he did not have one on call. And Todd was adamant that he did not want to go to the hospital. We knew that the hospital's COVID treatment protocols were extremely limited, restricting the use of natural therapeutics, a fact I later confirmed after Todd was admitted. With the vaccine newly approved for emergency use and widespread pressure to vaccinate every American, I felt uneasy about taking him in, fearing potential coercion by hospital staff. I felt utterly powerless.

I settled into the loveseat, wanting to get a good night's sleep, but knowing I would be up most of the night worrying about him. I was quite the worry wart. His coughing was getting more forced and the quiet in between them was minimizing. Sleep ended up coming quickly for me, most likely from the exhaustion of taking care of the house and yard work, only to be roused by Todd calling my name a few hours later.

"Lisa," he said out loud in the dark. "I think you need to check my oxygen levels," he said between coughs, his breathing labored.

Feeling my way through the dark, I found the side table and felt for the oximeter, placed it on his finger and turned on the light. After a few moments, the reading showed 89. I sighed. Not good. *Not good at all.* It was at that moment that I no longer felt comfortable waiting until the morning for him to get medical attention.

"I think we need to head to the emergency room," I said. He didn't fight my decision. I knew then it was serious. I knew he did not want to go to the hospital; he heard the stories, as did I. But he no longer had a choice, and I prayed it was the right one. I just wanted him to be well.

We gathered our things and headed to the car. I backed out of the garage, as Todd settled into the passenger seat, a mask covering his face, with only his brown eyes looking at me.

"I'm sorry," he said quietly.

I felt terrible for him, but he knew I was angry, not at him, but at the situation. Angry that we had reached a point neither of us wanted. We spoke about his health, and as the uncertainty settled in, fear rose in my chest, hardening my demeanor.

When I go into protective mode, I become hyper-focused and silent, only letting my guard down when someone else takes the reins, or when I feel safe. *Safe* was not in my vocabulary at that moment. I was in full protection mode, unwilling to speak too much for fear of saying something I'd regret. And I certainly wasn't comfortable handing control over to hospital staff.

Instead, I was preparing for the inevitable, the question I knew they would ask him in the emergency room. *The million-dollar question of the year.*

"Are you vaccinated?"

Chapter Five

OUR LONGEST SEPARATION (OR SO I THOUGHT)

While driving, we chose the hospital we felt would not give us as much pressure with that question, and I prayed that all the propagandist views had not permeated our chosen hospital's walls. It was located in the next town, the one I grew up in, about twenty minutes away. We drove to the hospital in silence. When we arrived at the emergency room entrance, I told Todd to go in while I found a parking spot. He waited for me so we could walk in together. The nurse on staff took his vitals, while he stood there leaning onto the front counter, his arm steadying his balance. He attempted to answer their questions as best as he could, and I answered for him when he could not. After the nurse finished asking her list of questions, she began to take his vitals, then ushered me out of the lobby. She advised me that I could no longer stay. COVID Protocol, she said. Of course.

I walked out of the hospital doors and headed towards the parking lot back to my car. With my car windows open feeling the hot, humid air of the summer hit my face, I sat in the driver's seat, waiting for Todd to let me know what I needed to do. My radio was tuned to the local Christian music station, and I let the lyrics of the songs wash over me to soothe the panic that was rising in my chest. I laid the seat back and closed my eyes, not wanting to fall asleep for fear of missing a text from him. After an hour of waiting, he finally texted me to say that he would be there a while and told me to just go home. I looked at the clock on my dashboard. It was after midnight.

By six o'clock the next morning when I awoke, I hadn't received a call or text from him, so I texted him to see how things were being handled and how he was feeling. He said he was still in the emergency room, and they were supposed to give him a breathing treatment. The breathing treatment never arrived, and he was now waiting for a room to be ready for him. He texted that he had an EKG, chest x-ray, steroids, an inhaler, cough medicine given and lots of blood samples given.

"So, you are being admitted?" I texted.

"Yes," he responded.

My worst fears were confirmed. I wanted to trust that he was in good hands, that God would protect him. It was hard for me not to worry because for the past year, the news filled our eyes and ears with the death toll of persons in hospitals around the country. News stories were shared of vans parked outside of New York hospitals to hold the overflow of bodies who succumbed to this virus. Nurses, behind the scenes, gave accounts of the grave conditions of the COVID floors via social media—only for their content to be removed due to sites deeming it as misinformation. The public was being fed so much conflicting information, and knowing Todd was going in without being vaccinated, I was nervous for his treatment and care. I clasped my hands in prayer.

I wanted to anchor my heart in the reality of God's awareness of this situation and have trust in HIM. He was in control, and I would not be shaken. "God, please protect and heal Todd, so he can recover and get back to me," I prayed. "As soon as possible,"

I added. I wasn't in the habit of making demands of our Lord and Savior, but desperation hit. I thought God would understand.

"My oxygen is back up to 94% on 4% oxygen," Todd assured me via text.

"Good. Do you want me to contact Tom and your parents?"

I didn't want to call his parents too early, even though I knew his dad would be awake. Todd's dad was going through cancer treatment and had one of his chemotherapy sessions the day before. I really didn't want to call him or my mother-in-law to worry about Todd being admitted in the hospital for possible COVID. So, I dialed our boss, Tom's number instead. When he answered, I explained the events of the evening. He said a prayer with me, told me he would let the office staff know, and asked me to keep him posted on Todd's progress.

To take my mind off what was happening, I went outside to the backyard to tend to the gardens and wait for Todd with more news from the hospital. The gardens have always provided peace and tranquility, and I busied myself by pulling weeds, watering the plants, and cleaning up the area. The hot summer sun was bearing down on me, but I didn't want to go inside. I knew I would only sit and ruminate on the situation at hand. Instead, I grabbed my glass of water off the patio table and went to sit under the Bradford Pear tree on the park bench that Todd had bought for me on Mother's Day the previous year, to escape the heat and cool off under the shade.

About that time, one of our neighbors spotted me sitting there and approached the fence. She looked at me, taking in my demeanor, and asked, "Is everything alright?"

"No," I replied. "Todd was admitted to the hospital last night."

She leaned on the fence, then raised one hand and pounded the top. "I wish he would have gotten vaccinated," she said.

I looked up at her, feeling my blood pressure start to rise. There was no expression of care or concern for Todd himself. Just a statement, void of empathy. As I sat there, I tried to keep myself calm.

The early days of COVID brought unity, but as time wore on, conversations shifted. People began judging one another, not by their acts of kindness, but by their choices regarding masks, distancing, and vaccines. And as I sat in my backyard, that division infiltrated my space.

This neighbor and I did not see eye to eye on vaccination. I believed in weighing the pros and cons of each vaccine before making a decision, respecting the uniqueness of our family's individual choice regarding vaccines. Over the years, she and I had maintained an *agree-to-disagree* stance on vaccination. And for the most part, we left it at that.

When the new COVID vaccine hit the market, Todd and I felt uneasy about it. Health authorities were pushing it aggressively, despite limited long-term data on its effectiveness. It didn't sit right with us.

I was reminded of a time two years before COVID entered our world, as I faced a difficult decision regarding vaccination. That time, it had been for our daughter.

In her excitement to see her boyfriend after some time apart, Anna bolted down the driveway to meet Jake, only to run straight into a wooden beam extending from the back of Todd's work truck. As we rushed to urgent care, she sat in the backseat, her boyfriend pressing a rag to the open, bleeding wound. Todd was driving, and I sat in the passenger seat, silently contemplating how to handle the inevitable tetanus shot recommendation. It was the standard of care for any puncture wound or open cut.

"Did that piece of wood come from a sanitary job?" I asked Todd.

With our work in underground utilities, I needed to know whether the wood had been exposed to fecal matter or other bacteria. If it had, I might reconsider withholding the shot. But if not, I knew that as long as the wound was bleeding, oxygenating the site, it was naturally killing bacteria. And at that moment, it was bleeding profusely.

"No," he said. "It came from the yard at work."

"Okay," my decision was made. Todd trusted me, and I appreciated that. The wound would be cleaned, stitched up, and we'd be on our way.

Or so I thought.

After three nurses and a doctor cycled in and out of the room, each attempting to coerce us into agreeing to a tetanus shot, my suspicions were confirmed—treatment for the actual wound seemed secondary. My daughter sat on the examination table, waiting, yet receiving no care. Their focus was more on administering an injection she didn't need than addressing the reason we were there. If anyone dared to go against the grain, a derogatory label followed, which during the pandemic meant being branded an "anti-vaxxer."

Throughout COVID, my neighbor and I remained on opposite sides of how we, as a society, should handle the virus. I stood by the belief that maintaining peak health, eating a nutrient-rich diet, exercising, and taking appropriate supplements, was key to resilience against illness. She, on the other hand, adhered strictly to CDC guidelines. And now, with Todd hospitalized, I could feel her wanting to prove her point.

Our conversation grew heated. "You say that if he had been vaccinated, he wouldn't be in the hospital. I say that if he had started prioritizing his health at the beginning of the pandemic, he wouldn't be here now. So, who is right?" I demanded.

I was angry.

We both held firm to our perspectives. And as I realized that neither of us would find peace in the discussion, I excused myself and went inside.

I didn't have the energy to argue.

Now, Todd and I rarely spent time apart. Not only was he my husband, but he was also my best friend. He even made going grocery shopping fun. He would go on fishing weekends to the lake or a week-long business trip occasionally, but for the most part we enjoyed one another's company and chose to be in it as much as we could. Leaving him at the hospital was the first time I knew I was going to be away for him for a period of time. Two weeks, possibly. The longest I had ever been away from him in 30 years. *I got this.*

As luck would have it, that night, a summer storm blew through the Midwest that left homes in our area without power for over 12 hours. I was still quarantined, so I spent the time by myself in the sunroom reading by candlelight, enjoying the quietness of the evening—because frankly, the noise in the world was so loud right now. Literally and figuratively, with everyone's opinions on the pandemic front and center, especially on social media, and even now in my own backyard.

Life felt so overwhelming to me, and unlike Todd, I didn't handle stress very well. When the electricity went out, it forced me to be still and unplug from the world around me and plug into God's Word.

As the darkness of life wanted to surround me at that moment, I would still choose to see the light. I meditated on 1 Corinthians 15:58 that says, "Therefore, my dear brothers and sisters, stand firm. Let nothing move you. Always give yourselves fully to the work of the Lord, because you know that our labor in the Lord is not in vain." I needed to have faith that the Lord would give me the strength to fight my husband's battles for him, since he was unable to do so himself.

The next morning, electricity was restored, and I went about cleaning out the spoiled food in the refrigerator. As much as I hated throwing out all the food in the fridge because of the outage, I found myself being grateful for that, too. I spent the morning scrubbing the fridge

> *I needed to have faith that the Lord would give me the strength to fight my husband's battles for him, since he was unable to do so himself.*

clean, ready to put all new healthy food back in, in preparation for Todd to come home and begin a new healthy eating plan.

While Todd was gone, our home became my sanctuary of sorts. Yet, every time I stepped out the front door, I was met with inquiring minds. If I ventured into the backyard, I was greeted by barking dogs or the hum of commercial mowers—no peace, no stillness.

I tried keeping busy, gardening in the mornings before the heat became unbearable, but it didn't bring the solace I needed to quiet my soul. Instead, I found myself anxiously waiting for Todd's texts; they became my small lifelines offering updates on his condition. I was careful not to burden him, knowing he needed to focus on healing. But as the hours passed, my restlessness grew.

A few days after he was admitted to the hospital, I decided to nap on the lounge chair outside. After an hour or so, I woke up and decided to take a walk, giving myself space from others coming along my path. I found myself very tired over the past couple of days and chalked it up to having the stress of Todd in the hospital, the kids beginning their new college semester away, and my quarantine. Regardless of the source, I forced myself to exercise because I always felt reenergized afterwards. My nose was running a bit that day, but since I have dealt with years of mold sensitivity, I figured that was the culprit to my nose issue. As I walked, I looked up the mold count and confirmed my suspicion. *Yep! That's it*, I thought. The mold count was extremely high in our area in the Midwest, so I continued on.

After my walk and being refreshed, I decided to harvest some different herbs from the garden. I love picking the oregano, basil, and thyme and smelling the aroma. This time, as I brought the herbs to my nose, I smelled nothing.

Oh, no! This cannot be happening! Todd and I were both getting ready to come out of isolation and quarantine, and I was so excited to be able to visit him in the hospital. But now I would have to wait longer to see him.

"I think I have COVID." I texted him.

"Oh, boy," he responded.

I was not concerned for myself. I had a runny nose, was a bit lethargic, and couldn't smell. Those were my symptoms. It was easy to go about my day, continue taking my supplements, exercising, and spending time in the sun to make sure I supported my body as the virus ran its course.

I was wavering on taking a home COVID test to confirm my result, and decided the loss of smell was a telltale sign of it. But I needed the test to confirm my suspicion, especially if I would be visiting Todd after my quarantine. The test came back positive. *Gosh, darn it!* I had to wait another five days before I could visit him in the hospital.

"I heard you are officially out of isolation. I can't come to see you though. Do you need anything that your brother or someone can bring up to you?" I texted.

The loneliness of being in the house by myself weighed heavily on me. Though it had only been four days since taking Todd to the emergency room, it felt more like four years. I couldn't imagine how isolated he must have felt, confined to a hospital room, separated from everyone, especially with COVID and not being vaccinated.

Later, when I read through his medical records, I discovered he had been feeling the same way. The hospital chaplain had visited Todd's room to pray with him. Knowing that my husband—strong, protective, and never one to ask for emotional support—had reached a point where he needed that comfort broke my heart. He was struggling, and I wasn't allowed to be by his side through any of it.

While watering my plants and mowing the lawn, my neighbor approached the fence again. I called over to her, saying, "Just want to let you know, I have COVID."

She immediately showed concern. "How are you feeling?"

I told her I was tired and sometimes nauseous, likely because I wasn't eating much due to the stress. But otherwise, I felt good. I gave her an update on Todd's condition, and we made small talk, both standing within respectable spaces, keeping our distance. Any tension from our previous conversation seemed to fade.

"Can I get you anything?" she asked.

I gave her a short list, and she joked, "If you start to feel really bad, I'll call you a taxi. I'm not the one taking you to the hospital!"

I laughed. "I don't blame you."

About an hour later, I stepped outside to find a bag of needed items and a bouquet of flowers sitting on my back patio table. Her kindness touched me. Regardless of our opposing views, we were still neighbors, and we treated each other as such.

I continued checking in with Todd over the next couple of days. If he didn't respond, I resorted to calling the nurses' station for updates. They gave me a rundown of his test results, which remained stable.

BUT THEN, THINGS CHANGED.

Todd contracted a bacterial infection in his lungs. Up until that moment, he had been holding his own against the virus.

Throughout the pandemic, I hadn't followed the treatments being administered inside hospitals. Realizing I needed to equip myself with a deeper understanding of COVID and hospital protocols, I knew it was time to start digging into the details.

I had spent years researching medical information to make informed decisions about my own health. Now, I needed to prepare myself to be an advocate for my husband, to be able to ask the right questions and better understand this virus.

First, I read about monoclonal antibodies. I wasn't quite sure he would have been a candidate at the hospital, where he was admitted. Based on the timeline of his illness, Todd was one day past the eligibility window for them, in my opinion, based on the literature I was reading. But at this stage, it didn't matter. *What's done is done,* I thought. Todd had already been in the hospital for almost a week, meaning he wouldn't receive the treatment regardless.

As I continued researching, I stumbled across a drug the CDC was using for COVID patients: Remdesivir. I had never heard of it. I printed out a case study detailing the use of Remdesivir, alongside four other drugs, on Ebola patients. Ultimately, the drug had been pulled from the study after 50% of patients died from kidney failure and cardiac arrest. *I don't feel good about that.*

After reading this drug, I sifted through Todd's text messages, searching for any mention of it in our conversations. All he had noted was that he'd been given an antiviral upon admission to the emergency room. I needed to confirm whether it was the same medication because if so, I wanted to be able to ask questions about it.

Determined to stay informed, I assembled a binder with my research printouts, a composition book for notes, and a list of questions I planned to ask the doctors once I was able to visit the hospital. In the meantime, I checked in with Todd's nurses multiple times a day and with Todd, making sure he was being treated respectfully despite his vaccination status.

I hated even considering the possibility that he might face discrimination over it. As an unvaccinated patient, he was considered "more dangerous" than others, and I worried about how that might affect his care. But each time I asked, he reassured me that he was being treated well.

I felt relieved, but also prayed that he was being honest with me, not just protecting me from bad news, as he so often did. I didn't press the issue.

The week Todd was admitted to the hospital became painfully mundane; daily check-ins with little response, nurse updates, messages to family and friends, remote work when I could manage it, and long stretches of time spent twiddling my thumbs. I felt anxious, waiting for anything new to develop. The frustration of having no real answers was wearing thin on my patience.

I felt powerless, unable to control anything in my life at that moment. The more I felt pushed, the more frustrated I became.

The weight of the situation became a perfect storm, and my family wasn't immune to the fallout. And as tends to happen in times of stress, my family was witness to the rawest parts of me.

While he was in the hospital, I was told that only one "care representative" at a time was allowed to see Todd. Wanting to preserve my role as Todd's designated family representative, I voiced my concern to my mother-in-law that if Todd's brother went to visit him, I wouldn't be able to see Todd myself. I understood how much his family wanted to see him, just as much as I did, but I felt like a gatekeeper. I was forced into a role I never wanted, and because of it forced to hold this boundary. This was my husband, and I hadn't seen him in over a week.

In truth, I knew I was being selfish.

The text messages with my mother-in-law went back and forth in a heated exchange until finally, I relented. "Let Todd's brother go to the hospital," I told her. At that point, my nerves were shot. I was trying to handle things as best as I could, but I admitted defeat, waving my white flag.

After sending the message, I stepped outside, sat on the patio steps and broke down. I wailed into the darkness of the night sky, unable to hold back my grief. I wanted to be strong. I *needed* to be. But the tears came anyway; tears of disappointment, anger, fear. I cried out to God, begging Him to heal Todd, to bring him home, to grant me the patience and peace to endure until he did.

I knew God was always with us. But at that moment, I felt so alone.

Just when I thought the night couldn't get harder, Todd's ringtone chimed from my phone. Wiping my tears, I glanced down at the screen.

He had finally texted me back.

This is Todd's nurse, if you could please give me a call.

Chapter Six

INTUBATION

When I saw the text, I immediately dialed. Todd's nurse explained that his breathing had become labored and was teetering in the dangerous zone on all of his stats. He was now running a 102-degree fever, and it was on the advice of the doctor to go ahead with the process of a planned intubation that evening. If they waited, it may turn into an emergency situation overnight.

Todd was so worn out physically, trying to focus on his breathing, with his oxygen saturation level holding at an 89. His oxygen was maxed at 100% because of his bacterial lung infection.

My deepest fear of him in the hospital was coming true with intubation. I heard stories of patients' lungs being injured due to excessive pressure settings on the ventilator during the intubation procedure.

I remained calm on the phone as she explained everything that they would do to put him in a medically induced coma to help

Todd rest his lungs so they could heal. I wanted to believe that was true. I needed it to be true.

She asked me when I was to come off quarantine. I told her my final day was in a couple of days. She was silent for a moment, then she told me Todd wanted to see me.

"How are you feeling?" she asked.

"I feel fine," I answered. My smell and taste senses had returned, and I felt like myself again, except for the heavy weight of anxiousness holding onto my body. She knew the severity of the situation and said, "Here is what I need you to do. Go through the emergency room doors and up to the desk. I will alert the attendant that you are coming, and they will bring you up personally." She strongly reminded me to wear a mask. They were going to let me see him before he was intubated and put into his medically induced coma.

"You can visit with him while we get the surgical room ready, which will be for about 15 minutes. How far are you out from the hospital?" She asked. She didn't know that I was already grabbing my keys and heading to the garage to get into the car.

"Twenty minutes," I told her.

I informed her where I lived, and that I was leaving now. As much as I am a rule follower, I don't remember what speed I was driving to get to see my husband. Excitement to see him after almost two weeks was overshadowed by the fear of his pending intubation washing over me. As my foot pressed further down on the gas pedal, my legs were violently shaking from the stress building in my body.

I cried out to God in the darkness that surrounded me.

"God, please don't take my husband. I need him. Our children need him. Please!" I cried out into the air.

I had never cried out to God in this manner before, not even when our son had his accident from the dog bite. I screamed out my prayers asking Him to spare my husband. I needed him healed. I didn't care what financial burden his care cost, I didn't care if we needed to sell everything but the shirts off our backs to pay for it.

I needed Todd healed and home. *"I am not ready for this God,"* I screamed out loud.

As I drove down the highway, I called my dad to let him know what was going on. He told me that he and my stepmom would meet me at the emergency room entrance.

I pulled into the parking lot of the emergency room a few moments later, to see my parents waiting for me at the ER entrance. I grabbed my purse, and mask, and ran across the pavement to hug them. They told me they would wait until I came back outside. With "I love you" said between us, I walked into the double door by myself and up to the receptionist desk.

When I walked into his room, Todd was lying in a prone position, on his stomach—a COVID protocol to enhance the oxygenation in a patient's lungs. The nurse tending to him handed me a clipboard that held the consent form for the mechanical intubation. Upon reading it, I went to sign the form.

"No," she said, stopping me. "He needs to sign it."

I held the clipboard for him, as I watched him write his signature as best he could.

I looked at Todd's nurse, who had called me.

"Thank you," I said.

"I am a wife, too. I understand. I will give you two a moment while we go prepare the surgical room." She quietly left the room, closing the door behind her.

I turned back to Todd. "Hi, Lovebug," I said, kissing the top of his head and his cheek through my mask.

"Hey, Honeybear," he said between shallow breaths. Since Todd was on his stomach, his left arm was by his side with the palm of his hand facing up. He moved his fingers, motioning for me to hold his hand, which I gratefully did. It felt so good to finally touch him. Hand holding was something Todd and I always did instinctively. Anytime we were in a parking lot, Todd's arm would stretch out to me, with his fingers spread so they could be intertwined with mine. I held his hand and stroked his hair with my other hand. I knew he was scared. I was, too.

"They told me it is to rest my lungs," he said, with his voice sounding very labored.

"I know, that's what they told me, too." I kept glancing at the clock. I felt I needed to make sure I said everything within our 15-minute time allotment. I wanted to believe with all my heart that this was not going to be the last time we would talk. I had hope. I was praying that God would bind up all his wounds and heal him.

I pushed my anxious thoughts aside and focused on only Todd at that moment. We decided not to call the kids yet. The hospital staff reassured us that this was a temporary situation, and once they saw improvement over the course of a few days, they would bring him back to a conscious state. I didn't want to worry Jacob and Anna more than they already were. They had just started their new semester at their respective colleges, and they needed to concentrate on their studies.

"When I get home, I'm changing everything," Todd remarked.

I knew exactly what that meant. This health scare reminded us of our own mortality. It had shown him how important it was to live a healthy life, reduce his stress, and manage his work schedule. I believed he would have made the necessary changes after this scare, and I was already mentally making plans to support the goals he would have when he was released from the hospital.

"We will be in our 80s, rocking in rocking chairs on the porch with our grandchildren and great grandchildren running around," he added, reassuring me.

"Yes, we will," I added, quite confidently, with a smile spreading across my face, although he couldn't see it behind my mask. We continued to hold hands and talk, as best he could, for 45 minutes. I was grateful for the extra time the staff gave us. I wanted to spend more time with Todd, but the surgical team walked in, interrupting our time together. They were ready for him. I squeezed his hand, kissed the top of his head, and said, "I love you, Mr. Fulshum," the usual greeting I had for him.

"I love you, too, Mrs. Fulshum."

They wheeled Todd out of his room and down the hallway, with me and his nurse following closely behind. The nurse expressed her fondness for having my husband as a patient, and reassured me that this procedure allowed his lungs to heal without Todd having to work so hard to breathe. I only nodded and prayed she was right.

She led me to the waiting room and told me she would come and get me as soon as they finished putting in his breathing tube. I sat down and took a deep breath. I couldn't imagine the thoughts going through Todd's head as they wheeled him down the corridor. What was he thinking about? I knew he was so scared.

I looked at my phone to see what time it was… 12:41 a.m. I texted my dad to let him know they just took Todd back to place the breathing tube in and begin the sedation. Dad let me know they were still downstairs waiting for me, sitting in between the double doors of the emergency room because they were not allowed in the waiting room. COVID rules. I sat back and rested my head against the wall. My thoughts turned back to Todd again.

This man rarely got sick, and seldom took a day off work. But in the few times he would succumb to the flu, it would take him down to where he would need a week to recover, usually with a prescription to clear the pneumonia or bronchitis that had developed in his lungs. I couldn't shake thinking about the cough he had been nursing for over a year. A forced-air kind of cough, and one that he would make throughout the day. I attributed it to possible allergies or a habit he developed.

After an hour or so, Todd's nurse returned and walked me to Todd's room in the Intensive Care Unit. His room was located at the end of the hallway to the left. Room 3106. That number is forever emblazoned in my mind. I entered his hospital room in trepidation of what I was going to see. I had never had to visit a loved one in the ICU before.

The first thing I noticed was that Todd no longer had a mask on, and then, I noticed his beard. It had grown out in the weeks since I had seen him last, and the salt and pepper coloring of it was quite pronounced; I guess I hadn't paid as much attention to it before. In actuality, it had been covered with a mask.

The sounds of the ventilator, with its rhythmic hissing, filled the room. I walked over to Todd's bed and looked down at him. I was afraid to touch him. There were wires and tubes attached to him for monitoring purposes, and a tube down his throat to keep the airway open for his lungs to receive oxygen. Around his neck was a strap to keep the tube in place. I looked down to reach for his hand to find that he had soft, padded cuffs attached to his wrists.

I looked up at the nurse, confused. She explained the cuffs were used to prevent self-injury or him wanting to pull the breathing tube out when the time came for them to lower his sedation and wake him up.

There was an infusion pump to the left of his bed that was administering the combination of Propofol, Fentanyl, and Dexmedetomidine. To the right of him sat the ventilator, the machine that would help Todd breathe since he could no longer do it on his own while he was sedated—the sedation drugs paralyzed his muscles. The doctor explained the process of Todd's intubation and asked if I had any questions. I was too overwhelmed and emotionally exhausted to think clearly of any questions to ask, so I simply shook my head no.

The nurses urged me to go home and get some rest and reminded me that visiting hours began at 8 a.m. It was made clear that I was not allowed to stay by his side. *I will be here*, I thought. I kissed Todd's head, whispered, "Goodbye for now. I love you." I gathered my purse and walked down the long hallway to make my way back to the emergency room.

I exited out of the double doors to see my parents sitting on the garden wall, still waiting for me. It was after 2 a.m. We were all exhausted and headed back to our homes.

Chapter Seven

ICU EXPERIENCE

I tossed and turned most of the night and was unable to shut my brain off, replaying the events of seeing Todd hooked up to the ventilator. It was August 26, 2021. And I was going on two and a half hours of sleep. Regardless, I was ready to go into battle. Putting on my armor and walking through a battlefield wasn't new to me.

Life had already thrown us a wicked curveball. In 2013, our son, Jacob, was attacked by a friend's dog and bitten in the face. He went through years of facial reconstruction surgeries, and our family learned to take each day as it came.

I remember that chapter of our life so vividly. I remember getting the call and thinking my son was gone. I remember handing the phone to my husband to gather all the details because my heart dropped to my feet, and my ears heard nothing but static. I remember the quiet drive to the hospital and the slow motion of the nurse stopping us as we headed to his room, preparing us for what we would see. I remember seeing my son's vibrant blue eyes looking back at me, as the rest of his face was bandaged. I remember kissing Jacob's forehead, just as I had done with Todd the previous night. I remember later, dropping him off at high school. I would watch Jacob walk in, and pray that his peers were kind to him. I remember driving to work crying and having to dry my tears to walk into the office. I remember his PTSD of being near dogs afterwards. I remember asking him at one point if he was okay emotionally, and if he needed to talk to someone; his response was "I'm good. I don't care what others think about how I look." He was more worried about me.

I remember the meticulous care Todd gave as he cleaned Jacob's incisions; an hour of patience in using so many Q-Tips to gently clean the areas after each surgery. I remember putting on my proverbial Mama Bear coat when we would go out in public, ready to protect my cub from unkind words and looks from strangers.

But I also remember the strength. I remember the resilience. I remember saying, "God if this is the only hurdle thrown our way, I'm good because we survived it, and I praise you that we survived." *Onward and upward* became our family motto. That experience strengthened our family, strengthened our faith, showed us our resiliency, and showed us the people who never left our side as we walked through that journey. The pain of that moment—the pain we thought would never leave—was now a distant memory.

But I remember it all.

I thought Jacob's journey would be the longest chapter of darkness and pain in my Book of Life. I stood corrected. I was learning that it is how we handle situations that bring us to our knees, even in sorrow, that makes us strong. If I had only known then that Jacob's situation wasn't going to be our family's largest battle. We walked through it together, gaining a few emotional scars from the experience, but mostly unscathed. I was quite confident we would get through this one with Todd.

I believe this is why God doesn't allow us to know the plans He has for us. Because in our Book of Life, there would be chapters we would want to skip, not want to read, or rip the pages out altogether. In our human nature, we wouldn't be able to handle it. I now wonder if all the journeys I have walked, including the one with Jacob, were preparing me for the one I was walking now with Todd.

I knew Todd was in the baby steps in healing, and I was firm in attempting to navigate this time with faith, trust, and keeping the spirits of our children up as they were doing for me. This was not what I had imagined their first week back to college would be. Jacob and Anna sent me texts and Snapchats between their classes and studying to fill my days with some joy, and I kept them updated on their father's condition. And we were surrounded with friends and family praying for us and Todd.

The next morning, my plan was to get to the hospital by the time visiting hours began, so I had a couple hours to calm myself and prepare friends and family with the news of Todd's current condition. I had spoken to my father-in-law when I came home the night prior, and I decided to wait a little later to call our children, more so for me in attempting to settle my soul and thoughts beforehand.

So instead, I called our boss, Tom, to tell him the news. I let Tom know that I would do what I could in handling my office responsibilities by working remotely by Todd's side. Not only was Tom our boss, but he and Todd were great friends. Tom would not hear of any of my suggestions about working, and advised me that my only job at that moment was to be by Todd's side. He did not want me to worry about anything at work, and Tom told me that our salaries would be covered until the two of us walked through the office door together. What an amazing gift he provided in lessening the financial burden and stress of trying to fit work in amongst the waiting by Todd's bedside, dealing with doctors and nurses, and keeping family and friends updated. I hadn't realized that it would be a full-time job for me. Tom and I finished our conversation with a prayer, and I went to get started on this new journey God set before me.

I spoke to Anna and Jacob on the phone and explained the situation. Their concerns brought a desire to come home and be with me and be by their father's side. I encouraged them to focus as best as they could on their studies, as their father would want them to. There was nothing to do at the hospital except to sit and wait, and Dad would not want them to do that. I promised them I would keep them updated on his progress and they could call and text me whenever they wanted.

After the phone calls were made, exercising done, and getting ready for the day to sit with Todd in his hospital room, I packed up a bag with my iPad, notebook, smoothie, and my papers about some of the research I had found about COVID and Remdesivir. I wanted to understand as much as I could about this virus and how it affected parts of the body and be able to make an informed decision for him, with me now being his advocate. I picked up my bag and purse and headed off to the hospital to spend the day.

When I arrived in Todd's room, the attending doctor was making his rounds and introduced himself to me. He asked me to step over to his computer screen to look at Todd's chest X-ray, and explained his x-ray should show a black area where the lungs were. But there was no black on the X-ray. It was all white as snow. This was not good news. Not only was Todd dealing with ARDS (Acute Respiratory Distress Syndrome) and a bacterial infection, but he had also developed pneumonia. A triple whammy and a lot for his lungs to heal from. The doctor explained they were not looking at day-to-day progress, rather a week-to-week progress, because the healing would be very slow. I needed to prepare myself for this process.

The doctor also explained that if Todd still required breathing assistance with the ventilator after two weeks, they would have to perform a tracheotomy, in which an opening is made at the front of his neck so his breathing tube could be inserted into his windpipe. Otherwise, Todd's vocal cords could be damaged if the tube was left down his throat for too long. At this point, Todd needed three times the amount of oxygen of an average person. He was considered in critical condition.

All of this information was a lot for me to take in. The doctor excused himself to finish his rounds with the other ICU patients on the floor—many others as COVID patients, and I turned my attention to Todd. He was still in the prone position, and it had helped get his oxygen saturation levels up. The nurse explained that Todd was in the inflammatory stage of COVID, which was good. It meant he was progressing through the expected stages of the virus. I was relieved to hear such news. I scooted the big recliner chair next to Todd's bed and settled into spending the day with him. I spent the day talking to him, watching our favorite HGTV show, *Hometown*, and fielding many calls and texts from family and friends. During my phone calls, my in-laws, my brother-in-law, Matt, and I were conversing with one another about their arrival from out of town to visit Todd.

We had to coordinate visiting times so everyone could have a moment to spend with him, since COVID hospital rules dictated only one person at a time could go up to his room. The attending nurse advised me that the family care representative was merely the name given to the person who was visiting Todd at the time; it did not need to be solely one person for his entire stay. If only I had known! Each visitor was given a special placard and a mask upon their arrival. We would take turns handing off the placard to those who came to visit. We would make it work so everyone could spend time with him.

While I was finishing up my calls, another doctor on Todd's care team walked in. He was the nephrologist, handling Todd's care for his kidney function. The doctor explained that the medications given to Todd to dry up the fluid in his lungs has caused his kidneys to become distressed. Another strike. I was learning how our bodies need a delicate balance, otherwise things can go awry very quickly. The doctor had been watching Todd's kidney function and explained that if they do not start producing output within the day, he would place an order for dialysis for Todd. If not, waste and toxins would build up in his system. It also meant my first of many forms of consent I needed to sign for his care because a procedure would need to be performed to surgically implant a catheter into the vein of his neck for access during treatment.

Another care team doctor was a physician from the Infectious Disease Department. He introduced himself and asked me if I had any questions.

As a matter of fact, I did. I began to pull my notes out on the clinical trials of Remdesivir, because it was quite clear from the last doctor that Todd's kidneys were having issues, and my knowledge of this drug being pulled from the study was due to half of the recipients dying from kidney failure. That result concerned me greatly. But before I was able to open my mouth to ask him, he informed me that he would not listen to any Google research or questions related to COVID that are not in the realm of CDC protocol. He shut me down in speaking about other treatments for my husband, not even any additional nutritional support, such as vitamin C therapy.

Well now. I decided immediately that he was one that I didn't care to have in my space, if he wasn't willing to be open to answer any questions I had about my husband's care. I found anytime I asked this particular doctor about some of Todd's symptoms or expressed my concern for them, he would simply shrug his shoulders and say, "It's just COVID." He chose not to discuss anything but the protocol the hospital set forth, and his arrogance towards our first meeting and the subsequent interrogation of Todd's medical choice of not being vaccinated left me with a bad taste in my mouth. I found myself quite disturbed. My husband was a human being, not a tic on their totals.

BECAUSE OF TODD'S VACCINATION STATUS, I felt I needed to tread lightly with the staff. I was afraid to push the envelope for fear Todd would be retaliated against and have care withheld, since I could not be with him 24-7. And Todd was not in the condition to be transferred to another hospital, much to the urging of many of my friends who worked in the medical field.

After the team of doctors left, I spoke to the nurse about my inquiries on the virus and Todd's care. I was trying to understand how the virus moved through the body, damaging organs along the way. I comprehended that part of COVID. What I didn't understand was that as each organ was affected, the timeline of damage each doctor perceived as COVID-related didn't jive with my thought process, and I needed to understand it fully for my own sake. So, I questioned the nurse, "If the doctors are saying his kidneys are affected because of the virus, does the virus hide in the body and attack the organs at a later time, kind of like a person ready to jump out from behind a door to scare someone? Does COVID burrow into the organs and hide to elicit damage later? Or was it the Remdesivir that caused the issue?" I personally felt it was the latter.

She honestly replied, "I don't know, but that is a good question that I haven't thought about. I will be sure to mention it to the doctors and get back to you." No one could ever give me an answer; only a shrug of shoulders. I was told, "It's just COVID." I don't think they knew either, or didn't want to go against anything set by hospital protocol. My confidence in the doctor's ability to provide me with information about it was waning, and we were only on day two in the ICU.

Todd's parents were in town, so I left the hospital a little earlier so they could have time to spend with him. I made my way home, exhausted but hopeful that healing was taking place, albeit slowly. I needed to remain strong in faith that Todd was in good hands, even as my trust in some of the doctors was being challenged.

Once I arrived home, I made myself an iced coffee and settled onto the front porch, hoping to de-stress from the day's events. My porch had always been an extension of my home, a place to watch the neighborhood come to life, wave to friends and neighbors out for a stroll, and even invite them to sit and chat from time to time.

But today wasn't one of those days.

I just needed to sit in stillness, to regain the strength to fight another day alongside my husband. My energy was draining quickly, worn thin by exhaustion and lack of sleep, still running on just a couple of hours from the night before. Mentally and physically, I was spent.

As I sipped my coffee, I noticed one of my neighbors visiting another home nearby. She stood wedged between the storm door and front door, chatting. COVID had recently swept through that neighbor's household. The wife had just returned from the hospital to recover at home. A relief, no doubt. I assumed she had stopped by to check in, as neighbors do.

After saying her goodbyes, she walked down their driveway, then noticed me sitting on my porch. She made her way toward my driveway, careful to maintain her distance, unaware of the whirlwind of events that had unfolded in the past 24 hours.

"Guess what?" she said, her voice bright. "They all got vaccinated, even the kids!"

I looked at her and nodded slightly, lowering my gaze.

"It still doesn't change the fact that there are no long-term studies," I replied softly. "I'll pray they don't suffer from any reactions."

I meant every word. I wanted nothing but health and safety for them. For everyone. But if she wanted to push me, I was prepared to push back, though. In truth, I barely had the energy for this conversation.

My response sent her into a tailspin.

"I can't talk to you right now," she snapped. She pointed her finger at me, her voice sharp. "You are *wrong*, Lisa. *Wrong!*"

Then, with a raised hand silencing any further rebuttal, she turned and marched out of my driveway without another word.

How had the world become so hostile over this virus? It was happening right in my own driveway.

I sat quietly through the altercation, sighed, and continued sipping my coffee in silence. That week's sermon on Matthew

15:18 echoed in my mind: "But the things that come out of a person's mouth come from the heart, and these defile them." Words reveal what is inside a person's heart.

God, please give me grace.

Opinions wouldn't change the circumstances, and they certainly wouldn't heal my husband. But what they had done was pull back the veil on how I now saw my neighbor.

And I chose to forgive her.

As a Christian, that is what I am called to do. I was trying to do it to the best of my ability given the situation at hand.

With my moment of stillness shattered, I went inside, took a hot shower, and got ready for bed, even though the summer sun had not yet set. Tomorrow was another day.

The following days held familiar updates from the doctors and nurses. There were no significant changes to report to family and friends, other than Todd being given medication to prevent blood clots and his kidneys continuing to decline.

When Todd had arrived at the hospital the previous week, his creatinine levels had been fine. But once he was transferred to the intensive care unit, his levels started to rise. The doctors suspected it was due to a reduction in his fluids, intended to "dry up" the wet pneumonia in his lungs. But in doing so, Todd's kidneys were affected.

I still couldn't shake my concerns about Remdesivir's role in his kidney failure, but no doctor would discuss it with me. Within days, Todd's output dropped to zero. Dialysis became a serious consideration. I voiced my fears, recalling the Remdesivir trial, as well as the procedure necessary to prepare him for dialysis. The nurses reassured me that this was a standard phase in the progression of COVID patients, that I shouldn't worry, as it was not unusual.

I couldn't help but wonder how many patients had been given this emergency-use drug, only to end up in the same situation. I wanted answers. I needed to understand the effects of mechanical ventilation on renal health.

But right now, I couldn't focus on that.

The damage had been done.

Instead, I turned my concentration to my husband's healing—praying, again, that by some miracle, his kidneys would begin functioning once more.

The nurses told me they had not witnessed one patient having issues with the surgery nor the treatment. The surgical team would make an incision near his collarbone to insert a tube. The procedure would be monitored closely to prevent a puncture of his lung, so the machine the tube was attached to could pump his blood out of his body, through the machine to filter and clean it, and then be pumped back in. Todd would only need a couple of treatments to wake up his kidneys. He would not survive without it. As the debris in the kidneys built up, the body would start to retain fluid, and one of the places it retains the fluid would be in his lungs. We were fighting an uphill battle.

Within a couple of days, I had my daily routine set. I kept my morning routine steady and treated my visits to the hospital like a job, arriving a little after visiting hours began so I could avoid the morning commute traffic. I had just sat my things down on the couch in Todd's room when two nurses and a respiratory therapist came into the room. One of them looked at me, but none acknowledged my presence, nor asked who I was—which I thought was a bit off.

All the staff prior to this moment had been cordial to me for the most part. Todd was still in a prone position, and they had come in to turn him over. I decided to stay in the room, and immediately regretted my decision.

One nurse commented jokingly about having to cover my husband's private area because she didn't need to see "any of that." No explanation was given to me as to how they were getting ready to do it.

They used the sheets to adjust, move, and flip Todd over, so he was now on his back. A 250-pound man, so full of life up until a few days ago, now appearing lifeless, being turned over by these three nurses with no care or compassion.

I stood and watched in horror. I was not prepared for the emotion that came over me, and tears fell down my face. I was speechless.

But that wasn't the worst of it.

One of the nurses began to brag about being excited in getting her second COVID shot and mimicked giving herself a shot in the arm. The other nurse laughed and commented how uneducated anti-vaxxers were, knowing full well that my husband did not receive the vaccine, as it was indicated in his file—and in all capital letters, I found out later.

My jaw dropped, and I could not form any words of rebuke from my mouth. My worst fears were confirmed. There was bias amongst the staff about the vaccination status of patients. Staff that were treating my husband. How was I going to be able to leave him each day, knowing he was being treated with as much compassion as any other patient?

My husband no longer had a voice. I was now his voice, his advocate, and I was not allowed to be by his side 24-7. I opened my mouth to voice my displeasure, and again nothing came out; only tears running down my face. The two nurses left the room, leaving me with the respiratory therapist standing across from me, with Todd in the bed between us.

Regaining my composure, with a shaky voice, I said, "Can I say something to you?"

I began to cry again and expressed my distress in listening to them mock my husband as he lay in bed intubated, unable to defend himself, all because of his vaccination status. I told her it was unacceptable and unprofessional. I continued to express my dismay in how the nurse commented about my husband's physicality, as I stood there listening.

The therapist apologized for the nurses' behavior and said the one nurse jokes around and says things like that to ease the tension on the floor, but assured me that none of it was directed at Todd. I begged to differ. At that point it didn't matter what she said, the emotional damage was done, and my trust in the staff treating my husband was fully fractured. One of the nurses who assisted in turning Todd over came into his room later to apologize to me. In hindsight, I wish I had filed a formal complaint about the incident, but I didn't, in the protection of my husband.

Lord, Hear my cries. I don't think I'm strong enough.

PART OF THIS BATTLE WAS not only in fighting alongside Todd for his healing, but also the spiritual warfare that was endured.

Our current world displays evil openly, with Satan leading the way; he wants us to doubt. He wants us to believe his lies. He no longer hides in the shadows; rather, he is sneaky in how he uses others to attempt to ruin us.

The judgment I faced throughout this journey was something I had not prepared for. Words, sharp as arrows, were hurled at me, not to offer comfort, but to bring me down, even though I was already at my lowest.

I endured condemnation for standing firm as an advocate for my husband, while praying for God to grant me the strength to withstand it all. I felt the condescension of doctors when I questioned protocol, though all I sought was understanding— truth and clarity. The oath to *first do no harm* no longer felt like an unshakable principle.

Had Todd died the previous year, before the vaccine rollout, the narrative around him would have been different. He would have been seen as *such a fighter.* But now, he was treated more like a leper.

In a world that prioritizes proving a point over compassion, people justify their words without considering the pain they inflict. And these actions, this lack of humanity, came at the expense of my husband's suffering. Possibly at the expense of thousands more like him.

It wasn't fair.

Chapter Eight

MAKING PROGRESS

By Monday, on the 29th of August, Todd was making progress in his ARDS; his oxygen saturation levels were steady at 97%. The ventilator was set at 40%, down from 60% two days prior, so he was not requiring as much help. The goal was to get the oxygen levels on the ventilator down to 21%, which is what we breathe in a normal setting, I was told.

He also had a PEEP score setting on the ventilator that insured the alveoli in the lungs did not collapse, as they are prone to do. He came into the ICU with it set at 18, and today, they had lowered it to 16. He had a way to go in this area, because the goal was to get him down to a 5-8, and the doctors decided to adjust it by stepping it down 1 to 2 settings every 16 hours.

The doctors reduced his Propofol and attempted to adjust one of his other medications, but it caused his breathing to not sync up well with the ventilator, so back up the dosage went. The doctors also changed Todd's nutrition panel to help with his kidney function while he was on dialysis. The doctor explained that dialysis would actually help his lungs heal even farther because it would remove excess fluid buildup that had accumulated during the past couple days. He had hopes to see continual progress in Todd's healing.

I was ecstatic! Everything looked like it was going in the right direction. There was talk about slowly weaning Todd off the sedation to see how he would wake up. They advised me they could not do it too abruptly because some patients get very agitated and scared, so they did not want to add more stress to the patient.

Again, I needed to trust and anchor myself in God's awareness of my situation, and pray Todd would continue to move in the direction needed to get him back home safely to me and the children.

Each day since Todd arrived on the ICU floor, I would walk past the following verse painted on the hospital wall: "Do not fear, for I am with you." Isaiah 41:10. Reading this gave me peace and strength to walk into his room each day. I was grateful for the small victories, and Todd was still taking small baby steps in the right direction. That was all I could ask for from God.

GRATITUDE FILLED MY HEART AS I thought about the people in my life who took care of me behind the scenes, so I could spend my time at the hospital. I had neighbors still dropping off care packages. My brother-in-law, Matt, and nephews were taking care of the yard for me. A friend stopped by daily to take care of our two dogs and filled my refrigerator with healthy food to sustain me. Many others sent messages of research to discuss with doctors, and others supported our family through encouragement texts and calls. I knew prayers were being sent up to God for healing, strength, and courage. None of the gestures went unnoticed. There was no "things-to-do" list to be done except for me to be still and focus on Todd's healing. I was grateful for the love surrounding our family.

Each morning, I would wake up and spend time in our sunroom that Todd and my dad built over a decade ago. It became my favorite room in the house. From my favorite chair in the corner, I could look out and have a panoramic view of the yard since three sides of the room were filled with floor to ceiling windows.

Today was no different, as I sat and drank my coffee and contemplated my day. The sun coming through the windows broke my concentration and I jumped up to get ready for my walk before the summer sun beat too hard down on me.

This morning, I was met with streams of light filtering through the clouds, as the sun shone brightly behind them. "God rays," I called them. It was the last day in August, and it was a beautiful day outside. As I walked, I listened to the many Christian songs in my playlist, again in an attempt to ground myself before leaving to go to the hospital. I texted my mother-in-law to tell her I felt that God shuffled my playlist to remind me of my strength in this storm and putting on my armor for my husband.

When I arrived at the hospital, the doctor informed me that Todd was making strides in a positive direction. Todd had already been intubated for almost a week, and the doctors continued to lower his PEEP score down to a setting of 14, and his oxygen levels were holding at 95. *Praise the Lord!* They decided to remove the Propofol fully and give him Midazolam, which he explained to me was the strength of dental surgery anesthesia. Todd's blood pressure was constantly being monitored, because if he became too hypertensive, they would not be able to pull any more fluid off of him during the dialysis treatment, scheduled for that day.

Shortly after, the dialysis technician came in for Todd's next treatment. The nurse handling Todd's treatment sat on the bench, watching Todd and periodically standing up to type in information into Todd's medical chart. He was constantly monitoring Todd's stats and adjusted his care, as needed. We both had a lot of waiting, so I asked him about the machines and how the dialysis machine worked. He explained that the big tank next to Todd's bed was a reverse osmosis tank to constantly cleanse the water before it traveled into the dialysis machine to cleanse the blood. The one on the other side of the bed filtered his blood. The goal was to pull three liters off during this treatment; so far 1½ liters were pulled and there was still an hour and a half left of the three-hour treatment. With nothing to do but wait, I settled into the chair next to Todd's bed, while holding onto his hand and watching the clock on the machine countdown to zero.

The technician began talking to me about his life. He was a military veteran who served in the Gulf War. We talked about our families, his siblings, about his father dying of cancer, and how hard it was losing his father. He was dealing with his own health issue, and we talked about everyone's opinions in this world during this past year. We had differing opinions on some things and agreed on others, and it was okay, because we were able to have a calm conversation based on our beliefs and backgrounds. I appreciated the company and the sound conversation, considering Todd wasn't allowed to have more than one visitor at a time.

While the technician and I were talking, another nurse came in and performed a Doppler scan on Todd's arms and legs since there was a considerable amount of bruising, swelling, and redness around the blood pressure cuff on his right arm. The arm was fine, but they found a deep vein thrombosis blood clot in his one leg. It was not too concerning since it was in an artery and not the vein that carries blood back up to the heart. They could not tell if he had it prior to coming into the hospital or after, but they told me it was superficial. To be on the safe side, the doctor was going to add a blood-thinning medication to his IV, and continue to monitor Todd to make sure he did not bleed out or begin to have excessive bleeding. If so, then another procedure would be performed to put in an IVC filter in his left leg to prevent a pulmonary embolism.

The doctor asked me if there were any issues with bleeding. Todd's nurses mentioned a nosebleed that resolved itself a few days ago and the bleeding that was coming from his IV entry and bleeding from his dialysis port earlier in the morning. The doctor nodded and reassured me that Todd was stable, and not to worry because all of this was a "keep watch" kind of situation.

"What are his C-reactive protein and D-Dimer readings?" I asked. D-Dimer was a marker for COVID patients in their prognosis. The higher the score, the higher the risk of developing thrombosis. The C-reactive protein test measures inflammation in the body. They would investigate the D-dimer test for me, and they said Todd had received multiple C-reactive protein tests with elevated readings. The nurse reminded me that the reading can be elevated when fever is present, so they would continue to monitor it as well.

The nurse began to prepare me for what would happen when they would begin waking Todd up from his sedation. She explained that when Todd was to be weaned off sedation, she would ask him to follow certain commands—and she told me to be prepared that he would be a little groggy. They would then begin to start a spontaneous breathing trial where they turn off the ventilator to see if he could breathe on his own. This trial, as explained, could take from 30 minutes to a couple of hours, and the machine would chart Todd's activity during the entire time. If it noticed that Todd was struggling, the ventilator would kick back on and take over his breathing for him. The nurse could also adjust the oxygen to accommodate if he was breathing too fast or things of that nature. When the staff was satisfied that Todd was holding his own, the intubation tubing would be pulled out of his airway.

The nurse assured me that if any of this took place while I was not there, she would call me to come be at his side, regardless of what time it was. I was thankful for that because I did not want him to wake up alone, with no one by his side. I was so ready to see his brown eyes looking back at me. It had only been six days since I had seen them last, but it felt like eternity. I went home feeling much better about the situation and prayed that each day I saw more strides in his healing.

THE NEXT DAY, WHEN I walked in for my daily visit, I was met with the dialysis machine filling half the room and the words "Wake

Up" written in big letters on his board on the wall. Today was a new day!

I maneuvered my way over to Todd's bed, carefully stepping over the tubes red with his blood that was being filtered, and kissed him on the forehead and said hello. The ICU doctor on call came in to tell me that Todd could possibly be getting one more treatment; he was not convinced that he was out of the woods with his kidney function just yet. I noticed that Todd's dialysis port was bleeding, so the nurse cleaned the area and re-bandaged it.

The nurse at his bedside was amazing. She was so meticulous in handling Todd in such a caring way. After an attendant came in to do a bladder scan, the nurse finished up cleaning Todd's port and lowered his Fentanyl to start the process of waking him up. If he didn't pass the breathing trial, he would remain on the ventilator to try again on another day. I noticed more measurable steps in his recovery, and although he had a long way to go, he was just trucking along. I was so proud of his progress.

When I went to bed that night, my head hit the pillow a bit more softly, knowing the kids and my in-laws were coming into town over the next couple of days for the extended Labor Day weekend. I would not feel so alone, being up at the hospital all by myself. I was looking forward to seeing all their faces and giving them hugs.

Chapter Nine

LIFE IN THE ICU

I woke up the next morning a year older. It was my 49th birthday, and honestly, it was not how I would imagine celebrating it. The only thing I wanted was to see Todd looking back at me. I wanted nothing else. All I needed for this birthday and all birthdays for the rest of my life was for him to be successfully weaned off the ventilator, to hear him call me "his old lady" for the next twenty-two days. An odd request, I know, but one that was so important to me.

Being called his old lady was only allowed for a small window between our birthdays. Todd and I shared September as our birthday month, and I was older than him by a mere twenty-two days. It was a joke we shared when we first began dating, and he was relentless in making sure he filled the air with those words each time he got a chance—always looking mischievously at me as he said them. It was our thing. Maybe by the end of the day, he could call me his old lady once again. When I arrived at the hospital on my birthday, the doctors told me they would try to make it happen and wake Todd up. *Hallelujah!*

Oh, how the ending of my 48th year sitting in a hospital room was not what I had planned in my life. But then, would anyone? We can do all the planning in the world and think we are in control, but God's plans supersede any of the ones we desire to have.

I had viewed this past year as my half-life. The year 48 wasn't to be a climax in the movie where once reached, it's a rollercoaster down. At least I didn't think so, even as I stood next to Todd's hospital bed. No! I was only halfway through my Book of Life, and I wanted to make sure the rest of the chapters in my story were as exciting and filled with love, happiness, joy, and health, as most of the first half was.

I prayed Todd would be by my side experiencing all of this with me. I did not take my life for granted, and I was so grateful for all the blessings that came into it. I wanted to continue to work hard, bring Todd home and rebuild his health, and close this chapter as a lesson in taking care of one's body. I wanted Todd and me to be an example for our children of how one should be living their life. Todd and I talked about growing old together, celebrating our children's life events, meeting our future grandchildren and great grandchildren, and preparing for a future retirement that we could enjoy and live vibrantly in, not bogged down in health issues.

The year 2020 had been wrought with sadness, hindrance of one's free will, as one would see it; but for me, my 48th year had been one of my best years yet, until this last month. The final month had been sitting in a hospital room, next to my husband as he fought for his life. This was not the year I had imagined.

I walked into Todd's room and checked the monitor showing his stats. His oxygen saturation was sitting at 98%, and he was still at a 40 on his oxygen setting. The PEEP score remained at 14. His sedation was set down to a 1, which meant plans were being put in place to wake him from his coma. I had waited for this day to come! It was the best birthday present ever, in my opinion!

Unfortunately, overnight Todd began to run a low-grade fever. The nurse took off the calf pressure cuffs and boot and placed a cool, wet washcloth on his forehead to cool him down. While she tended to Todd and removed the catheter that ran from his bladder, we chatted about the upcoming weekend.

Over these past few days, this particular nurse and I talked about many things. She was very easy to talk to, and I appreciated the patience and care she took when dealing with Todd. Her care and compassion settled any concerns I had from last week's episode with the other nurses.

The subject of the vaccine mandates surfaced, and she admitted that she may be losing her job. She was newly married, and she and her husband wanted to start a family, and she was not going to get the COVID shot. For her to continue working, she explained that she and a fellow nurse on the ICU floor had to receive constant COVID tests with a negative result in order to work their shifts. Everyone working on the floor knew which two nurses did not get vaccinated, and as she revealed how stressful it was to be ostracized by her peers, she began to tear up. I gave her a big hug and told her that I appreciated her honesty and thanked her for caring so much in making my husband as comfortable as he could be, given the situation. I encouraged her to stand firm in her decision for bodily autonomy.

As I sat in the chair, watching this young nurse be vulnerable in sharing her story with me, I pondered about how much humanity suffered during this pandemic. We are all people. We all make choices that fit our health and our lives. We make choices that are best for our family, because we know them best. We love, we hurt, we cry, we get frustrated. We are all human. But this pandemic had divided us and took away much of the empathy each of us could receive or give when it came to protecting our own health. I was thankful to see glimpses of it at the hospital. My heart went out to this young nurse in her difficult situation.

I shared with her that it was my birthday and if Todd woke up and could see me, it would be the only gift I would want. The only gift I would have ever wanted in my lifetime. She wanted to make this gift happen for me but advised that due to his kidney not being able to filter out the sedation medications as efficiently as if it were working, Todd waking up was going to be a long process. I needed to be patient, she reminded me.

Patience seemed to be a common word said to me lately, and I found I was not as patient of a person as I thought I was. But I had all day to stand by his side.

At 9:24 a.m., they turned the sedation off and the machine that dosed Todd's heparin medication. We waited.

And waited.

While we waited, a physical therapist came into the room to work with Todd. She explained that physical movement in the early stages of intubation can shorten the duration—although I was praying today would be the end of him being on the ventilator. They also wanted to protect against muscle weakness and joint contracture. She began showing me some exercises I could perform to help him along with his healing during the times the therapists were not available. I was an eager learner. I wanted to do anything I could to help Todd's healing process become smoother for him.

While still waiting for his sedation to wear off, I spent most of the day responding to family and friends with thank you's for birthday wishes. I sent texts to family and friends, updating them about Todd's progress. All the while, I watched Todd intently, waiting to see any signs of movement. But there was nothing.

His blood pressure remained at a good rate, with his saturation dropping down to 96% and his oxygen level on the ventilator being raised to 60%. Still, there was no response from Todd, and he was now becoming unstable. The doctors decided to place him back on sedation and pain medications.

I LEFT THAT DAY WITH another dialysis being performed, and without seeing Todd's eyes looking back at me. I had been so hopeful. But now, I was heartbroken as I pulled out of the hospital's parking lot. Another day down, with my birthday wish not fulfilled.

I woke up the next day with renewed strength to carry on as I headed back to the hospital. It was Friday, so the kids would be heading into town after classes to spend the long weekend with me. It had only been a couple of weeks since I had seen them, but with everything going on, it felt like an eternity.

When I arrived at the hospital at my usual time, I walked into Todd's room and noticed a bag of blood sitting on the counter. I asked the nurse if it was for Todd. It was, she said, as she handed me a consent form to approve a blood transfusion for him. I took the clipboard from her. Here I was, standing at the end of Todd's bed, and I hadn't even had a chance to set my purse and bag down, nor kiss him on the forehead yet. *Breathe, just breathe.*

I looked down at the form attached to the clipboard. Would he want a blood transfusion? I didn't know how he felt about it; we never talked about any of our health concerns before this happened.

I looked up at the nurse and asked her why he needed this transfusion. She explained during a recent blood panel, it showed he was low on red blood cells, which oxygenate the blood. His blood volume should be between 11 and 13. His level was at a 7. I took a deep breath, knowing he needed it by her explanation, and signed the form. She took the clipboard from me and told me that she needed to gather some supplies and left the room.

I stood there, looking at Todd, and began to sob. With each signature, I prayed I was doing the right thing for him. But consenting to a blood transfusion for him felt all too much for me today. I was wiping my eyes when the dialysis technician came in to do another dialysis on Todd.

"What's wrong?" he asked. We had become quite comfortable in conversations, considering he came into Todd's room often for three-hour long dialysis treatments. I explained to him about walking in and seeing the blood transfusion bag on the counter and signing the consent form. He was shocked and seemed irritated that no one had informed me that it was going to take place, because it was noted in Todd's file. I shook my head. By now, I understood some staff were really good at communicating with me on Todd's care, while others were not.

God, please give me strength because I haven't been in his room for more than an hour and I am already faltering in making it through the day.

I found with this journey, Todd may take two steps forward, but one step back—and it happened daily. But today, this felt like a huge step back to me.

THE ATTENDING DOCTOR CAME IN and decided to turn off Todd's sedation once more and do another attempt to wake him up. Todd was running a slight fever again, so blood cultures were being run and an antibiotic was added to his IV as a precaution. If he passed his commands test and spontaneous breathing trial, I was really hoping that today, he would be strong enough for this progression to possibly remove his breathing tube. It was coming down to the wire to hit the two-week deadline in Todd needing a tracheotomy. The only thing standing in his way was that he had to wake up first. Also, I hoped he would be awake when the kids came for their visit.

To calm him in the waking up process, I brought his iPod loaded with all his favorite songs. I gently placed the earbuds in his ears and found one of his playlists. He loved Van Halen, Big Head Todd and the Monsters, and Chris Stapleton. In the weeks prior to his hospitalization, he mentioned that he wanted us to attend Chris Stapleton's concert scheduled in town for later that month.

Todd's iPod was full of his songs, and we would listen to them when we would travel to go see the kids at their respective colleges, or while driving to the lake to visit his parents. I remember sitting on the patio one night last summer when the song, "Simple Song" by Chris Stapleton came on. At the chorus, Todd sang out the lyrics.

After the song finished, Todd looked at me and said, "You and the kids are all I need."

He was such a simple man; simple in the way that he didn't need much of anything. Maybe a classic car to rebuild—that was his dream. We had recently begun to look at property to build a large garage for him to do so. In the meantime, he enjoyed working with our son, Jacob, on his 1971 Chevelle, and they would take weekend drives in it. He liked his BBQ, his Jack Daniel whiskey, and being surrounded by me and the kids. He had such a humble and caring spirit about him.

AND TODD WAS AMAZING IN how he cared for me. Memories flooded back as I sat next to him in his hospital bed. There was a song, a quite popular song from the 70s that was on Todd's collection. It evoked a certain sadness from my childhood anytime I heard it. It comes on the radio on the classic rock station quite often, and it was part of his song collection. When I was alone and the song came on the radio, I would simply change the station. If Todd and I were together, I would start a conversation to focus on something else until the song was over. It was no big deal after all these years, and it was something I did to deal with this trigger from childhood memories.

One day a few years ago, Todd and I were hiking in the woods and got to talking, and the subject of songs came up. I brought up this particular song, and the actions I took to not listen to it. Todd had no idea. He gently asked why I never shared this with him in all the years we were married. This was my own idiosyncrasy, and it was hard to explain, only it had to do with my mom. I tried to do so with words, but couldn't find them. He understood why and didn't need me to go any further with my attempt to explain. We had been together for over 30 years. He knew every facet of my life, including struggles in childhood, he just didn't know about this song.

We continued with our walk and the conversation was forgotten about until a couple days later. He showed me his iPod, and there was my own playlist on it, titled "Lisa's Playlist." We would listen to the playlist on mornings as we drank coffee in the sunroom or on the patio. He made a playlist of all of my and his songs meshed together, but it did not include this song. So, any time we were listening to music together, the song would never play in my presence. That was the kind of man Todd was.

So, as the music from his playlist played gently in Todd's ears, I watched TV, waited, and prayed for the man I loved. I found sitting there, waiting patiently for the process of the medication to wear off, was wearisome. And this day ended again with him running a slight fever and the port site of the dialysis catheter beginning to ooze. His nephrologist decided to continue dialysis daily and then give him a break on Sunday. A day of rest. Still nothing about him waking up, and I went home feeling defeated in this battle yet again.

Labor Day weekend was upon us, and Todd's parents and the kids came into town to visit him. We each took turns going up to the hospital room, so most of my day was spent sitting outside the hospital front doors catching up on life with family members. My days had been spent traveling from the hospital to home, and back again.

When Anna arrived at the hospital, she immediately wanted to go up to see her dad and wanted me to accompany her. I felt it was a reasonable request, so I asked the nurse if I could do so because of my daughter's fragile emotions. It was the first time she would see her father in such a compromised state. And I was told no, due to COVID rules.

Anna looked at me with tears in her eyes. She was scared, knowing what she was going to see. Her dad was her hero; she saw Todd as I FaceTime video called her, but seeing her father in person was going to affect her profoundly. I knew that.

As a mom, I stood there wanting to say *screw any COVID rules,* because my job as a parent was to protect my children. But my internal rebelliousness was overridden by my fear of possibly being kicked out of the hospital and told not to return.

I had to be an advocate for my husband right now. He was my priority. His care was my utmost concern, but I felt defeated in my own ability to protect anyone at that moment. I was angry. I gave Anna a hug and called her on FaceTime. As she left my side, up the elevator, down the ICU hall, and into her father's room to visit him for the first time since he had been in the hospital, I was with her, talking softly to her through a phone screen. *God, please be with her and give her the strength she needs right now.*

After some time, Anna returned to the lobby, handed the authorization card to her brother and sat down without a word said to anyone. She remained quiet. The emotional toll the rules of the pandemic was having with the patient's family could be seen on the faces of the people standing outside of the hospital doors, which now included my daughter.

But through hardship come the fighters. I found a community of people within the outer doors of the hospital. We gave one another support as each of us waited for our loved ones to heal. Spending many days at the hospital, I began to recognize the same people sitting on the benches outside of the lobby, as I have, when other family members or friends wanted to come up for a visit. I began talking with a young couple. The husband's mom was in the room next to Todd's in the same diagnosis and condition. We prayed for each other's family members and gathered strength and comfort in being able to speak in medical terms we were now proficient in.

I recalled the sermon at church was a much-needed listen for me in remembering that even though there were setbacks, after setbacks, after setbacks, and we have every reason to be discouraged, upset, or frustrated, all things will be restored. I needed to hear that.

I had to have faith and patience that there was a staff of amazing doctors and nurses who would provide Todd with the necessary support so he could heal and come home. It is on God's time, not mine—nor Todd's.

Today, the wife of this young couple walked up to me to give me a hug, and I noticed her shirt said, "Y'all need Jesus." That statement just so happened to be that same statement on the front of my church bulletin that morning. God coincidences were not unnoticed.

When the time came for her mother-in-law to be called home with the Lord a few days later, she texted me asking if I was in the hospital because she needed a hug. I immediately left Todd's room to find her, comfort her, and be by her side. Since there was no reason for them to stay at the hospital, I wasn't sure if I'd ever see her again after we said our goodbyes.

Later in the day, the nephrologist checked in on Todd again and explained they were going to attempt to pull more fluid and try to balance his electrolytes. He also put Todd on blood pressure medication because it kept dropping during the last two sessions. It seems that Todd was not tolerating having too much fluid taken off his body, and by the look of his arms and legs, he was beginning to swell considerably. One more concern added to my list.

But we had little joyous cheers as Todd stirred a bit and moved his head, or lifted his arm. One of his eyelids would flutter, like he was trying to open it. We were all encouraged to talk to him during this time. Family and friends took turns going up to Todd's hospital room to visit and pray for him.

UNFORTUNATELY, THE HUSTLE AND BUSTLE of the weekend and excitement of bringing Todd out of his induced coma was too much for him, and his body became agitated. His blood pressure shot up to dangerous levels. The nurse decided to turn off the lights and pull the shades on the windows to reduce the additional sensory overload he was experiencing. At one point during one of Anna's visits with her dad, the nurse told Anna to keep her hands off of him, not to speak to him, and turn off the football game that she wanted Todd to see Jake playing in. *He was not to be touched*, the nurse demanded.

More setbacks, but this time with my children witnessing them. Up until this weekend, Anna had only seen Todd through her phone screen. To Anna, holding her father's hand and feeling it grip hers, even though it was involuntary, meant everything to her.

She FaceTimed me from his room, visibly shaken by the nurse's bluntness. As she held her phone, she explained what she was being told. I spoke gently to her, trying to soothe her anxiety, but I could feel the anger bubbling up in me again. How have we become a society where we are separated from our loved ones in their most dire time of need, and then not able to soothe them with our touch? My mind was reeling with what our world had become with this pandemic.

AS THE AFTERNOON MOVED ON and evening was upon us with visiting hours soon over, I gave my hugs and said my goodbyes to family. I went to Todd's room to gather my things and head for home. The dialysis team had already begun his treatment, and Todd became unstable, his blood pressure rising yet again. The same nurse advised me that visiting hours were over and it would be best if I went home while they continued to work on him. She assured me if there were any downward changes, I would be contacted. I walked down the hallway defeated; it was becoming a pattern that I didn't feel good about in his recovery.

How can I leave him in this state of being unstable? I wanted to be there. My fear was that I would get home and then get a call that I needed to return to the hospital. But I knew there was nothing I could do for him now. And, I wanted to believe that the doctors were doing their best to stabilize him. But as his wife, I felt I needed to be there for him, for him to have someone by his side, holding his hand. After the scolding Anna received earlier in the day, I knew in my heart it was not to be. I knew that.

The one glimmer of hope that I held onto was when he responded to my voice by turning his head towards me. I would hold on tightly to that moment and be grateful to be able to witness it. My mind went through the day's events as I laid my head down on the pillow, escaping the reality of my world, and drifted off to sleep.

I WOKE UP TO THE sun streaming through my bedroom windows. Again, today was a new day, and I prayed we could get Todd back on track and moving forward again. Thankfully, no call came through the night, and I arrived at the hospital with Todd placed back on his sedation with more medication added to his protocol. Another attempt for a dialysis treatment was scheduled later in the day.

Right now, it felt like three steps back and a baby step forward. But the doctors continued to remind me that healing comes in weeks, not days. Each day brought a new challenge, and today was no different. Todd's attending doctor came into the room to discuss their plan of action for his tracheotomy.

Todd was slowly reaching the end mark of having the breathing tube removed and a tracheotomy performed, and I was advised that I needed to make the decision to consent for this procedure. The doctor added that they also wanted to place a port in his stomach for his feeding tube, rather than having the tube go down his throat. Otherwise, the feeding tube could create issues with his vocal cords and possible infection.

His blood volume reading showed another blood transfusion was needed. *So many procedures.* How can his body heal when it is in a constant state of stress and inflammation from new surgeries? There was always a risk of infection with any new procedure, so I mentioned our family history of our livers not having the ability to detox chemicals, like acetaminophen, from our system as efficiently as others. I voiced my concerns, and asked if they could test him for homozygous MTHFR. I was, by no means, a medical professional, but I witnessed the reactions brought on by this issue, including neurological ones, so I felt my concerns were warranted to be considered. She advised that she would text the infectious disease doctor on his thoughts of this, but she would not have an answer immediately because of the extended weekend and he was not on call.

I wanted to make sure that Todd's system was supported with medications his body could handle. I signed his consent forms for the tracheotomy, scheduled for the following Tuesday, and the feeding tube port, scheduled sometime next week. The ENT doctors would assess Todd's condition up until the surgery to make sure he was a good candidate for the procedure before they would proceed. If they felt he was making progress in the coming days, the surgery would not be performed and the doctor's order would be canceled. I was really hoping that would be the case.

The doctors, again, attempted to lower Todd's sedation to allow him to wake up. His saturation levels were good, holding at a 96, and his PEEP score was continuing to be lowered, which now showed a 10, and needing only 60% oxygen.

Todd was trying his best in fighting to wake up. I knew it in my heart. *Come on, Babe, you got this!* As I sat there watching him through the day, he moved an arm or leg, and whenever I would speak to him, he would turn his head toward my voice and attempt to open his eyes. I just needed to see his eyes focus on mine, and I waited patiently for it to happen.

Unless I was signing paperwork or updating family, I didn't know what day of the week it was, nor the date on the calendar. Every night when I returned home, I would peel off the visitor sticker from my shirt and place it along the door jamb of the door in the family room that led out to the garage. Today, my stickers reminded me that I was heading to the hospital on the thirteenth day of Todd being intubated and in the ICU. Almost two weeks. Through the coming days, his progress continued to stay steady in all his statistics, and I was so grateful for it.

No news was good news, and the nurse on staff even commented, "He is having a good day." Despite everything that had happened over the Labor Day weekend, they were seeing progress in all his stats compared to last week. I was told Todd was the strongest ICU patient on the floor.

The doctor reassured me that she had full faith Todd would recover. She wanted to give me a hug, but instead said, "COVID." I nodded, and began to cry. I wanted to celebrate these small victories, but I was so mentally exhausted. His victory meant he was stable, and if he was stable, then he could rest and heal without any issues arising that his poor body needed to fight. And boy, did Todd have a fight in him!

But the stress of holding all my worries and fear were mounting, and I expressed I was having a hard day in preparation for Todd's upcoming tracheotomy scheduled for later in the day.

"Would you like for me to call in the chaplain for you?" She asked.

I could only nod, as tears dripped down my cheeks and onto the hospital room floor. She reassured me everything would be fine, and she would make sure the chaplain would be up soon to meet with me. I needed someone I could talk to that wasn't involved directly with Todd, nor with his care.

I attended church every Sunday, even with Todd in the hospital, so I could renew my faith that God would get us through this. But my strength was faltering, and I wasn't allowing myself to set my fears down at God's feet. As much as I was celebrating these small victories, I was afraid if I celebrated too early, the next hammer was going to fall.

And it did.

After the chaplain spent time with me praying for strength for me and healing for Todd, a case manager walked in and introduced herself. She was handling Todd's care file and came in to discuss LTAC, which meant Long Term Acute Care, for him upon discharge.

Discharge? I expressed my concern, as I felt he was not there yet. She agreed, but said they needed to be prepared and have all the paperwork done beforehand. She explained that due to Todd's condition, he would need to step down in his care prior to coming home, which meant the LTAC was the next step in his recovery when he awakened.

After that, Todd would need intense physical therapy to regain his ability to walk, speak, and possibly to feed himself. But all of that would be assessed in the future, once he woke up. We were in this for the long haul, she explained, with Todd possibly not returning home until around Christmastime. How can one not be able to do any of the things she mentioned by being intubated for only two weeks so far? It boggled my mind.

She handed me the file with four locations nearby, and advised me that due to the limitation of beds in many of them, Todd would most likely be placed, depending on the bed availability. She mentioned that I could request a location close to my home. *Of course*, I thought, because I would be planning on being there every day until he came home with me. I prayed that Todd would not need this option, and that all his motor skills would be intact when he woke up. But the case manager reminded me again that they wanted to prepare for it. I took the folder from her and thanked her, making a mental note to call the locations and make an appointment to tour them. As if I didn't have enough on my plate already.

Shortly after our meeting, Todd was wheeled back into his room, and I got to see his face fully without straps or a tube protruding from his mouth. His beard, now a color sprinkled with a hue of salt and pepper, was growing thick over the course of the past few weeks. He usually shaved it into a goatee, but it had grown into a full beard while in the hospital. The pads placed on his cheeks that protected the skin from pressure injury had been removed, revealing ulcers underneath. The nurse was tending to these wounds with ointment.

Two respiratory therapists walked in to check on Todd, and one of them noticed there was leakage in the vent tube. One stood on one side of Todd's bed, as the other one stood on the other side, both taking turns listening and trying to find out if the leakage sounds was an issue with the ventilator machine or Todd. One therapist was listening to his lungs and asked the other one, "Do you hear that?" They discussed that they may have to order a CT scan, and left the room with no further explanation.

The days continued with the discussion of the ability of removing Todd from mechanical ventilation before transferring him to LTAC. Moving him to the new facility seemed to be in the forefront now, with pressure being placed on me to decide which location I wanted to choose for him, if available.

The week seemed to be filled with surgeries to only accommodate his move. A surgery to place a feeding tube. A surgery to place a port for his dialysis. All these surgeries were not necessary for his healing, I felt. They were simply done to prepare him, so he could be moved from the ICU to make the bed available to another patient. It didn't seem fair he was being pushed out like this. Did he have no value? Because every life is valuable and precious, from the womb to the tomb. But I was realizing that my sweet husband was just a commodity to them.

I began to find myself sitting in his hospital room when, so many times, his alarms would be beeping. I would sit in my chair next to his bed, the anxiety rising as the beeping continued. And continued. To the point that I would have to walk down the hall to look for a nurse to help him. My husband was in the ICU, so he should have had a nurse stationed outside of his room to always monitor him, but that was no longer the case. So, what happened to him when I was not there to handle this task? I felt in my heart that they were giving up on him.

By now, it was the 10th of September. I found myself still holding out all hope that Todd would wake up. As I walked into his room to start the day, a nurse came in behind me and noticed that his oxygen was at 100%. She didn't know why, so she lowered it back down to 85%, without another word said to me. I was feeling the energy in the room had changed by all I was witnessing. I felt in my heart his care had changed.

The next day, I walked into Todd's room to find a new dialysis nurse, not the usual technician, handling the scheduled dialysis. It was a young woman. As I sat in my usual spot, the machine kept making beeping sounds because she needed to change out the filter in it. The nurse assigned to Todd's room began yelling at her to shut off the alarms. In the haste of moving the tubes around the machine, one of the tubes, now full of his blood, caught on a metal piece on the side of his bed.

I gasped as I watched the horror show happening in front of me.

I was waiting for the tube to release from the machine and witness his blood spilling all over the floor. And then, what would they do? What would I do? I wanted to scream that this was my husband, the love of my life that they were caring for, not just some lifeless body lying in a bed.

But tears formed instead. I was too devastated to speak. The young nurse quickly fixed the position of the tubing, turned off the alarms, and went back to typing Todd's statistics into the electronic chart, as if it was a usual occurrence. I had to walk out of the room. It was all becoming too much to handle at this point. Once I settled myself, I came back and gripped Todd's hand to calm the overwhelming sense of dread climbing up my back.

THE HAMMER WAS BEGINNING TO fall again. Todd was no longer syncing with the breathing machine and his breaths were like baby breaths. The doctor decided to remove Todd from the current sedative and replace it with a heavier one. Since the tracheotomy and other surgeries, he explained Todd was only able to handle one thing at a time now. *Of course, he can't!* His poor body was fighting numerous surgeries and attempting to heal from all of them, including the reason he was there in the first place! He was making progress until all of this happened!

I felt they simply were giving up on him.

I asked the nurse if the CT scan revealed any issues, and she advised me that the leak sounds the respiratory therapists heard had come from around his tracheotomy placement and incision, and it had been resolved. The MTHFR test that I requested still had not been done. When I asked the doctor again about it, his response was simply, "Why does it matter now?" *It mattered. My husband mattered!*

By the end of the evening, Todd was stable again, and I was growing weary with the stress of daily ups and downs of his treatment. My brother-in-law's girlfriend surprised me with a dinner in the parking lot, complete with table and chairs, to help relieve a bit of the stress that was building in my body. She wanted to give me a little glimpse of normalcy in my life, while Todd's brother spent time visiting Todd in his room for the evening. The September nights were still hot and humid, but I relished being able to sit outside for even a moment, and talk about life outside of the hospital.

I RETURNED HOME A BIT refreshed, and when I walked through the garage door, I peeled off my hospital guest tag from my shirt, and placed it along the door jamb. Seventeen stickers lined the doorway so far. After a quick shower, I collapsed into bed, ready to tackle another day by his side.

The next day was Sunday. That meant church, and I was looking forward to spending time in God's Word to give me the strength to continue this fight alongside my husband. I turned off the lamp next to my bed, said my prayers, and drifted off to sleep.

Chapter Ten

TODD'S PASSING

September 12, 2021 started off like any other day while Todd was in the hospital. He had been in the intensive care unit for eighteen days. The night before, I had left him in fairly stable condition. Throughout the day, the nurses had commented numerous times how stable he was, with his blood pressure in normal levels, his PEEP score at 14, and oxygen level in the 90s, and that "he was having a good day today." It allowed me to be hopeful after the past few days that he had endured. That night, I had left him with a slight fixing of his hair, a smoothing of his beard, a kiss on his forehead, and an "I love you and I'll see you tomorrow," whispered into his ear.

Yesterday, I spent it as usual, sitting next to him, watching online as our daughter's boyfriend played in his college football game, relaying plays as best as I could to Todd as he laid in the hospital bed, with the sound of the breathing machine in the room filling the air with a noise of a steady rhythm. Todd and I looked forward to watching Jake play. While we knew we may not be able

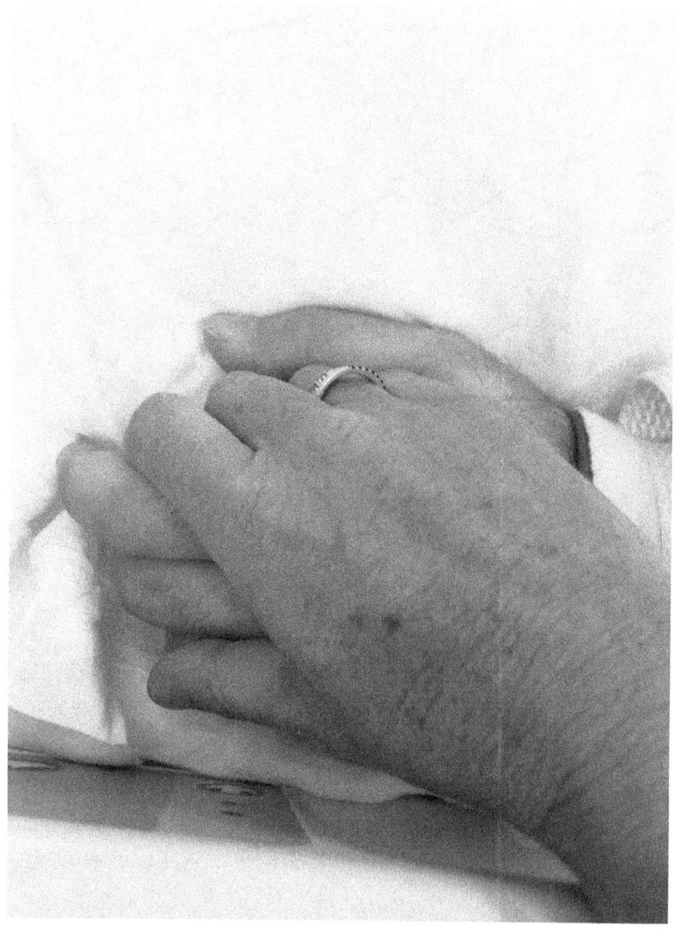

The last photo taken with him in the hospital holding his hand

to watch him on the field in person this season, we were surely ready to watch in person during the next one.

As always, I woke up that Sunday, glanced at my phone, and was relieved to not see a missed call or text from the nurse on call. I got up and prepared to go to church. Since Todd had entered the hospital, the only places I went were to see him, and to attend church on Sunday, mostly attending alone which I found ironic considering a year prior, I was afraid to sit in a pew by myself. But now, the congregation was aware of our family's crisis, so I welcomed the care and concern given when I walked through the church doors. But I made sure to keep my head down so others couldn't see the tears flow throughout the service. Going to Sunday morning services allowed me time to sit with God and settle myself to go into battle each day for my husband's healing.

When the service ended, I left the parking lot with renewed strength and headed to the hospital, refreshed for another day of sitting next to him and holding his hand, and giving family and friends updates of his daily progress.

I also had an occasional stop at my parent's house, since they lived a mile from the hospital. They would encourage me to stop by, I think mainly so they could make sure I was eating and taking care of myself as I was taking care of Todd. They usually had dinner waiting for me or sent me home with a care package, with my mom reminding me each time that my smoothie and "rabbit food," which was her nickname for my homemade trail mix, was not enough to sustain me. I would kindly nod and agree, but knowingly in my heart my appetite wasn't there to eat food anyway. My stomach had been in knots for weeks from the stress of Todd's hospitalization. As I carried my goodies to the car while saying my goodbyes to them, I remember one time jokingly saying, "I have never lived by myself, and I have had enough of it; I am ready for him to come home now." My mom just laughed and reassured me he would be home soon enough, so enjoy my alone time. I nodded and got in the car and drove home.

As I walked down the ICU hallway, with its monotone gray walls and carpet lined with doorways that I always glanced into, I would always glance at the Bible verse painted in large letters on the wall, Isaiah 41:10 that said, "So do not fear, for I am with you." Those words still gave me the peace I needed. I had walked this same hallway for weeks now and that Bible verse reminded me that I was not alone, for God was with me during this battle.

But, as I made my way to the end of the hallway where Todd's room was located, life was forever going to be changed for me. I didn't make it down the hall. One of Todd's nurses rushed up to me to block my path, as if she had been waiting for me to arrive. They knew my schedule by now. I immediately felt something was not right because the look of concern in her eyes told me what she was going to say was not good news.

"Mrs. Fulsom, you can't go in there. They are stabilizing him," she said.

I took a deep breath, and asked, "What happened? He was fine when I left him yesterday and never received a call overnight to share any concerns." I placed my hand against the wall to steady myself, and fearing her next words were going to become the reality I most feared.

Her response was almost robotic, having probably said these words to many other families during this pandemic and prior to it, she stated, "He went into cardiac arrest. It took the doctors and nurses six minutes to get a heartbeat back. They are currently stabilizing him. You can see him once they are done."

"Six minutes?" I knew what that meant. My head began to reel from what was being said to me about my husband. His brain had not had oxygen to it for more than six minutes. *His brain had not had oxygen to it for more than six minutes.* Like a letterboard playing across my brain, these words flashed through it.

I could not comprehend this. So not only were his lungs damaged, possibly needing a kidney transplant, numerous surgeries performed on him to prepare him for the long-term care facility, I had to sit with the fact that I now had to worry about his brain being permanently damaged, due to lack of oxygen. I looked down and started shaking my head in disbelief.

"Yes," she continued. "And in performing CPR to revive him, six of his ribs were broken." I immediately prayed that one hadn't punctured his lung.

I felt myself drop my bag as I slowly slid down the wall. I burst into tears. My world was crumbling right before my eyes, and there was nothing I could do about it. *God, please help me!* I prayed silently.

The very person I needed to lean on in times like this, was the very one I was holding out all hope for, the one that was lying in a hospital bed, down the hall. The hall I wasn't allowed to walk down in the attempt by the staff to protect me from seeing the traumatic events unfolding in my world. I tried to listen to the nurse explain everything the doctors and other nurses in Todd's room were doing to save his life, while I was holding my head in my hands, rocking back and forth, as my sobs filled the hallway. But all I could do was think about those six minutes and my life with this man, my husband.

Six minutes.

MY HUSBAND WAS A MAN who was a leader in his own right in his career. He prided himself on never asking for a handout, of being so humbling of all the knowledge he held in working at the same company for 25 years. He was smart. He could multitask like no one's business. He was quick witted and so funny, with his boisterous laugh filling the room. As the nurse continued to talk, I looked up and interrupted her.

"What about his brain?" I asked. Everything else can heal, I thought. I had already prepared myself for the long road ahead of recovery with him. The long-term care facility was chosen, and I knew we were in it for the long haul… but his brain. There was no way to recover from that kind of damage.

"That is not the utmost concern right now, Mrs. Fulsom. We need to get him stabilized first." She knelt, taking hold of my hand and said, "What I can tell you is that after four minutes without oxygen, permanent brain damage can occur. After we get him stabilized, we can start accessing his brain activity." *Permanent brain damage?* I can't believe this. How is he going to live a life like this? My thoughts immediately began processing what his future life would entail. What my life would now entail, as his wife, in caring for his needs. Our life. I began to mentally prepare for it.

The nurses continued to stand with me until the doctor came out of Todd's room to address me on the situation. He repeated to me what the nurse had explained and added that overnight they attempted a CRRT, continuous renal replacement therapy, which is a method of slower continuous dialysis, but it failed, due to the filter becoming filled up with blood clots. He added that based on his labs, it looked as if Todd was going into multiple organ failure.

"Mrs. Fulsom, he is in critical condition," the attending doctor advised. "I believe that in the state that he currently is in, we suspect that he will have another cardiac event by the end of the day. You need to prepare yourself, and maybe begin calling family members."

"And what about assessing his brain activity?" I asked. I knew I was grasping at straws, but I prayed the doctor would say something different than what the nurse had advised me.

"We cannot assess that at this time, but it has been compromised," was his answer. I bowed my head and nodded, feeling fully defeated. I watched as an orderly wheeled in a new ventilator into Todd's room. I looked at the doctor. "Why are you bringing this in?" I asked.

"We just want to make sure the machine isn't malfunctioning." I just stared at him, a feeling of mistrust filling my head. It seemed the damage had already been done. A couple days earlier, with Todd experiencing a leak in his tracheotomy tube, I wondered if something like that happened overnight that I was not being told about which may have caused this cardiac event. Lack of oxygen, even while using mechanical ventilation, can cause cardiac arrest. But I couldn't think of anything else except to get to my husband, who was 20 feet from me—but felt miles away.

The doctor excused himself to go back into Todd's room.

I can't do this alone.

I grabbed my phone and immediately called my parents to tell them what was going on, and that I needed them. I then called

Todd's brother, Matt, and told him to come up to the hospital, and for him to call his parents to begin the four-hour trip back to town because the news was not good.

I also had the task of informing our children. I needed to call them and tell them the news. As my heart was breaking from the turn of events, little pieces of it broke off, knowing I had to call our children and hope they would make it to his bedside to say their final goodbye. The outcome was grim, but I was still holding out for a miracle.

I DECIDED TO CALL ANNA'S boyfriend, Jake, first. My thought process was intact in thinking I needed his calm personality to handle the heaviness this type of call entailed, and I knew he would get to my daughter to comfort her. At the same time, I felt horrible that I was putting this kind of weight on his shoulders. He was only nineteen years old. The phone rang numerous times. No answer. I FaceTimed Anna next.

"Hello?" Anna said tiredly.

"Anna, It's Mom. I need you to listen to me and listen carefully," I said, trying to keep my voice steady. She immediately sat up and said, "What's wrong?"

As calm as I could make my voice sound, I said, "Dad went into cardiac arrest. He is stabilized right now, but I need you to get up, get dressed, grab your phone and laptop and get to Jake. I tried calling him and there was no answer. Can you do that for me?"

"Mom! What's going on?" Her voice pitched to a shrill. *Oh, Babygirl, I don't want this for you.*

"Just get to Jake and start driving. DO NOT go home; come straight to the hospital. Okay?" I spoke.

"Okay," she said.

"I love you. Talk to you soon," I said.

"I love you, too," she said and hung up.

NOW IT WAS MY TURN to call my son. He attended school an hour away, compared to three hours away for my daughter. The conversation was the same, in telling him to grab his things and make his way to the hospital. We said "I love you," and hung up.

As I ended my call with Jacob, my strength dissipated, and I found myself sobbing again, rocking back and forth on the hospital floor on my knees. I felt two nurses pick me up under my armpits and heard one say, "Get her in a chair." *I guess I am making a scene.* I pushed myself out of the office chair and said "No, I need to get downstairs to my parents." I glanced into Todd's room, unable to see him; two doctors were standing by his bed, so it blocked my view of him, and I was informed that I was not allowed to go into his room. Standing in the short distance between him was unbearable. I grabbed my things and ran down the hallway corridor to the elevators, praying the whole time that my parents were in the lobby. I couldn't do this alone.

My parents lived close by, but because of the rules of only one person in the room at a time, they were prevented from coming up to meet me. A few minutes later, I exited the elevator and rounded the corner of the lobby, and I spotted my dad and stepmom walking through the glass doors; I ran to them and collapsed into my father's arms.

"I'm losing him, Dad! I'm losing him!" I cried out. The full feeling of desperation overcame me. He was holding onto me as hard I was on him, with my stepmom cradling both of us, with her words of reassurance cooing into my ears.

"He's going to be okay," she assured me. What else could she say to me? Yet, I think she knew.

EVERY MINUTE FELT LIKE AN hour. We stood for what seemed like a lifetime, and I calmed myself just enough to explain what the doctors told me. Then, out of the corner of my eye, I spotted Matt coming through the hospital doors. I let go of my dad and ran to him, sobbing again that I needed him. As I was explaining what happened when I arrived at the hospital, a chaplain walked up to me and asked if I was Mrs. Fulsom.

"Yes," I replied, knowing full well I was headed back upstairs for another episode. A chaplain in a hospital doesn't just come looking for a family in a lobby if there isn't bad news attached to it.

"We need you upstairs right now. Your husband is in code blue again."

I looked at Matt and grabbed his hand. I didn't care what the rules were at this point, and decided I wasn't going to do this alone. It was all too much for me to bear by myself.

Waiting for the elevator to open was brutal. I had no patience for watching the light above the elevator door to come on, and jabbed the up button with my thumb, hoping the doors would open sooner than later. We finally made our way back upstairs within a few minutes, only to be stopped by the nurses again, telling us that we could not go into my husband's room while they were working on trying to stabilize him for a second time. She looked at Matt. Thankfully, she said nothing about him being present.

He and I just held each other in the hallway outside Todd's door, clinging onto whatever hope we had in wanting God to spare Todd's life and heal him from all the destruction that was happening to his body.

But I knew in my heart what this second cardiac event meant. The doctor had warned me. My world was shattering around me, with its shards piercing my skin into my heart. I felt powerless in defending myself from the pain of my reality. My husband of almost 30 years was planning on leaving this earthly realm, and there was nothing I could do about it.

God was calling Todd home. And, by a shred of a miracle if he survived through all of this, he would not be the Todd I knew. He would only be a shell of the man I loved with all of my heart and my soul. Regardless, I was ready to put on my armor. Whatever battle God wanted of me, I would oblige. Through sickness and in health. I just wanted my husband well and whole again. I needed him home, and I couldn't bear the knowledge of the pain he was experiencing.

Matt and I watched doctors and nurses rushed in and out of Todd's room, with their arms full of supplies. After what seemed like hours, the doctor finally walked out and talked to us.

"We have been able to revive him and get his heart started, but it is very weak, and he is in pain."

"We had to remove all medication and he is in pain," he repeated. "Your husband is not in good condition, and I need you to start thinking about the decision to consider removing him from life support. I strongly suspect that he will not be recovering from this." He said flatly.

NO. NO. NO. NO. NO. NO. My mind was screaming!

These words kept ringing in my ears. This can't be happening. Our hopes, the hopes of us rocking in rocking chairs when we were old, surrounded by our children, grandchildren, and great-grandchildren were dissolving right in front of my eyes.

There was nothing I could do but pray. I prayed that Todd wasn't in the pain the doctor said he was experiencing, and that he could just hold on for Jacob and Anna to be able to say goodbye to him. I wanted him to be able to hear their voices one last time telling him they loved him.

I knew in my mind what the doctors were telling me, but my heart was trying to bargain in trying to keep him here with us in any way possible. Deep down, I knew the truth of Todd's reality. Todd was dying, and I was going to have to let him go to his heavenly home, regardless of my selfishness in wanting him to stay here. Feeling this level of desperation in that moment was indescribable, and I found myself wanting to bargain. But with whom? God?

I whispered prayers for healing, offering anything I could in exchange for more time, more moments, more of him. I prayed for a miracle to be bestowed upon Todd, not just silently, but with every fragile thread of hope I had left. I prayed for this slow shut down of his organs to shift upward, so he could become stable, to give doctors more time to work on him, and for God to intervene on his behalf. But beneath the praying was the ache in my soul of pure helplessness, was the quiet devastating knowledge that sometimes miracles don't come.

A short time later, the doctors allowed us to enter Todd's room to be by his side and speak to him. While he was intubated, the nurses had explained that although he is in a medically induced coma, he could hear our voices. With all medications stopped, I didn't know if he could fully comprehend me and Matt standing there. I ran up to the side of the hospital bed, cradled his face into my hands, leaning in from forehead to forehead, and told him I loved him and needed him to stay here with me and the kids. I told him the kids loved him and that they were on their way to be by his side, and to just hold on, but I added that if he was in too much pain, and he needed to go, I understood. *But please hold on.*

I stepped back for Matt to talk to him. His response, in a voice as boisterous as Todd's, was of love for his brother in needing him to fight this battle and fight hard to stay here. Because we all needed him.

I looked up at Matt when he finished talking to Todd. "You understand what is going to happen, right? If they cannot stabilize him, we are going to have to let him go. He will not be able to handle much more," I expressed through my tears.

The doctor asked us to step into the hallway again to go over the plans for the day. As he was speaking, "Code Blue, Room 3106," echoed through the hallway. Todd's room. It hadn't even been ten minutes. Todd was going into cardiac arrest again.

I was feeling myself beginning to collapse onto the floor, so I held onto the wall for stability. *I can't take this. My heart can't take this.* I felt like I was standing on railroad tracks as a freight train was coming full force at me, and all I could do was stand there and be ready to be hit with blunt force. The doctor rushed into Todd's room and came out a few moments later and looked at me.

"You need to make a decision, and you need to make it now. We can no longer stabilize him!" His voice was full of urgency and demand.

If there was any moment in my life that felt like it was happening in slow motion, it was this one. Make a decision? How in the world is this happening? He had such a good day yesterday. He was the strongest patient in the ICU, I was told. I had secured a long-term care facility for him to be transferred scheduled for the following week, so he could continue his healing. I was prepared to sleep on the floor in the family room and care for his every need until we walked back into work together. I was preparing to donate a kidney to him, if need be, praying I would be a match. I was making a plan, and this was NOT part of my plan.

As Todd's wife, I would have given him anything. Our marriage vows etched in my heart: "In sickness and in health." I was preparing. But I was not ready to let him go. And our children weren't here yet.

The doctor's words knocked me back into reality.

"MA'AM, I NEED YOUR DECISION NOW! HE IS IN PAIN," the doctor urged, his words reverberating in my ears.

I looked up at my brother-in-law with only my eyes telling him what needed to happen. Todd was not going to come out of this hospital regardless of how badly I needed him to. His body was failing, his organs shutting down, and his brain activity was compromised and possibly non-existent. He was dying. And as his wife, I was forced to make the ultimate call to have them turn off the ventilator.

No one ever can prepare you for the emotions in having to make such a hard decision, especially when it is unexpected.

I nodded my head in defeat.

The doctor nodded back to me, turned, and rushed back into the room, with us closely following suit. I barely reached Todd's side to hold his hand, for the worst sentence to ever be muttered in my presence.

"Time of death is 10:21 a.m."

Chapter Eleven

TELLING THE KIDS

Time stands still in moments like this. My soul was shattering into a million pieces. I knew my life would never be the same. I watched Todd, my husband, my best friend and confidant, take his last breath. The man whose laughter could fill the room, was now silent.

The hospital staff left his room, stepping over the scattered medical debris, remnants of their failed attempt to revive him. I cradled his head in my hands, whispering countless *I love you* into his ear, praying he heard them all as God called him home.

Gently, I laid my hand over his eyes and closed them; I couldn't let anyone see them. They no longer held life, no longer able to search for me or our children. These were the eyes that once glinted mischievously as he ran toward me, ready to tickle me with that sheepish grin. The eyes I looked into when I needed comfort. The eyes that, just eighteen days earlier, met mine as he told me he loved me.

I stood there, staring at Todd, as one thought echoed through my mind—*What have I done?*

THE CHAPLAIN MUST HAVE BEEN called again, because he brought a chair to me to sit in while I held onto my husband's hand. I could not let go, as my cries of sorrow filled the room, and my body began to shake uncontrollably. I had never felt so much pain in my body as I did then.

Matt sat with his head in his hands on the couch behind me. I was not in the condition to walk over and console him, and nor was he to me. We were each in our own, dark world of despair. Minutes passed and the realization of the moment was mounting. I stood up and walked over to him and sat next to him on the couch.

"I don't think you feel I made the right decision, do you?" I asked.

"You did what the doctors told you to do," he replied.

I understood. I knew it was a response coming from hurt and pain, because he knew the love Todd and I had for one another. I knew he was not ready to say goodbye to his baby brother. The weight of sorrow in the room was heavy.

I stood and returned to the other chair; my gaze fixed on my husband's face. I knew I couldn't turn back time. *What is done is done.*

This was a decision no one should ever have to make. I had spent weeks making choices on his behalf, praying that each one was the absolute best, signing my name through tear-blurred vision. Each signature was a plea for mercy, for hope.

I knew every inch of his body. For 28 days, I had watched him fight for his life, his organs failing one by one. His body bore six broken ribs from resuscitation attempts. And now, in the middle of his third cardiac event, his heartbeat lost, the weight of his life rested in my hands with this one final decision. Even as I willed myself to take full care of him if the time came to bring him home, I knew the truth.

I knew my husband. I knew what the nurse said, what the doctor said. *So why did I feel I had made the wrong choice?*

God, forgive me.

AFTER WHAT SEEMED LIKE HOURS, Matt made his way over to the other side of the bed to tell me that he needed to go downstairs to the lobby because Stephanie had arrived.

I nodded my head and looked up and said, "I need you to do something for me. I cannot have you tell anyone Todd has died yet. You can tell them whatever, but his children deserve to hear from me that their father died before anyone else downstairs."

He nodded and left the room.

After Matt left, I held Todd's hand and stared at him. I hope he knew how wonderful of a father he was to our children.

Jacob and Todd walking hand in hand

This man LOVED his children with all his heart and soul. As any father knows and understands, a man will do anything to provide for his children. Todd took pride in working the hours he worked in order to provide for his family.

Our children never needed anything because of him.

He was proud… so proud of them. There was always a gleam in his eye when he spoke to others about the accomplishments of his children: what they were doing, where they were going to university, and the goals they were making for themselves.

As I SAT THERE WITH Todd's hand in mine, a rush of memories washed over me. Todd was such a big part of Jacob and Anna's lives and their decision making. He raised them to have a strong work ethic. Jacob started at a job at the same company we worked for when he was fourteen, and Todd reminded him, "You are my son, and you are a reflection of me. I am going to expect more from you and your work than anyone else in this company." That was just how Todd was. He guided his son in learning his job, and that was the difference.

He taught our children responsibility. He wanted to make sure they grew up to be able to stand on their own two feet. But he wasn't against rewarding them either. His rule was when they were doing what was expected of them, he would continue to reward them above and beyond anything expected. He always delivered. When Anna was a teenager with a new-to-her car, we taught her how to write a monthly check to us to help pay for the car. After she showed responsibility and paid it off, Todd told her that money was saved and would be given back to help her pay college tuition.

And Todd was the purest example of how a man should treat the woman in his life. The kids witnessed daily the protection, the love—the simple things he did to make sure I was well taken care of. They even witnessed the very rare moments of us having a bad day, and saw how we resolved it together. They witnessed every time he came home, the way he walked straight to me to give me a kiss hello. If I wasn't in the kitchen or family room, he would seek

Todd loved taking rides in Jacob's Chevelle

me out and find me. He was the epitome of a gentleman, and I am so thankful my children were raised by a man that held the importance of "honoring your wife."

Todd went to all their concerts, all their sports activities, competitions—even the many photoshoots of homecoming and prom dances, even though he would have wished to otherwise spend it watching sports on the television. Todd was there for it all.

He made sure every morning from the time they were itty, bitty babies to go into their rooms before he left for work, to kiss their foreheads. It was EVERY MORNING without question. As they grew older, Todd would go in and simply tussle their hair or give a squeeze of the toe, just to let them know his love for them. He once commented on how much he would miss that when they left for college.

When the kids came back home for a weekend from college, he would send them back with something he recently concocted in the kitchen, whether it be salsa or hot sauce. The Sunday "big breakfast" as he called them, created the word "big egg." Our children began calling fried eggs "big eggs" because they thought only adults could eat them, while the children had to eat scrambled eggs.

He loved taking drives with Jacob in his Chevelle. Every Father's Day, it was his pick of a movie at the movie theater driving up in the Chevelle, with us in tow. Game nights were a must on the weekends. If you were a friend of his children, he made sure you didn't have to open your wallet in his presence; Todd always took care of it.

He always reminded Jacob and Anna how much he loved them with an "I love you, buddy" and "I love you, Babygirl" each time they left his side.

He was the purest example of a father. And I was now given the task of telling his children he was gone.

THE RULES CHANGE IN THE hospital once a patient expires, ironically. Instead of only allowing one person in the room, we were now allowed three people, with a security guard standing by to make sure no one broke hospital rules. I thought, *He's dead, what is he going to spread?* The rules were so ridiculous, but I would not let the bitterness of them break me. I would not allow myself to be hostile at this moment.

Regardless, I stayed in Todd's room while Matt waited outside at the entrance to the hospital for my son, my daughter, and his parents to arrive from out of town, and came up periodically to check on me. My parents kept vigil downstairs. As much as I wanted to go be with them, I could not let go of my husband's hand. I didn't want him to be left alone, with the possibility of his body taken away without my knowledge. I wanted as much time as I could with him; to take in this silent time of realization of how drastically my life was going to change. The weight of knowing he wasn't going to be part of it was incredibly heavy.

I waited, mentally preparing myself for what was to come when Jacob and Anna walked through the door of their father's hospital room.

The first to arrive was our son, Jacob. This young man has been through more in his 22 years in healing from numerous reconstructive surgeries to his face from his dog bite encounter. He was my stoic one, and Matt went down to the lobby to bring him up to me. I stood outside Todd's hospital door waiting to tell him the news that no parent should have to tell their child. How am I going to tell him that his father died? I saw them make their way down the long hallway to me.

God, please give me strength.

Jacob could see the sorrow in my face, so there was no hesitation in telling him what I needed to tell him. We walked into the room, us holding each other's hands as tightly as we could, as I broke the news of his father's passing to him. I have never heard the most gut-wrenching cries come from this child ever in my life.

My heart, not having recovered from witnessing Todd's last breath, now was trying to hold together in trying to console our grown son, who waved goodbye to us just a month prior, excited to start his senior year at college. Life was good and exciting when he left, and now… it's all changed. Todd's brother left us alone in the room, so Jacob and I could have a moment together.

Anna and her boyfriend, Jake, were still on the road traveling back from their college three hours away. Anna is like her momma; she wanted to know all the details so she could plan accordingly. My little planner. My mini me. Nothing was going to prepare her for this. I texted her to ask how far away they were in their travel.

"I'm an hour and a half away," the text said.

"Have Jacob or someone call me and let me know what's going on," she texted.

I can't, Babygirl.

I could not let her find out the news of her father's passing via text or a phone call. I needed to protect her as long as I could, until she reached my sheltering arms.

"I can't right now, Babygirl." I responded.

She wanted Jacob to call her, and I texted back to her that I knew she needed answers right then—but I just needed her to come straight to the hospital so I could explain to her what was going on.

My heart was not going to be able to take much more. She attempted to call me, and I could not bring myself to answer her call. Many more calls ensued, and I left them unanswered. It was gut-wrenching to see her name flash across my phone screen and not swipe to answer it.

"Just get here," I finally texted her.

As we were waiting for Anna, Jake, and Todd's parents to arrive, we sat in Todd's room. The time spent waiting was a blur to me. I do not remember anything we talked about. Maybe we were all in such disbelief that none of us talked. I remember just staring at Todd's body, which now lay lifeless.

This man, the love of my life, now wouldn't see either of his children graduate from college, Todd would not walk his daughter down the aisle on her wedding day, nor welcome his grandchildren into this world.

Why, God… Why? Please help me understand.

MEANWHILE, I WAS TRACKING THE arrival of Jake and Anna to the hospital on Life360. As I saw they arrived, I walked to the elevators to watch from the big picture window as she and Jake exited her car. *I don't want to do this again.*

Our daughter was Todd's baby girl, that was her nickname given by him. She went to him when she was sad. They spent their weekends with Anna leaning up against Todd on the couch, scrolling through social media, as he watched a sports event on the television. She was Daddy's girl, through and through, and here I

Todd and Anna fishing at the dock

was watching her walk into the hospital knowing the news I was going to share with her would leave her broken beyond repair.

Matt went downstairs to bring Anna up, while Jacob and I waited by the elevator doors. I stood there, bracing myself, knowing the words I was about to say would shatter her heart forever.

Then the doors opened. She ran into my arms, and I broke the news to her that her dad had died. In my heart, I knew she already knew. Maybe she just needed to hear it out loud, to make it real.

Honestly, I don't remember much after that moment. Only that, with my children on either side, we walked hand-in-hand, down the hospital corridor, toward my husband, their father's room.

THE ICU STAFF GAVE US a few hours to say our goodbyes. We each took turns spending time in the hospital room, waiting for Todd's parents to arrive. To pass the time, I began to slowly gather up Todd's things; his New Balance shoes, his gray athletic shorts, his phone and charger, and all the photos I had taped onto the cabinet for him to look at when he woke up. Pictures that now served as a memory of our perfect little family.

As I was putting things into the plastic bag the hospital provided, Anna asked where Todd's green t-shirt was. This green t-shirt, a St. Patrick's Day-inspired St. Louis Cardinals t-shirt, was one of his favorite things to wear, all withered and worn from wearing it for so many years.

"We need that shirt," she said. I asked the nurse where I could possibly find it, that maybe it was left in his previous room; the room that I had only spent an hour in eighteen days ago. The room that we had said our goodbyes and "I love yous" in, not knowing they would be the last ones spoken to each other.

The nurse excused herself to go look for the t-shirt, but she had no success. She advised me the emergency staff must have cut it off of him while he was being treated the night I brought him into the hospital. I disagreed, because he sent me a photo of him in it the days after he was admitted, but I didn't have the energy to push the subject.

Another nurse came into the room and said, "I hate to interrupt, but have you decided what mortuary you would like to pick up your husband's body?" *My husband's body. Was his body now only a shell to them?* That statement seemed so surreal. *I don't know*, I wanted to scream. Instead, I just stared back at her. She patted my arm, and said, "When you decide, let me know." I managed to give her a nod.

Within the hour, Matt came in to tell me that his parents had arrived. *I am not ready for this. Not again.* The kids and I went back down the hallway to meet them at the elevators.

We waited for the doors to open once more. And when they did, my mother-in-law, still wearing sunglasses to hide her swollen eyes, enveloped all of us into a hug, as we all cried. The children and I excused ourselves to go back down to the lobby to sit with other family members so the three of them could be alone with Todd. I watched as Matt took his parents down the corridor to see their beloved son. As I was reeling from the loss of my husband,

I could not imagine the pain of a parent losing a child. I looked away just as the elevator door dinged and opened for us to step in.

Jacob, Anna, and I made our way down to the hospital lobby and out the front doors to meet with my nephews, nieces, brothers, friends, and parents. They were keeping a vigil outside, waiting for all of us to finish saying our goodbyes. By this time, they all knew of Todd's passing.

I excused myself and walked alongside the front entrance of the hospital to sit on the concrete stairs so I could catch my breath. These stairs had been my quiet space for three weeks when I needed to take a break to eat, or allow one of the many friends, family, pastor, or co-workers to visit Todd, again, due to the hospital's protocol.

I needed to call our boss, Tom. I dialed the number, and it began to ring. One ring, and he answered.

"Tom," I began to cry. "We lost him."

"Nooooo, God no," I heard the cries coming through the phone. Todd was one of Tom's best friends. It is hard to hear the agony of this man's pain. He had walked this same path in losing his wife a few years prior himself. Through my quivering voice, I began to share with him the last hours of Todd's life. I choked out the words in explaining how Todd went into cardiac arrest three times that morning, and how, on the final one, it became too much for his body to fight. I didn't know what else to say and sobbed into the phone. Tom took over at that moment and began to pray over me and my family. I told him I didn't know when I would be returning to the office, but that I would let him know any details I had in the coming days about Todd's funeral. I hung up the phone feeling the weight of the world sitting on my shoulders.

Taking a deep breath, I stood up and joined the rest of the family at the front entrance. By this time, Matt, my mother-in law, and father-in-law made their way out of the double glass doors of the hospital entrance. We all just stood there, not knowing what to do next except to head for home. As I was gathering up my own things, I realized I had not let the nurse know my decision for the mortuary.

"I need to go up and tell them where to take his body," I told Jacob.

"I'll go up with you," he said.

NOW, I TRULY BELIEVE THERE are moments when God steps in to relieve a pressure valve of sorrow. He does this by inserting a bit of lightness, if one can say that, within a horrible situation. I was not expecting the valve to be released before we even left the hospital—but it came in the form of a little old lady, in our case.

After all final notifications were made, Jacob and I stepped out of the elevators at the lobby floor, and we were met with an elderly woman struggling with the large doors that led to the emergency room.

"Do you need help, ma'am?" I asked, motioning to my son to help open the door for her.

"No, just making my way to the cafeteria," she quipped, her frail, little legs shuffling a mile a minute to move her wheelchair forward. She looked up at my son, and then down at him holding my hand.

"Is that your gentleman friend?" she asked ever so sweetly, with a glint in her eye.

What? I thought, a bit bewildered. *Did I hear her correctly?* Not a question that I was expecting to be asked. Can she not see my red, swollen eyes, and tear-streaked face? *Give her grace,* I thought. *Give her grace. She does not know.*

"No, it is not. This is my son," I answered, being as kind and patient as I could muster, as he and I began making our way through the lobby to the main doors. She clearly had not heard what I had said.

"IS THAT YOUR GENTLEMAN FRIEND?" her voice bellowed through the lobby again. Her words stopped me in my tracks.

This can't be happening, I thought, as I shook my head and quietly sighed with a slight chuckle at the lunacy of the situation.

"No! This is my SON; my husband just DIED," I yelled back. *Sorry, God,* for I was not very graceful in my delivery.

"Oh!" she said, shocked. "Prayers to your family," she hollered back, as she bowed her head and immediately began kicking her feet to continue her shuffle to the cafeteria.

I thought, *Thanks, Todd. You're already trying to put some lightness in our paths to help with this pain in whatever weird way you can.* I took a deep breath and kept walking, still holding onto my son's hand.

Jacob and I walked through the lobby door, and I promised myself that I would never walk through them ever again.

No one is never prepared to say goodbye and certainly not prepared for walking out of the hospital room for the last time and leaving your loved one behind, nor leaving in the most unexpected ways of exiting the hospital, as we just did.

I expected to walk out of that building, with Todd in tow. But now, I walked through the doors with only a bag of his things in my hand.

And me, with the newly acquired title of widow.

Chapter Twelve

COMING HOME

As I walked into our home, knowing Todd was not going to follow behind me, I felt an emptiness I knew would never be filled.

The house was quiet. I stood in the middle of the family room, looking around as if I was waiting for him to walk around the corner to greet me with his, "Hey, Honeybear," greeting. I could picture him sitting on the couch. It was so vivid; I felt I could reach out and touch him. This house was our home for 21 years, and although he left for the hospital 27 days ago, I could still feel his strong presence in it.

We bought this home to build our family. The memory of walking into it for the first time and seeing the bookshelves I pictured being filled with the many books I would read to our children, flanking the fireplace—I knew this was the house for us. The backyard was parklike, with its gradually sloping up hill, perfect for sled riding in the winter months.

I had also dreamt of having a two-story house, one where I could hide our daily messes upstairs if company stopped by. To me, it was perfect. Our son, Jacob, was sixteen months old when we moved in on an autumn day in late September 2000. Three days later, I found out I was expecting our second child. We waited to find out if she was a boy or girl at the first cry when she entered the world. We named her Anna, after my paternal grandmother. Our family was complete.

Life runs pretty fast when babies and toddlers are in tow. At that time, I was finishing up my bachelor's degree in Elementary Education at one of the local universities, with a few more semesters left to finish.

Todd cradling Jacob as a newborn

The years we spent building onto and decorating the house made it our home. Todd and I both loved spending weekends lounging in the sunroom, drinking coffee on Sunday mornings and discussing our life. Todd had designed and constructed his dream outdoor kitchen, fitted with a drop-in grill he lovingly called "Bessie," with the inside joke that if he called Bessie hot, I knew he wasn't talking about another woman. Todd loved that grill, with its stainless steel cover and rotisserie features.

Our home was the hub for all of our children and their friends to converge on during the weekends and holidays. There wasn't one weekend during our children's adolescent and teenage years where we did not have an extra place set at the table, but usually more than one. Todd was such a masterful cook that he always made more than we could eat, and their friends were all welcome to have a seat at our table. Many of them would stop by the house on a Friday night to hang out with us until Anna or Jacob returned home from a football game. Our home was open to their many friends. I recalled one friend who showed up with a bowl full of cereal, asking if we had milk. Their friends knew they were always welcome. We built memories and love in this home.

Todd and I would spend weekends in our backyard, enjoying each other's company while discussing our future, hopes, and dreams. And sometimes—the hardships.

HARDSHIP COMES WHEN A MARRIAGE lasts as long as ours. We had seasons of it that we affectionately called our "dark years." They were the couple of years where, by the grace of God and forgiveness, we were able to make it through. We knew those seasons only made us stronger in our love.

One of these hardship-type discussions was a few weeks before he became sick. I was noticeably quiet one afternoon, mulling over my thoughts and concerns about his health. Todd was the kind of man who put everyone else first, and his work in the forefront of everything else. He was the quintessential workaholic.

To say that he had a lot of stress on his shoulders being the vice-president and operations manager of a family-owned company was an understatement. His stress level was always running high, but no one would ever guess by looking at him.

Todd's motto was "It is what it is." But his body knew. I knew. I think he did, too, but he didn't know how to verbalize it. He did not sleep well, usually running on 4 hours of sleep at night, waking up before his 3:30 a.m. alarm, and arriving at work by 5 a.m. His 12-to-14-hour workdays were filled with constant calls pertaining to jobs and inquiries from staff. He did his job of over 20 years with ease, rarely taking a break for vacation. He simply did not want to have to come back to a pile of work that would cause him more hours in the office.

After dinner, Todd usually spent time watching television to wind down, only to fall asleep on the couch by 7 p.m. Sometimes, he would make it to 8:00, but never to 9:00. I would leave him on the couch to sleep while I went to bed. Many times, he would ask me why I did not wake him up to join me in our bedroom. As much as I desired him lying next to me in bed, I knew he needed that time of uninterrupted sleep. If I were to wake him, I knew he would be tossing and turning for the rest of the night.

IN APRIL 2020, WHEN NEWS of the pandemic started to weigh down on our community and the world, my husband went into action. It added additional stress to his already-heavy workload, due to new safety rules set in place by municipalities.

A stay-at-home order was being put in place effective on an upcoming Monday, so on Saturday, Todd was on the phone non-stop until dinner time, talking to the crew foremen, other employees, his contacts at city and county utility companies, and local county governments, to get clarification of the new order. He got the required permits for our company to be able to work. He worried about crews, worried about their families, worried about which job may or may not be completed. He talked to suppliers and subcontractors. He needed to make sure his men stayed

Todd and Anna looking at a video on her phone

working to support their families. All the while, he was concerned about leaving me to handle household weekend duties and dinner.

After many hours on the phone, Todd finished his list of necessary calls and came into the kitchen, gave me a hug, and said, "I'm sorry I didn't get stuff done around the house that I was planning to."

"Umm… what?" I scoffed and then laughed, as I lovingly swatted him on the arm with my tea towel. My job as his wife was to attempt to ease his stress and get things done around the house, while he took care of the work family. That's what we did. We were a team, a well-oiled machine of a couple.

But, Todd held the additional stress of the past year in his body. I noticed he was beginning to show outward signs of the stress.

"I know something is bothering you," he said, while we sat at the patio table late summer in July 2021.

"You might as well tell me," he urged. I have always struggled to share my feelings or concerns when it may hurt the other person. I would rather hold the burden and not say anything. I wasn't sure how he would react, because not only was his stress showing physical signs, but behavioral signs were also beginning to surface in Todd's reactive behavior. He was always a calm, levelheaded person, quite joyful, and had the patience of a saint. But the past year, with all the frustrations that the pandemic brought to the surface, he became short and dismissive not only to clients, but to me and the kids. We found ourselves walking on eggshells around him often. But I knew I could not hold in my concern any longer, regardless of his reaction to my words.

"I'm worried about you," I admitted, and began to cry. He knew why. I didn't need to tell him anything other than that I was concerned. He was not taking care of his mental or physical health. It can be hard to acknowledge a hard truth, even when it is staring you in the face. Todd became emotional, and with tears in his eyes, he simply stated, "I feel trapped."

"I have so much on my plate, and everyone is relying on me," he shared. "I don't know what to do," he admitted, looking up at me for guidance and reassurance.

"The first thing I think you should do is find a doctor, have lab tests to see where you are health-wise, and then we can go from there," I reassured him.

He knew I would be all in with helping him to achieve the goals in his health that he wanted to make. We talked about his sleep schedule and his diet, and we decided he needed to make an appointment for a sleep study. After an hour or so of discussion, we put a plan in place. We decided he would call my doctor to make an appointment, with both of us praying that she would be accepting new patients. We continued the afternoon, enjoying grilling and being in the backyard, while discussing things that were happening at work and in our world.

But Todd never called and made the appointment. He became so sick, just three weeks later, that it landed him in the hospital.

I WAS JOLTED BACK TO my reality as I walked through our garage door and into the family room with full consciousness that Todd would never again walk through that door, would never again arrive home from work to come straight to me and give me a kiss hello, never go through the routine of hanging up his keys and plugging in his phone. It was mind numbing to me. None of this seemed real.

I closed the door to reveal seventeen hospital visitor stickers lining the door jamb, reminding me how many days I had sat next to his bedside, praying Todd would walk back through this door with me. The stickers were a stark reminder that I was now living my worst nightmare.

I looked down to see his sandals, the permanent place he put them next to the door as he would jokingly chide me if I moved them up to our closet while cleaning. "Woman!" he would exclaim. "Where did you put my sandals?!"

Your sandals will stay right where you left them, I thought, as I closed the garage door behind me.

THE AIR IN THE HOUSE was thick with grief. I don't think any of us knew what to do. I quickly realized that, while our home was my sanctuary while he was in the hospital, it now became my prison in his absence.

But in these times, God has a way to bring comfort into your life through friends and family. Shortly after we arrived home, there was a knock on the door. Co-workers from the office had come to give their condolences.

Our work family. Tears and embraces were shared as we all sat, dumbfounded that we would never hear Todd answering the phone, his deep voice coming from his office. Todd had such a deep, boisterous voice. If he left his binder and coffee cup on the receptionist's desk, we all knew whose it was, as he was preparing to leave the office to check on jobs or go get permits. Todd always noted his time on the board as to when he would return to the office, and none of us knew how he could magically estimate the time that he wrote of returning back, but it was always spot on. He had built friendships with the men he led out in the field and the staff in the office. The loss was more than just losing a coworker. They lost a friend. We were family, and their faces reflected the pain of loss as I pulled out of each of their embraces.

As we said our goodbyes and the stress and pain of the day left me exhausted, I excused myself to go upstairs and retire for the night. After I completed my nightly routine and walked to my side of the bed, I passed the large wedding photo of us on the wall. I stood there, gazing at it. We were both so young, I thought.

What am I going to do without you?

I could feel the day's events weighing down on me. My body was no longer braced for battle, but now sagged under the weight of grief and the uncertainty of my tomorrows. It was as if every muscle surrendered to the defeat of the day's events, and the weariness of the reality of my life felt like wet sand had filled my limbs. I knew my only escape was sleep, to slip into something beyond the pain and struggle I was feeling.

I began to move the decorative pillows from my side of the bed and piled them up like a wall onto his side of it, and then climbed in. I wanted to wall off any view of the empty space, as if shielding me from the ache growing in my heart. I couldn't bear to see the space where he should have been. As I laid there, I felt his absence fully. I thought of the nights he would come upstairs to sleep instead of choosing to sleep on the reclining couch downstairs to help his sleep apnea; in playful retaliation, I would jokingly respond to him by pretending to steamroll over him and claim my spot and say, "What? This is my bed!"

I WOULD HAVE GIVEN ANYTHING to see him lying there on his side, smiling at me. I prayed that sleep would come fast, not only for rest but for mercy from the pain I felt, and that I would survive this first night alone. But, the silence in the room became too loud, and my sobs pierced the dark, releasing any strength I had left in me. I cried until my body gave in, and somewhere between the tears and the darkness, sleep finally took me.

Chapter Thirteen

PREPARATION

The next morning, I dragged myself out of bed, feeling numb. My eyes were swollen from crying, and I couldn't remember if I had even eaten anything the day before. I didn't have an appetite anyway, so I made my way downstairs to make some coffee. But I didn't want to make it myself. Todd always made it for me. That was our thing. One of his many "love taps," as we called them.

I stood there in our kitchen thinking about Todd and I. We treated our relationship like it was a house; we gave it a good, stable foundation that started with God. He knows that the only true foundation for love, blessing, peace and prosperity to exist in any other area of life is under His loving guidance. And then we had the bricks: loyalty, commitment, trust, love, faith, passion, and so on. They were important too, and they were built onto the foundation. And then we had the mortar. The mortar was the cement that kept the bricks in place. It was the small spaces that needed to be filled in or the house would fall. These love taps were the cement mortar in our relationship. The small spaces of mortar between the bricks aren't given much notice when one is looking at the entire house, but he and I both knew they were just as important. Like the mortar on a house, the daily, intentional, love taps we gave one another kept the foundation and bricks of our relationship in place.

Making coffee for me was one of Todd's love taps. It was the mortar. Coffee was always ready, and if it was the weekend, he would have a cup sitting out there for me to fill. If a holiday was approaching, he always chose a themed coffee cup, because I was a collector of many mugs, and found joy drinking out of them. No one could tell me that coffee in a themed cup doesn't taste better! It absolutely does!

I LOOKED AT THE COFFEE maker and began to cry; something so simple as making coffee was no longer the same. I stood there, realizing that I was preparing to face a lot of these little gut-wrenching moments. I found out later these moments are called "triggers."

We were scheduled to visit the funeral home later in the morning to go over the arrangements for Todd's service and burial. It was the same funeral home where we had my mother's visitation twenty-five years earlier, so I was familiar with the layout. They advised me over the phone that I could bring the clothes that Todd was to be buried in, so I would not have to make a separate trip. I was thankful for that option.

I needed to prepare for this meeting, and my widow's brain went into overdrive thinking about all the things I needed to pack for him so they could dress his body in his forever clothes, as I called them. I felt it was the duty of being his wife that I do this task on my own. So I placed my empty coffee cup in the kitchen sink, walked upstairs into our bedroom, and opened the closet door.

Todd's clothes were on the right-hand side of our closet, and I walked over and buried my face into them, trying to capture his scent. But all the clothes were clean, as I had done the laundry during the weekend when he was sick at home. There was nothing that smelled of him. I tried to smell as deeply as I could into the fibers of the cloth, but none of Todd's scent lingered.

I rifled through his suits and dress pants and chose the one he wore to most events we attended when he needed to be dressed up—which wasn't very often. Todd was a shorts and sweatshirt or t-shirt kind of guy.

Before I chose a pair of pants for him to wear, I checked all of the pockets to make sure there was nothing he had left behind. I don't know why I did this, but they were empty. Maybe I was stalling. I decided on the dark gray dress pants that he wore recently to a wedding we attended. Now the shirt. He did not have many button-down dress shirts either, so I chose a yellow one that he wore many times when he and I would need to dress up to go to a dinner or event. I grabbed his nice leather belt, and looked at the box up on the shelf that held his prized leather shoes that he bought when we were engaged to be married. He spent a pretty penny on those shoes almost thirty years ago, and they still looked as good as new. They were the shoes he wore at our rehearsal dinner, and for nice dinners while we were on our honeymoon. He kept them meticulously cared for, always placing the wooden shoe forms into them and carefully placing them back into the shoe box each time after he would wear them.

I took the shoes down from the shelf and pulled them out of the box. Bringing them to my chest, I began to cry. I didn't want to part with them. *Does he really need shoes laying in the casket?* No one was going to see his feet. I argued this point back and forth with myself for a minute or two. I contemplated even placing his Okeefe's Working Hand lotion into the bag to place in his casket, because he applied it on his feet every day. I certainly had no need for it anymore. And what about socks? *Maybe I will just bring socks to cover his toes.* A grieving brain really does go through weird thought processes during such times.

I decided against keeping the shoes, and placed them into a bag, but kept the box and shoe forms. I nixed the lotion idea, too. I walked over to his dresser and opened the drawer where he kept his socks. I grabbed a dressy, black pair and closed the drawer.

I could hear his voice in my head, complaining about wearing fancy socks. *Should I pack him a pair of underwear?* I thought. Todd would think it funny if he went commando. I quickly nixed that idea, too, and decided no, he needed them, and I plucked a pair out of his dresser drawer. A tie finished off the wardrobe.

I opened the top drawer of his dresser to reveal his wedding ring; he rarely wore it except on special occasions, due to the nature of his job and being on construction sites. I took the ring out of the drawer and slid it onto my finger next to my wedding ring; it was too big to wear on my finger, so I removed my gold necklace around my neck that held the diamond cross he bought me, threaded the ring onto it, and clasped it back around my neck. Albeit heavy, having his ring around my neck gave me a closeness to him that I needed.

I gathered all of his things and carried them downstairs to take with us to the funeral home. Another task done. *One step at a time.*

THE NEXT MORNING, THE KIDS and I met Matt in the parking lot of the funeral home. As we followed the funeral director down the hall and into the room, I made sure I focused on my breathing. What I wasn't ready for when we arrived to make the arrangements for Todd was that the meeting was being held in the same room that my mother was laid in-state so many years prior. She died, as well, at 48 years of age. The same age as Todd. *Both were so young— too young.* The director motioned us to a small table with four chairs in the front corner of the room.

For a moment, I thought about my mother.

The footsteps of unhealthy living through smoking, alcohol, and drugs ultimately led to her death of a massive heart attack. My memories of her life and her funeral intertwined with my thoughts of having to plan Todd's funeral.

WHEN MY MOTHER DIED, I was a young 23-year-old, sitting along-side my two brothers and stepmom in the same situation: making plans and wondering if all her wishes would have been met by our choosing. I didn't know a lot about her. She was young, made bad choices in life, and left her young adult children to handle all the financial burdens of this task. Regardless, we loved her and wanted her to have a proper funeral.

Because of my mother's transgressions in life, it unknowingly taught me many things in my own life about making good choices; choices that tended to be opposite of her own. I never understood it as a child, but I did as an adult.

As I looked over at my own children, stoic in helping me navigate decisions for their father's burial, I realized my mom taught me how I should live and be a good mother. And it began the first look at the pregnancy test that flashed positive in my hands with my firstborn. My mother taught me how I should raise my children and be an advocate for them. She taught me the significance of being present in my children's lives, as she was hardly present in my own. She taught me how important it is to take responsibility for my own health and well-being. She taught me grace and for-giveness, even when it took me years to do so—because I know deep down that she only knew what she was taught. I don't believe she was equipped to know how to be a good mother, and she bat-tled her own childhood wounds.

Upon her funeral and saying goodbye, I realized that is how I could honor her when Todd and I decided to start our family so many years back, because that was something she was not able to provide me, due to her own upbringing.

And sitting there in that same room, 25 years since her passing, all the memories of her visitation rushed back.

I COULD STILL PICTURE MY mother in this room, so I purposely po-sitioned my chair to keep my back to the pink lights positioned against the back wall that would flank a casket. Instead, I tried to focus on the task at hand… my husband's funeral.

The stress of the past couple of days was beginning to take a toll on me, as I tried to listen to the director go through the pricing of the funeral. I didn't have to worry about the cost, because my father called me earlier in the day to tell me that he would take care of all of the funeral expenses, until everything was settled. I felt like this was another God-provision moment. I was able to breathe with this provision of payment made. I was so grateful for my dad's generosity, and planned on repaying him once all the financial affairs, like the life insurance policy, were settled in the coming weeks. But still, the cost gave me a bit of sticker shock.

I asked Matt to join the kids and me in making arrangements for Todd because I needed his support and wanted his input in decision making. He chose the poem that went on the back of the funeral card, and we discussed options for the floral spray that would be placed across the casket. Ultimately, I decided to call a different florist and held off including it into the price.

I signed the contract with the dates and cost of the funeral, handed over my credit card to pay for it, and then it was time to follow the funeral director to the basement to pick out Todd's casket. He led us to an elevator that would take us to an area which held the caskets that we could choose from.

The elevator doors opened into a huge room of dozens of caskets. Now, Todd was not a showy man. I don't think he would have cared what we would have chosen for him, but I wanted to make sure it was nice. His body was going to reside there. That is what I kept thinking about; somewhere in this building, his body was lying, by himself, all alone. I shook my head, keeping those thoughts out of my mind, all the while grasping his wedding ring around my neck, rubbing it between my two fingers for comfort.

I allowed Jacob and Anna to make the selection for their father's casket. I felt like it was a final act of love for them. My heart ached as I watched them walk from one casket to another, their eyes scanning each one meticulously for their own unspoken requirements, with each touch of the polished woods, each glance at the lining, feeling sacred. They didn't speak much, only moving quietly among the caskets. I stood back letting them take this lead, though every fiber of me wanted to shield them from this pain. I had stood in this same room many years ago having to make the same decision for my mother, so I saw the way grief had aged them in a matter of days. They were too young to be having to make such a decision, yet they carried themselves with strength that shattered me.

They chose a casket with a deep, dignified black finish, with silver handles that lined each side. It was elegant in its simplicity, and a final vessel worthy of the man who would reside in it. We agreed to add a bronze cross and medallion to hang at the upper hinge of the casket lid. The lid itself held soft creases in the fabric designed for loved ones to tuck prayers, letters, or thoughts to be buried with their beloved. In that moment, we chose to write letters and place them there after the funeral. It felt like one last act of connection for each of us before letting go. And though the grief was heavy in the room, the thought of those letters resting close to him brought me a measure of peace. After the meeting ended, and saying our goodbye to Matt, the children and I made our way home to end the day watching episodes of *Spongebob Squarepants* to deafen the noise of sorrow.

THE VISITATION WAS SCHEDULED IN three days, so I needed to make arrangements with the cemetery and contact our pastor to make sure the church was available for the following Friday. I handed Todd's clothes to the director, and we left.

Our plan was to have the family come over the following evening. We would order Todd's favorite food, Imo's pizza, and go through photos to make collages for his visitation.

We made our way home so we could take a break and prepare to meet the caretaker at the cemetery that afternoon. I had dealt with him a few times before today's meeting, since the company that Todd and I worked for was commissioned to dig graves for them each time a person was laid to rest at the cemetery. The caretaker would call the office, and many times I would take down the information to give to our boss. I had never met him in person —until now.

We chose this cemetery because it was located down the road from our work. I had passed it so many times on my way to the office, never paying much attention to it. But I wanted Todd's final resting place to be nearby, so we could visit him when we felt we needed to be close to him. It was quaint and provided solace for us; the location was on a quiet road, away from the hustle and bustle of the world.

When the kids and I met with the caretaker, he immediately extended his condolences, and said that he wished Todd would have been vaccinated. I ignored his remark. I knew he meant well, but the timing or audience wasn't appropriate, I felt. These are the moments that God lightly placed His hand on my shoulder to bring calmness back into my being.

This man had known Todd from his many job-related dealings with him, so I knew the comment came from pain, not malice, so I wasn't angry with him.

As the caretaker pulled out the paperwork and plat map for where we could choose where Todd was to be buried, he said the burial dig was going to be handled by the company Todd and I were employed at for no cost. I wept. I knew who the main person was to perform such a delicate task, and all I could think about was the honor of the plot being dug by him. It was just one more special detail I could hold onto, knowing Todd was in good hands and taken care of, even in death.

As I was completing the information on the paperwork, the caretaker asked me if I wanted to purchase the plot next to Todd. I looked up at him bewildered. *I wasn't ready to make that decision.* I thought to myself that I would live many more years and didn't know where I would be when I died. Would I be like my Maw Maw, who lived out her life single when she became a widow herself at the age of 54? Or would I remarry, because I knew in the deepest part of my heart that I loved being loved and could not imagine living life without a loving partner by my side? A husband.

I didn't know what life would bring. I was barely taking one hour at a time, not thinking about the future. But, if I said no in front of my children, what would they think of me? For me to make such a decision seemed odd, and I immediately felt guilty in thinking all these thoughts. I loved Todd with all of my heart. I had spent weeks making hard decisions, saying the hardest goodbye in my entire life. And now, I was asked to make a forever decision on my own mortality. I wasn't ready, and simply asked out loud, "Do I have to make that decision now?"

"No," he said. "But you only have a couple of weeks to make it, because I can only hold it for so long." *That many people are dying?* I know, such an odd thought being released from my brain—and luckily not through my mouth. I understood and nodded back to him.

Jacob, Anna, and I chose a beautiful area near a tree for shade. The kids felt good knowing that their dad would be near a tree that could shade him and give him a view of beautiful colors in the autumn time. Of course, we wanted this more than him; his body was only there. We knew his soul was in Heaven, and he probably witnessed more vibrancy of color now than we could have ever imagined. Before leaving, the caretaker gave me a business card for someone to call to make the headstone, and we headed home.

Today was all too much to handle, and the kids and I spent the rest of the evening watching *SpongeBob SquarePants*, simply to escape the world and watch something that would not remind us of our current situation. We were numb from handling all of the decisions of the past couple days.

THE NEXT MORNING, ANOTHER BUSY day was ahead of us as we needed to find clothes for Jacob and Anna to wear for the upcoming days of services. Jacob had outgrown the last suit he wore, and as a pallbearer, we needed to find him a new one. I decided this would be a day that I could concentrate on my children to help drown out the sorrow in my heart.

Unfortunately, others had a different idea. As I stood, leaning up against a shelf while waiting for Jacob to finish trying on his suit at the store, Anna let out an, "Uh-oh, Mom."

"What?" I questioned. I didn't need anything else on my plate right now.

"People are starting to post about Dad on Facebook," she commented.

I wasn't too concerned. Todd wasn't on social media, and I had already posted about the arrangements of his funeral, so I knew family and friends would post about their love for Todd. He was a great guy. And I hadn't been on my phone since earlier that morning, so how much harm was there? I thought.

"Mom, one of them talked about Dad in their post and urged everyone to get vaccinated," she said.

It seemed people we knew were using my husband's journey to push their opinion on social media and make him an example for all the world to see; some even adding hashtags to get their point across. *Well, here we go.* I didn't have time for this, and my voice revealed my frustration in the nonsense the world has brought into my space.

"Are you kidding me?" I said exasperated and then sighed, feeling defeated. I couldn't take much more. I felt the unnatural, vile monster of unnecessary pain and hate that didn't belong in my world standing over me, teeth bearing with its spit dripping over my head. I waited to be devoured.

"Don't worry, I'll take care of it," Anna said with determination. She quickly sent a message to the family member to request they remove the post and asked to respect her father's legacy—not the reason for his passing.

One wouldn't post about someone passing from lung cancer and tag an announcement as to why it is important to not smoke, so why would a person feel it was okay to do that because it was COVID? It seemed the pandemic affected people's empathy for humanity, and it was pushing through into our tiny bubble in a very big way.

Anna became Todd's protector in the electronic world, and I willingly left her to the task of taking care of respecting her father's legacy. She advised me of another one, this time from a person in our neighborhood, reminding others about the importance of vaccination while speaking about Todd's passing. Good grief! Can we just remember the one who has passed and not push an agenda? But again, that was the world we were living in, and everyone had to have an opinion.

We had another person post about him on our town's Facebook page, a man who didn't even know my husband personally, but felt it was his duty to announce Todd's death to the community. It was all too much for me. *Anna, please take care of it.* I did not have the energy or strength to handle anything else.

While I was on my knees at the feet of God, praying out loud and begging for my husband's life to be spared, I felt others kept shooting arrows at our family. And now, my children suited up and spared many of these arrows from hitting my heart. But they couldn't catch them all—some hit the bullseye. All at the expense and suffering of my husband and others in his situation. I simply wanted to spend a day with my children before the visitation and funeral.

By this time, Jacob had found a suit, and Anna wanted to go to another store because she needed a dress to wear, so we headed across town to another shopping center.

As Jacob was driving, I turned on my phone to see if I had any messages. There were two, both from the neighbor that had made a post on social media about Todd. Hours earlier, she had texted me asking for my parents' phone number. The first one from her was a text about how she and her family wanted to extend their condolences for Todd's passing, and wanted to help with the food for our family during the visitation. I felt this gesture was incredibly thoughtful. I was so appreciative of the generosity, regardless of the differences we had on how we each felt COVID should be handled. *Let bygones be bygones.*

But then I read the next message from her, sent to me sometime after Anna had requested that she not use Todd's passing as a public health announcement. Her message simply said that she felt it was best if their family withdrew the providing of the food for the visitation. I burst out crying. I didn't understand what was happening. How could one offer such a gracious gift and then take it back so easily?

I quickly dialed my dad's phone number and bawled into his ear about what had just happened. I didn't know what to do. The stress of the past days was mounting at an enormous rate, and I wasn't sure I was going to be able to handle much more. I was drowning! My dad said some choice words, then calmed himself down enough to tell me that again, not to worry, he and my stepmom would take care of it all.

He advised me to text my neighbor as such. I ended the call with an "I love you" and hung up, attempting to text her back with shaky hands. As kindly as I could, I told her how thankful I was that she and her family were doing this for us, and that I was drowning in grief and could not deal with any more stress at this time. If this is what she chose to do, then so be it, and that I would love and appreciate her always. I needed to give her grace yet again. I hit send and turned off my phone.

My sanity was hanging on by a mere thread, and I could not make one more decision. Is this what a nervous breakdown feels like? If so, I was there. I just wanted to go home, cover my head with a blanket and shut out the world that no longer had my husband in it. It had only been two days. How am I going to do this life without him?

The afternoon ended with a visit from the pastor to plan the funeral. Our pastor had known Todd and his family for many years, and he officiated our wedding. He knew Todd well. We spoke at the kitchen table about the schedule of the funeral service and what scripture and songs I wanted to include during the service. I made sure I included not only Todd's original confirmation verse, but I also included our children's verses from their confirmation since all of them completed the ceremony at our church.

After our pastor left, our boss, Tom and his wife, Sheila, came by the house to check on the kids and me. They had recently celebrated their first wedding anniversary, the one that Todd and I attended that precipitated my baptism commitment. Both were widows, losing their beloved spouses a few years prior. They understood the pain that I was feeling in losing Todd. Tom was a very spiritual man; they both were. While Todd was in the hospital, he and Sheila would call nightly to pray with me for Todd's healing and for my strength.

As we stood in the kitchen, talking about the upcoming funeral, Tom said, "God tells us to take care of widows and orphans, and that is what we are called to do."

He knew both Jacob and Anna were working on their bachelor's degrees, Jacob having a year left, and Anna with an additional six months behind him. Both of our children had worked at his company while in high school, and Jacob acquired his CDL to haul equipment to job sites while taking classes at a local community college before transferring to his university to finish his mechanical engineering degree. To say Tom knows our family well was an understatement.

Looking at both kids, he simply said, "We want to pay for your schooling until you graduate. I want you to continue to strive to succeed, and not worry about the financial burden of it. But I expect you to work hard and keep your scholarships intact."

My hand slowly raised to my mouth in astonishment, and I tried to stop the sob starting to form in my throat. Immediately, tears began to form in my eyes as I looked at my children and witnessed them with the same reaction as mine. The kids and I looked at one another, bewildered at such an amazing gift.

Over the past few days, I had walked through a fog of uncertainty as to how I was going to handle all the financial burdens that were being placed upon me, including my children's college educations. And in that moment, I was reminded that God always provided, however He seemed fit. This was a gift of provision. All of us stood together, hugging one another, and thanking them repeatedly. Jacob and Anna followed suit with an outpouring of gratitude. It was an incredible gift given to us in honor of my husband, and I was so very thankful for it.

Tom and Sheila left after saying a prayer, reminding me to call them if I needed anything else and that they would be near our side in the coming days.

THE FINAL DETAIL WAS TO put together the collages of photos for Todd's visitation. The next evening was a reprieve from being out in public and dealing with all the aspects of funeral preparation. And as hard as it had been during the past week in all the decision making, in choosing just the right things to honor Todd, and the planning, I carried the weight of it with quiet resolve. I tried to hold up the ones around me, as they were doing the same for me. We leaned on each other, each of us grieving in our own way.

By evening, I allowed myself to breathe. To give myself a moment of gratitude. I looked around and felt deeply thankful. I was thankful for my children, my in-laws, Matt, and my nephews. Together, we had taken the time to choose the best photos to display Todd's life on four different poster boards.

We ordered Todd's favorite pizza from Imo's and spent the evening going through hundreds of photos, choosing ones that captured his life beautifully—the birth of his children, our wedding day, birthdays, holidays, childhood memories, lake life, his favorite things, his favorite people. I wanted to celebrate his legacy.

Todd lived an amazing life. And as I looked at the photos we collected to spotlight him, I felt incredibly blessed to have spent 31 of his 48 years with him. He was so loved. I hope he knew that.

His family honored him, not just with photos, but with intention, presence, and love. At one point in the evening, I sat on the couch, in his spot, looking around at everyone and thought, *You should be here.* We cried, we laughed, and we ate, because if you knew Todd, you knew he wanted to make sure you left with your tummy full. I would like to think we all ended that night also with our hearts full; at least I know I did.

As the evening wound down and I said our goodbyes with hugs and kisses, we all went to bed knowing how difficult the next day would be. No one will ever tell you how to prepare yourself for the things that go into getting ready to say goodbye to a loved one. One thing that I can say on repeat is take the photos, make the videos, however silly they may be, and enjoy every moment with the people God has placed in your life.

Chapter Fourteen

SAYING OUR GOODBYES

The day of Todd's visitation was a typical Midwestern day. Hot and humid. I forced myself to remain focused on staying busy enough to keep my mind from ruminating on what the evening would bring in seeing Todd again.

When we were making plans at the funeral home earlier in the week, we had decided to allow for an open casket. I was trying to settle myself, knowing these last two days would be the last time I would see his sweet face in the flesh for the rest of my life. No one can prepare you for the realization of this moment. It felt like years since I had seen him, when only it had been days.

Although I knew his spirit was with our Lord, I desperately needed to see him in physical form. I can't explain my need for this except that maybe I needed to be reminded of this horrible reality I was in. Because at this moment, it just felt like a nightmare; one that I desperately wanted to wake up from. I wanted to be assured all would be well, that he would just walk through the door and come give me a kiss on the forehead as he would always do. I shook off my thoughts and made myself busy to get through the day.

Most of the last few days had been spent filling time with preparing for this very day; saying our goodbyes and walking through the fog of grief that such a tragedy brings. I needed to make sure that I forced myself to be present and aware of every moment of how these two days would present themselves. I felt the need to try and keep as calm as I could for my children, although they seemed to be the ones holding me up.

We don't really witness the strength of our children, especially in hard times of loss. My children have been there for me through all of it. And I prayed to God to give them strength to endure these trials. My children. These precious beings God placed in my life to care for and raise, have grown into adults who lifted me up amidst their own grieving. A selfless love towards their mother.

While Todd was in the hospital, they called, FaceTimed, or texted daily, even multiple times in the day. Annie called me almost nightly to make sure I was okay. She sent encouraging texts to Todd and talked about things going on at school, and maybe a photo or two of a plate of yummy food because that's what they did. All of it was there for him to read when he was able.

When the children FaceTimed me at the hospital, they talked to Todd and encouraged him, told him they hoped he was having a good day, and told him how much he was loved. I listened and prayed he heard each of their words. Anna made videos showing Todd how she learned to shuffle playing cards, so she could show him when he came off life support.

As soon as Todd went into the hospital, the kids both wanted to come home from their colleges, but I reminded them that wasn't what their father would have wanted. He wanted them to stay and focus on their studies. He never wanted to be coddled over, especially when it came to them.

I was so thankful they were able to come home Labor Day weekend to spend time with him, hold his hand in the ICU, encourage him, and let him know they were there. And since that moment, they had been by my side. They witnessed my raw emotion and all they wanted to do was protect and shelter me. Jacob would just hold my hand because he knew I needed it. If he heard me crying, I would feel a hand on my shoulder or immediately be enveloped into a hug. My son continued to tell me not to worry because he knew worrying was a superpower of mine.

Anna had been my protector, shielding me from any negative that came into our space that wasn't a natural part of grieving for my husband and her father. She made sure I ate. They both did. She made sure I didn't forget things or handled them herself because the grief brain settles in quickly and without warning.

Jake, Anna's boyfriend, went back to school to gather things Anna needed. She left with only her phone and the clothes on her back on the day Todd died. Jake made sure he did what he needed to do so he could stay by Anna's side, and he had never left since.

These next two days were going to be tough for Jacob and Anna. They loved and adored their father. Losing him was the hardest thing they had ever endured. But despite the grief they were experiencing, they carried themselves with grace and maturity beyond their years.

To keep my mind busy that morning, I made a big breakfast for Jacob, Anna, and Jake. Jake stayed at the house with us the entire week, rather than coming back and forth from his family home located fifteen minutes away, so he could help with anything that we needed. His parents were so helpful in providing us with support during this awful time, as well; his mom had dropped off a cooler of food for us to eat and more to take to share at the luncheon that was scheduled at the house after Todd's funeral the next day. While making breakfast, I knew my job was to make sure my children were supported in care and doing so brought comfort to my morning.

Final preparations were mostly finished prior to coming into this day, so all I had to do was count down the hours until we drove to the funeral home. And we would write our letters to Todd.

Each of us wanted to write a personal letter to him that would be tucked into the folds of the casket fabric. Private letters. Letters that only the author would know of the words written on them. My letter entailed words of love and commitment that were built over thirty years of our love story. There were so many things I wanted to tell him. I knew he already knew.

I reminded Todd how he left a legacy of love to our family, as our family will grow into more generations, and I asked him to watch over us as we navigated this life without him, now and into the future. I told him I would be counting down the days until seeing him again. I signed it, *Forever and Always, Your one and only Love, Lisa.*

I finished my letter, placed it in an envelope, sealed it and set it on the kitchen table. As I went through the afternoon, I noticed the kids had placed their letters on top of mine to take them to the funeral home. I stood, staring at the pile, wondering what words they chose to write to their father. I don't think any word could have ever expressed the love they had for him, nor the sorrow they were experiencing in his absence. We all kept to ourselves, each of us lost in our own grief and trepidation of the evening that would soon lay before us. We got ready for the visitation in our own time, and I made sure not to rush them because I needed to be as calm as I could be for them, knowing how difficult the evening would be.

As we were all standing in the kitchen, dressed and ready to leave for the visitation, I looked at them and said, "Let's take a picture." I don't know why I suggested it, but I am glad I did. When I look at it now, I see strength and the permanently altered life we were getting ready to walk through. Our core family would always be a family of four.

We arrived at the funeral home as the rest of Todd's family was arriving. We had an hour before other visitors were going to come

The kids and I before heading to Todd's Visitation

to pay their respects, so we could have a private moment with immediate family. The funeral director made his way to me and asked if we were ready. I nodded, took a deep breath, and stood up. Jacob took my hand, and we entered the parlor, with Jake and Anna standing behind me, and Todd's parents, his brother, and my nephews following suit.

We entered at the end of the room, and I immediately glanced up to where Todd lay in state, and then quickly diverted my eyes. *I can't do this.* As much as I wanted to see him, the moment of realization hit me. I scanned the room for something for my eyes to focus on and my mind to settle, when I noticed the flowers and plants sent by loved ones and colleagues; they lined every inch of wall space, and the scent of carnations filled my nostrils.

I have hated carnations since smelling them in the air at my mother's funeral. The smell of them made me queasy. I squeezed Jacob's hand for stability and led him over to the tables and easels set up in the back of the room for the photo collages we brought, our wedding album, and a TV set up for us to play a looping video of photos of Todd's life in still form. I knew I was stalling. I also knew everyone in the room was looking to me for guidance. *God is my strength*, I said to myself. I placed my purse under the clothed table, took another deep breath, turned and looked at my children. I took both of their hands into mine, and we made our way up to the casket, my feet feeling like bricks trying to keep me from moving forward.

Standing at his casket, each of us lined up alongside it, we collectively looked down at him. He looked like himself, like the Todd I knew. Not the one hooked up to tubes, with his face covered in an unshaven beard. I unconsciously reached for his hand, with it resting on top of his other hand on his stomach and placed my hand on top of them. They were hard, cold, and still. Not the warm, familiar ones I reached for when I needed comfort. I wanted to wrap my fingers around them for reassurance, but I knew they wouldn't squeeze back.

Rather than quickly jerking my hand away, I quietly pulled it back, careful not to startle the kids. I didn't want to disrupt their moment with Todd, and I didn't want my own grief to spill over and drown theirs. They deserved this time with him, too. Feeling a whimper beginning to escape my throat, I swallowed it down, stepping back which allowed them to move closer to where Todd's head lay.

I watched them, standing in a space I couldn't protect them from. Their shoulders drooped, and their eyes were heavy. They stood, looking down at their father in heartbreaking silence.

I needed a moment, just to breathe, so I turned to look at all the flowers arranged around the room. *Breathe, Lisa.* I took in some deep breaths and let the air flow out of my mouth to allow a moment of whatever calm I could muster to wash over me. A pause to gather the piece of myself before others entered the room to pay their respects.

Earlier in the week, I had prepared the kids for the large number of people that would be coming to the visitation. Their father was well-loved and respected. As the doors opened for others to pay their respects, I took my rightful place next to Todd's casket, with Jake and Anna standing beside me.

As Todd's wife, my job now was to stand next to him to receive and acknowledge the hundreds of people filing into the room, patiently waiting their turn to come up and hug or express condolences to us. I refused to leave his side. I was now his protector.

Throughout the evening, people filed in and out of the room; many I knew, but so many others I did not. I was honored by the colleagues of his, whom he had built business relationships with over the years. They introduced themselves and shared a sentence or two of their fondness in working with my husband.

Todd was so much more than my husband and Jacob and Anna's father. He was well-respected in the community and the words "respected" and "enjoyed working with him" were spoken too numerous to count. One of the greatest expressions of appreciation for his work ethic and dealings came from a well-known businessman in our area, whom Todd had dealt with many times; a man who had high expectations in business dealings.

He said, "Todd never told me no; he would always say, 'I will see what I can do.' As a businessman, I appreciated and respected those words."

That night, my children not only witnessed the love of their father by so many people, but also the respect from others he carried in his career. I was saddened that sometimes it takes a funeral for others to see the impact one has on the world. I hope Todd knew that of himself. He made a difference.

It was because of Todd's humbleness that he never shared his achievements at work. He took care of people and didn't need any fanfare to remind him why it was important.

I remembered a few years back, when he was heading into work at his usual early hour of five am, he came upon a young man stranded alongside the road. Todd explained that this man didn't look much older than our son, so he pulled over to the side of the road to assist him. The lad was driving to work, but lived an hour away, and thought he had run out of gas, and his car stalled in the middle of the road. It was cold outside, so Todd helped him push the vehicle to the side of the road and took him to the local gas station, which was about 5 miles away.

Once they arrived back at the vehicle, the gas wasn't the problem; something else was wrong with it. Did he leave this young man stranded? Of course not. He took the young man back to the gas station to wait for someone to pick him up. He said he would hope others would be so kind to help our children out if they needed it in the future. Todd was unassuming and kind, always seeing the best in people. It was just who he was, a good and faithful servant.

Many family and friends came to pay their respects that night. We exchanged heartfelt memories, and our family was provided words of comfort and prayer. I was shocked to see the young couple who I had met at the hospital come to pay their respects. I hugged the wife upon seeing her and thanked them for supporting me, even as they were dealing with the loss of their family member. A shared grief.

The evening ended with all of us exhausted from intense emotion. We each retreated to our own bedrooms, not looking forward to what the next day entailed... saying our final goodbye to Todd.

Chapter Fifteen

THE FUNERAL

The day of Todd's funeral began with the sun bright in the sky, and the summer heat registering in the 90s before 7 a.m. I woke up and again, prayed to God for strength to get me through this day.

God was hearing a lot from me lately. I longed for Him to tell me why I was walking through a day such as this, and why the pain I was experiencing was for some purpose. A purpose that, even if I knew, was probably one I would not want to acknowledge. Why would God take such a good man from his family?

Those questions would have to wait, because I knew they would not ever be answered in my lifetime. I finished with an "amen," kicked off the covers, and climbed out of bed.

The funeral was scheduled in the morning, so there was not much time for me to think. I focused on the clock and mentally broke down my tasks based on the hands resting on its numbers. I did not want to forget anything. I stood in our master bathroom, fully dressed in a side-tie dress patterned with a dark blue and paisley pattern, and black pumps. As I stared at myself in the mirror, the reflection staring back spoke to me:

I am a widow.
I need to be strong.
I can do this.

I sighed back at the image. Who was I kidding? As I looked at the woman staring back at me, tears welled up in my eyes and the mascara I just applied mixed with them, causing a black trail to run down my cheek. I didn't care. This was the last day I would be able to look at my sweet husband's face on this earth except in photos and my memories.

How can one prepare for the pain and sorrow in saying such a goodbye?

I looked at the clock on the wall. It was time to leave to head to the church. I wiped my tears off my cheek and headed downstairs to gather the kids.

EARLIER IN THE WEEK, JACOB had asked if he could drive his restored 1971 Chevelle in the funeral procession in Todd's honor. I could not think of a better way for a son to honor his father than to drive the car they spent many hours fixing together, cruising, and talking about.

With my permission, Jacob spent hours the day before the funeral washing the exterior to make sure it was pristine for this day. Its cobalt blue color with silver stripes on the hood and trunk shone like a mirror.

And Todd loved the Chevelle. He loved the fact that he could live vicariously through Jacob, enjoying car shows and Sunday drives with his son until he could find the time and space to be able to own his own classic car to restore.

During this past year, Todd and I looked at different properties with large garages, so he could fulfill his dream of restoring his car, and land large enough for a humongous garden for me. When the first property we looked at turned out to be too good to be true, we decided that if it was God's will for us to move, He would make a way and His promises would hold true. So we decided to hold off continuing our search until the kids graduated college. God seemed to know the reason why that property was going to be out of reach for us; I didn't know then, but I was realizing it now.

After buying the car at age fifteen and passing his driver's test in the rain on his sixteenth birthday, determined to gain his license to have the freedom a car gives to a teenager, Jacob would ask Todd if he wanted a ride somewhere. There were many weekends, he would tell me, "We are going for a drive," and off they would go, with me listening to the rumble of the engine to announce their return hours later. On Father's Day, we would all climb into the car looking like the *That 70's Show* intro, and Jacob would escort us, with Todd sitting in the front seat and the rest of us in the back, traveling to the nearest theater for Todd's annual movie day. It was always his pick of what movie we would watch, and we would usually end the day with a run to our favorite malt shop. These are the memories I would hold dear to my heart.

I ESCAPED MY THOUGHTS AND looked up at the clock to see what time it was. It was time to head to the church. I gathered the children, and we headed out the door. The Chevelle rolled out of the garage with Jacob behind the wheel. He stopped to let me, Anna, and Jake get in. I took my place in the front, Todd's place, sitting next to Jacob on the bench seat, taking a moment and thinking of the hours Todd sat in the same spot on car rides with his son.

I am quite sure there were a lot of father-son conversations that have permeated into the fabric of the interior. "You ready?" Jacob asked.

Not really, I thought, but nodded.

He put the car in drive, and we headed toward the church. Our family church was located less than a minute from our home. Todd attended there as a child with his parents, received confirmation as an adolescent, and took me there when we began dating. We said our vows of matrimony there, baptized our children there, and our children completed their confirmation there. I was baptized there last year, with Todd and all the occupants in this Chevelle, by my side.

So many memories are stored in the church building that it only seemed fitting to have Todd's service there, too. Our pastor, who married Todd and me, would now close the circle of "'til death do you part."

Jacob pulled into the parking lot and parked near the hearse. The parking lot was beginning to fill with cars of people attending to pay their last respects to my husband.

I walked into the lobby holding onto Jacob's hand, seeing a line of family and friends ready for us to take our place in the receiving line. I glanced to the right of me towards one of the sets of double doors that led into the nave of the church. I caught a glimpse of Todd's coffin situated at the front of the church, centered in front of the pulpit.

"Mrs. Fulsom?" A voice spoke.

My name being called jerked me back to reality. I looked over to see the funeral director looking at me. He needed a moment to discuss the procedures of the service, then excused himself to gather the pallbearers and discuss the happenings of placing the coffin in the hearse afterwards. Jacob let go of my hand. He and Jake followed the funeral director, along with Todd's brother, our two nephews, and Todd's best friends, the same friends who stood as his groomsmen on our wedding day.

Once they were done, the kids and I, along with Todd's parents and brother, lined up along the wall to receive the attendants.

The church began to fill to capacity with people coming to pay their final respects to Todd; equivalent to the church filling on Easter or Christmas morning.

The immediate family reconvened alongside the wall on the right side of the church to receive visitors. Many people who could not attend last night's visitation came with hugs and condolences, each of their faces distraught with grief. The line went out the door, so I knew we would be standing here for a while before the service began.

In between the people walking through the line, I took a quick moment to check on the kids, even though they were an arm's length from me. I looked up to Jacob and over to Anna standing next to him, he in his suit and she in her black dress, and I was in awe of their strength. All these people walking through this line, expressing their loss of Todd as an uncle, nephew, co-worker, fishing buddy, or friend, suffering with grief, as I see both of my children standing, again, stoic in receipt of the grieving, all while holding their own grief, as wide as an ocean, tucked inside their heart, to wade in later. *Todd would have been so proud of them.*

A while later, our pastor walked up to me and gently said that it was time to begin the service. The rest of the line disbursed and found available seating, as we took our places at the front pews in front of Todd. I sat down and just stared at him.

This man was…

My protector
My soulmate
My high school sweetheart
My maker of coffee every day
My spoiler of gifts to the nth degree
My creator of "Lisa Eve"
My "Hello, Mr. Fulshum" (my daily greeting to him)
My cohort in the kitchen
My garden guy, as he patiently waited for the jalapeños to ripen
My children's amazing father
My best friend
My "it is what it is" philosopher
My comedic one-liner and stress-reducer
My lover
My warmer of blankets for me
My cheerleader for my health
My rock

My can-do better laundry than me do-er
My soft spot to land on when days were hard
My so much more
My everything…

For better, for worse
For richer, for poorer
In sickness and in health
To love and to cherish
Till death do us part

My husband. He was my everything. I didn't want to stop being a wife, or any of the other things that he made me. I was not meant to be alone. How was I going to navigate this life without him?

And here I was, sitting in front of his earthly shell. While his soul was rejoicing in Heaven, our souls were crushed in saying our final goodbyes to him here on earth. As I stared at him, I felt every one of those attributes he was in loving me forever lost now, never to experience again.

As Pastor Dar shared stories of Todd and our family, and the love we held for one another, photos of Todd and his life flashed up onto two big screens. My Todd, always with a smile or a cheeky grin on his face. He was so photogenic. As I listened to the Pastor share about Todd's younger years and our life together, I let the tears roll down my cheeks. I didn't know so many tears were stored in this little body of mine. I knew I was strong, and God would not give me more than I could handle. But the current situation felt like being pushed into a lake with a boulder tied to my ankle as I sank to the bottom of dark waters, never to resurface again.

I knew Todd would want me to be strong, especially for our children. But the emotions I have gone through each day since his passing, and today bringing them to a close, sent shock waves of remembrance of him. He was the love of my life.

I sat there thinking "Husbands, love your wives well. And wives, love your husbands well." I was so blessed to have this man by my side for over 30 years. He loved me fully, even in our hardships; his love was unconditional. There was no denying that fact.

As the service continued, Pastor Dar spoke of Todd's confirmation verse and the kids' confirmation verses to remind us of God's love for us, even in grief. The congregation stood in prayer, and we finished it with the Lord's Prayer. I stood there, head bowed, and recited it verbatim, the way Todd taught me so many years ago, so I could say it as my mother's ashes were spread.

For the rest of my life, every time I speak out this prayer, my thoughts will turn to Todd.

THE SERVICE ENDED, AND WE were allowed to walk up to his casket to say our final goodbyes. I looked down at Todd's body and reached out to touch his hair, moving it slightly to the side. I moved my hand down to touch his arm; the arms that held me close when I was having a bad day. I took the letter I had written to him and tucked it into the folds of the white fabric inside the lid. I stepped back to allow Jacob and Anna to do the same.

An elder escorted us and Todd's family to the prayer room, so the funeral director could take care of the final arrangements in closing the lid, which we were told could be too overwhelming for the family to witness. I appreciated not being there for that. Once finished, he wheeled Todd's casket up the side aisle and past us, and we followed behind him and back into the lobby.

We made our way out into the summer sun, and lined the walkway with family, as the pallbearers took their places alongside the casket. I could not have chosen better men to hold this honor today.

"We are going to be okay," Anna whispered into my ear with a squeeze of my hand in hers. I wasn't so sure at that moment. The very attempt to ever imagine my life being joyous again was too far reaching. How could it be?

"I know," I whispered, not believing my own words, and squeezed her hand back.

The pallbearers placed the casket into the back of the hearse, and everyone disbursed to their cars to prepare for the ride to the cemetery. Jacob started the car, and I noticed the funeral director walking towards us to speak to me, so I rolled down the window.

"We are going a certain way to the cemetery. I want to reassure you that I know where I am going. Please trust me," he said.

I didn't know what he meant by "a certain way," but I nodded, anticipating what he was going to do. The hearse pulled forward, with us following behind. Each car in the parking lot slowly took their place in line for the drive to the cemetery, which was about eight miles away. It would take approximately 15 minutes to reach Todd's final resting place.

I had driven this path for so many years on my way to work or to run errands, but it felt so much longer on this day. As we made our way up the two-lane highway, my mind was numb. My body was numb. I didn't want to feel any more anguish. I kept my gaze on the back of the hearse, seeing a peek of the coffin through the back curtained window. My life did not feel real at that moment. No one ever can explain the feeling of walking through the moments of the final goodbyes of a cherished spouse, unless one has walked through it.

I needed this day to be over because the sorrow was almost too much for me to bear. But in my heart, I knew the coming days and weeks were going to be far worse, once the kids left to go back to school and I was alone. Truly alone.

As the hearse neared the intersection of the street where it should have turned, instead it continued straight.

"Wait! This isn't right! He needed to turn back there," my voice rising to a shrill. My anxiety levels were at an all-time high, and my nervous system could not handle even the mishap of missing a turn.

"Mom, he said to trust and follow him," Jacob comforted me. He reached for my hand to calm me.

I sat back and watched the hearse; the funeral director drove through a couple of roundabouts and merged onto the divided highway, heading west, which ran parallel to where the cemetery was located. I relaxed a bit and sat back. Looking into the rear-view mirror, I witnessed a line of cars behind us following suit and merging onto the highway.

"I wonder why he is taking us this way?" I asked out loud, directed at no one in particular.

"Maybe because of the number of cars?" Anna responded, looking behind her as she sat in the back seat.

"That makes sense," Jacob said.

As we drove down the highway, I anticipated the turning of the procession onto the next street on the left, but the hearse did not slow down and kept going. *Where is he going?* And then it hit me, as the hearse slowed down and made a left onto the side street near our work. I didn't have enough time to collect my thoughts and instead burst out crying.

"He's driving past our work," I sobbed.

As we made the turn on the street where the company we worked for and the cemetery was located, the hearse slowed down in front of our office and stopped. The place Todd worked at for the past 25 years, the place he had worked his way up from a part-time welder to vice-president, was the last place he would pass on his way to his final resting place.

Through my tears, I looked over and saw our UPS delivery driver standing next to his truck in the parking lot, with his hat covering his heart as the funeral procession passed by. The company was closed for Todd's funeral, and he stood there and waited until the procession passed. I didn't think my heart could take much more. I gave up on holding my composure for the rest of the procession, which only had less than a mile left. The hearse slowly carried on down the street.

Moments later, it turned into the cemetery and made its way to the blue canopy placed for the graveside service. A sea of red company trucks followed and lined the narrow lane in front of the burial plot and weaved into the next lane. I had never felt more love and dedication from the men Todd mentored and led at work than I did today.

These were his men. The men who I later found out met at the local restaurant down the street after the graveside service to toast to Todd with a shot of Jack Daniel's whiskey, which was his favorite. As each man toasted him, he called out the nickname Todd had given him, as a show of respect. He was loved by many.

We took our seats under the canopy as the pallbearers placed Todd's coffin onto the riser. The service was short, with a prayer spoken. And when it was over, I stood up and quietly pulled one of the jalapenos out of the floral arrangement on top of the cas-

The company trucks lined up in honoring Todd at his burial
(photo credit: Jan Karsten)

ket. Most would not understand why jalapenos were present amongst the flowers, but Todd loved all things spicy. Asbestos tongue, I'd call him. The peppers were a tribute to him. As I held it in my hand, I stood there, feeling lost, not knowing what to do next.

A LUNCHEON WAS PLANNED AT our home for the immediate family, but I didn't want to leave. If I left, then that meant I was leaving Todd there. And I couldn't do that. But I knew I had to. Because I knew… once I left, that meant it was final.

People came up to us, enveloping us in hugs and speaking words of strength into our ears. I didn't know how much longer I could be strong. I felt everyone was looking at us to see what to do next, so I excused my family to head back to the house for the luncheon, knowing many family members would soon follow. I needed a reprieve from this pressure of loss.

The kids and I climbed into the car, and Jacob looked at me, with a twinkle in his eye, said, "Can I do it?" I knew exactly what he was asking.

"Yes," I said. "Your dad would like that as a final send off." I smiled and nodded.

Now, I am the kind of person who does not like attention brought onto me and will go by any means possible to avoid any kind of behavior out of the norm. I was a straight shooter. A follow-the-rules kind of gal. But my son's last call of love to his father burst forth, and I was along for the ride. With a grin just like his father's, Jacob started his Chevelle, and opened the headers with a flip of a switch, allowing the sound of the muffler to reverberate into the air. He drove through the cemetery lanes respectfully, with the car rumbling along. As he made his way out of the church parking lot and onto the main street, he punched his foot onto the gas, causing the wheels to squeal in delight, leaving a black mark on the pavement 50 feet long.

I could only imagine hearing Todd laughing up in Heaven as Jacob straightened the fishtail motion of the car, and we made our way back to the house.

That was all for you, babe.

Chapter Sixteen

GRIEF IS NOT MY FRIEND

Two days after Todd's funeral, Jacob and Anna headed back to their respective universities. I knew they didn't want to leave. Yet even while experiencing their own enduring pain, they were worried about me. And their worry was warranted, because honestly, I was scared to be by myself. I attempted to hide my feelings so as not to scare them, but I wasn't ready for them to leave. I was scared for my children, too.

I knew once the next day came, Monday, they were expected to behave, study, and be good students, even as their hearts were breaking and they were mourning the loss of their father.

Upon notifying their professors of the events of the past week, many of the teachers understood and modified the lesson plan assignments for the kids, or allowed them to skip them entirely. But a couple professors paid no mind that my children were grieving. It was a hard pill for a young person to swallow: sometimes life pays no mind to hardships. *Put your head down and keep going* seemed to be society's motto.

No adult, let alone a young person, should have to go through the grief that my children were experiencing, and also have to carry themselves as if this was not happening in their lives. My children were expected to continue performing at the level that they had before their father went into the hospital and then ultimately saying goodbye to him.

Even with the blessing of the gift received from our boss and his wife, my children had scholarships to keep up. My heart was breaking for Jacob and Anna. I prayed God would give them the strength to find the focus needed for their studies, and the comfort to lean on Him when grief filled their minds, which I knew it would.

Once they left, I found the house to be eerily quiet, more so than the night we came home from the hospital after Todd died. I found myself wandering aimlessly from room to room, not knowing what to do with myself. The house felt so empty. I was paralyzed in fear of what my future was going to hold. I no longer felt that I fit into this world. I knew who I was before Todd passed away. I was a wife, and a mother. We had a perfect family unit, and we still did, but one member was visibly absent, and my fledglings were off at college.

With my former life, I felt comfortable in my own skin. I had someone by my side who stood by me through thick and thin. Someone who would encourage me to pursue my passions. Someone who protected me from whatever life came my way. Someone I could lean into. Someone who I planned on walking arm in arm with, into a new chapter, called empty nesting. Todd and I looked forward to going on adventures together and doing things that we wanted to do because we knew we had done our job as parents; we raised our children to be independent and to live their lives fully. It was supposed to be our time.

And then he died. I felt like I hit the slide in the Chutes and Ladders game of life. I was back at the starting line, living this life solo. I no longer knew where I fit in. The job title of wife that I held so dearly and honored fully in life with him was gone. I should be relishing this time and wanting my children to live their own lives. I didn't want to be selfish with them, feeling they needed to give me attention. Although, I desperately needed it.

During the first few weeks after his passing, I felt the full effect of despair grip me tightly. I had not slept a full night since he died, or even while he was in the hospital, and my body survived on coffee because I did not have an appetite for anything else. I physically could not eat. Family members would stop by with food, and I was grateful. I attempted to eat a meal with them, with all my might, but usually one or two bites was all I could muster.

The psychological aspect of grief was beginning to take a toll on me. I knew I needed to lean on God in knowing that everything was going to be okay. But I preferred my life whole, and I could no longer believe my life was ever going to be as good as it was. I felt it was now permanently fractured.

This was not what I planned, and the fear of uncertainty hung onto me like a vice grip, because frankly I could not see even a week ahead of me, nor years.

I didn't want to do this life alone. Some nights upon arriving home, I found myself pulling into the garage, sitting in the car, debating if I should just close the garage door and leave the car running. My desire to be with Todd and escape all this pain at times became too heavy for me to hold. When these intrusive thoughts started, they would only last for a second, thankfully, because I knew the responsibility I had as a mother overrode any of my selfishness in wanting to be with their father. I did not want any more pain thrust upon my children.

Also, I knew I shouldn't be playing God in choosing my own expiration date. In my heart, I knew He still had plans for me, and they would be good. But my pain wanted to tell me otherwise. I held strong to God's promise. On those nights, I would shut off the engine, close the garage door, and go into the house to head to bed. I prayed that sleep would come soon, so I could escape my nightmare, even if it was for a few hours.

Grief and depression didn't play well, especially in those moments. I was quite aware of the darkness looming deeper into my soul, and I was ready to reach out if the pain became too much to handle on my own. I had been there before, only it was by means of a reaction to a medication a decade before.

The enemy was bearing down hard, wanting me to succumb to this darkness. I had to trust that God would carry me through it and bind up the wounds gaping open in my heart. Only I needed Him to do it as soon as possible because this pain was too great.

I knew I should fear not, for He is with me. God doesn't give us a spirit of fear. When my emotions of fear wanted to overtake me in this deep valley of grief, God reminded me of Psalm 27:1: "The Lord is my light and my salvation—whom shall I fear? The Lord is the stronghold of my life—of whom shall I be afraid." He is the light, and the stronghold in my life, so when the "what ifs" of my future consumed me, God has commanded me to be strong and courageous, for He is with me wherever I go.

The pieces of my life were scattered, but I had to have faith that God would eventually put them back together, however He deemed necessary. I was trying with all of my might to trust that it was His plan and be still. Some days, it was harder than others.

Grief envelops you like a slow rolling, thick fog.

Many of my friends and family reminded me that I needed to only take a day at a time, and on the days when it was really bad, an hour at a time. In the couple of weeks I had until I returned to work, I attempted to keep myself busy, filling my mind with tasks.

Well-meaning people sent texts and called me to check on me, but I was too overwhelmed to respond to them. I did not have the energy to express my pain, nor hold onto theirs as some were asking me to do, so the messages were responded with a "thank you," and the calls were left unanswered. I hoped they understood. I was trying to cope the best way I knew how. My nose was barely above the water in this pool of grief.

It didn't help that a week after his passing, I was faced with my first "year of firsts," as the widow community calls them. They are reminders we face that are specific, noted days that have meaning or celebration attached to them.

My first "first" was Todd's birthday. He would have turned 49 years old. He didn't even get to celebrate the big 5-0, one we could have joked about when AARP mail arrived in our mailbox on a random Tuesday. While Todd was in the hospital, I had plans to send out a message to friends and family, requesting birthday cards to be sent to me, with the intent to fill his hospital room with them, so when he woke up, he could see the outpouring of love to give him the strength to get back home. The kids and I had given him his birthday gift early, a set of the best chef knives, that he was able to use one time. I couldn't wait to see what kind of meal he would have whipped up using them. Todd was a master in the kitchen.

He used to call me his "old lady," with me being 22 days older than him. He always had the privilege of rubbing it in, which was funny. It was our thing.

This birthday was the first time I was not going to celebrate it with him by my side since he was 17 years old. This first in my "year of firsts" was a brutal reminder of Todd's absence. I wasn't looking forward to the next one looming ahead, just a week later. Our wedding anniversary.

We would have celebrated 28 years of wedded bliss together. We were married on October 2, 1993. A beautiful, autumn day, chosen because I loved fall and everything about it—the changing of the leaves, the cool weather, and the beginning of heading into all the other holidays that I also loved.

I was still on a leave of absence from work for bereavement, so when this anniversary day came, I had the day to sit and reflect on the love that he and I shared in almost three decades of marriage.

From the moment we started dating in high school, our love never wavered. I always said I would only wear two rings on my fingers: my engagement and wedding ring on my left hand, and the promise ring Todd gave me two years into our relationship. The Christmas prior to him leaving for Heaven, he changed my stance on that and surprised me with a ring that had a row of emeralds on it, to signify the birthstones of our children. We knew we had set the example for our children on how marriage was supposed to be: one filled with love, faith, laughter, selflessness, and commitment.

A couple years back, a co-worker who was celebrating a new marriage asked Todd how many years we had been married. When Todd told him, the man said that it is rare these days of long-lasting marriage such as ours, and by the time a couple reaches this milestone of years together, many of them find themselves living as roommates and not lovers. These were the words Todd said to him:

"You have to have trust, and also understand that you will have differences. But you have to learn that sometimes you are wrong and other times she is wrong, and you apologize and work through it."

We worked through a lot of stuff through the years, as many couples have done, especially being married as long as we had been. When he shared this conversation with me, I told him he had set the bar high on how a man should treat the woman he loves.

I was proud of the beautiful life we had built together. But now, I felt so heartbroken because I knew we were given this once in a lifetime kind of love, and it was cut short. I wondered if, in the future, would God grant me this kind of love a second time around, when there were so many others praying for ever having one moment of what Todd and I experienced in our marriage? I didn't know. I couldn't even fathom loving a man other than my husband, and it felt selfish of me to think I deserve a second chance at it. Still, I felt cheated. I was angry at Todd for leaving me. I knew it wasn't his fault. He fought a good fight, but I was still mad. I learned anger is part of the grieving process.

I was mad at the world we were living in, and how people treated one another, too. I was mad at the hospital for following government current protocol and the mighty dollar, because I am sure they had their hand out waiting for some government subsidy given for COVID patients, especially the patients on ventilators, who then perished like my husband. I was mad at myself for not advocating more for him than I did, fully knowing I would have done it a million times over if I knew he would have come home to me.

When anger from the world's ways came knocking on my door, I found those were the days that I wanted to throw things, smash plates onto the floor, or walk into the woods and scream the most guttural scream I could, just to release some of the pain I was feeling inside. But I remembered Proverbs 18:5 teaches, "It is not good to be partial to the wicked or to deprive the righteous of justice."

I prayed most of the hospital staff didn't overlook the atrocities the protocol brought to families like mine, and that they were only doing the best they could. I hoped they would have spoken up, protecting their patients, and that the few unfavorable hospital staff members that I encountered during Todd's stay were miniscule. I knew I would eventually request his medical records. I just wasn't ready yet.

And I was mad at God because I felt He took the love of my life away from me. He took a father away from his children. I could not understand anything that was thrust upon me and my family. After Todd passed, our son Jacob said that he would have endured a thousand times the pain of his reconstruction surgeries just to have his dad back.

I wanted to ask God, "Why? Why Todd? He was a good man. He was a good husband and father." It wasn't fair.

But is life ever fair?

I was also learning that a grieving mind plays nasty tricks. Not only was I paralyzed in fear of finances, I was also paralyzed in fear of the current situation in our world, and how volatile it seemed. I no longer had my protector. For almost thirty years, I could lay my head down on my pillow, knowing my husband was there to protect me and our children if danger ever came our way. I no longer had that.

Many people in town knew that my husband had passed away, so I felt exposed. There was a hedge of protection and comfort knowing that my children were in the home with me during the week between his passing and the funeral. But now, it was only me, by myself, in this big house. I felt vulnerable. Every night, I became obsessive in making sure all the doors to the house were locked before I retired to my room for the night, shutting and locking my bedroom door behind me. As I laid in bed, I thought about how I could climb out my window if an emergency loomed in front of me. We lived in a nice town and neighborhood, so I should not have worried. But my brain was in such grief that my thought process was in a survival-type mode, and not computing anything relating to feeling secure. Simply, I no longer felt safe.

It didn't help that my anxiety was fueling the fire of these thoughts. During the day I was fine, but at night, my mind raced with thoughts of somebody wanting to take advantage of the situation at hand. I would only pray that sleep would come fast. Unfortunately, many nights it did not. I would lay in my bed and stare into the darkness. Inevitably, I would roll over to face what would have been Todd's side of the bed, and attempt to picture him looking at me with his brown eyes, and smiling with his impish grin.

I felt so empty and alone. When I did fall asleep, the sleep was not restful. Many nights, I found myself waking up at the same time Todd would be waking up for work—3:30 a.m. As soon as my eyes opened, my thoughts turned to him. I knew in my heart I was strong and that God would not give me more than I could handle. But the motions I was going through each day of this loss would find me sobbing myself back to sleep.

Many times during those nights, I would send my prayers up to God about my fears and loss. This untethering of the life I knew was unsettling to my soul, and I lived with an ever-present pit in my stomach. So, I talked to God often during those nights. What else was I going to do? Before Todd went into the hospital, I would have my daily talks with Him, and now, I made many requests to Him—requests of peace, strength, and comfort.

THE NIGHT TODD WAS INTUBATED, I had cried out to God while speeding down the highway. I begged Him not to take my husband because I was not ready to lose him. As I fought alongside Todd in the ICU, I asked God to heal him so he could come home to us. And while standing in the hallway as Todd coded, again, I asked God why, knowing full well I would never receive an answer.

I asked Him to help me, because I couldn't do this alone. And over the course of the days in preparing for the visitation and funeral, I prayed to God and asked Him to give me strength. The supersonic kind of strength to stand tall and to give me courage as I stood in love, in faith, and steadfastness with our beautiful children by my side as we said our final goodbyes. I know He listened to it all. And God was still listening… but I felt broken.

My weight was already beginning to plummet. I don't even remember how much I slept. I just knew in the first couple of months that I slept to escape from my reality, as best I could. Friends and family continued to check on me and my children called daily, sometimes with numerous calls in a day. I was anticipating having to return to work in the coming days, as I hadn't been there since the middle of August when Todd went into the hospital.

I was also dealing with the guilt of having to make the decision to turn off the ventilator. I had the heavy weight of feeling responsible, even though the rational side of my brain told me otherwise.

ONE NIGHT, A CALL CAME from a parishioner who had lost her husband the same week as Todd, and in the same situation. She called to give me condolences. As we spoke of God's will and promises, it was then that I spoke with her about my feelings of what God thought of my decision and allowing the doctors to turn off the ventilator. My decision was weighing so heavily on my conscience, and I felt safe in sharing with her the guilt that I felt about it. She reassured me that God knew what he was doing. God was already preparing to take Todd regardless of what was happening. He knew the pain Todd was enduring at that moment. I did not. There was too much damage to his body, and he was not going to recover. God knew that. And in my heart, I knew it too.

Our talk settled my soul a little bit.

But I still sat in a darkness I could not shake.

The events of the night leading up to Todd's death were not sitting well with me. I knew I eventually needed to find the answers, but it would have to wait. What I did know was that when God called Todd home, His arms were stretched out wide, welcoming Todd. And when He surrounded my husband in His arms, God simply said, "Well done, good and faithful servant. Welcome home." God needed him for something bigger than I will ever understand. And this, I wouldn't question, as much as I wanted to.

Although the darkness of life wanted to surround me at that moment, I chose to see the light.

THE
JOURNALS

October 12, 2021

Dearest Todd,

It's been a month since you left me and the kids to go to heaven. I cry every day. I want you home. I am still in disbelief of how all this happened. I would have done anything to bring you home.

I don't know what to do with myself. The kids are at school and I am alone in this house surrounded by all of your things. I feel so alone. I go to bed alone. I wake up alone.

I am slowly getting all of the paperwork done. It is a lot. I went back to work into the office. I expected you to come downstairs like you always did. I can't bring myself to go into your office. It's just too hard. I miss you so much my heart hurts. I constantly ask why this happened. I didn't deserve losing you— you had so much more life to live and I am mad you didn't get to spend it here, with me and the kids. They miss you terribly but you would be so proud in how they are handling themselves.

I will never be the same. You were part of me—we were one. I pray for strength every night and hope you are whole and doing great things in heaven. I wish you were here with me though.

Until we meet again

Your Honeybear,

Lisa

Chapter Seventeen

THE MONTHLY JOURNALS

Upon the first month anniversary of Todd's passing, I decided to open up what I now penned as "Todd's Journal." It was a small, grey, soft-bound book that I bought while he was still in the hospital, with anticipation to fill it with all my notes and thoughts of his journey from the hospital to home. I wanted Todd to read it when he was ready, so he could see how much he endured and conquered.

But it was not meant to be. I had since transferred all my hospital notes into it, along with the daily stickers I wore when coming to visit him in the ICU. One thing missing was the photos that I took. They were taken more for him, as the nurse suggested, so he could see them when he returned back to health. There were not many photos, and I didn't think I needed the visual reminder of his ordeal, so I left them out.

I wanted to begin writing personal letters to Todd, telling him my thoughts, talking about our lives as we tried to acclimate to life without him, and how the kids were doing.

Todd used to write me letters, too. Lots of letters. Letters of love, as did I to him. So, this book became my love letters to him in Heaven.

Because I was a writer by hobby, I felt it would give me a sense of comfort and healing to have the ability to move forward from this tragedy. I knew it was going to be a one baby step in front of the other kind of process, but it was also going to be the start of me being proactive in my healing process. I knew it was likely to be a long one, too.

God strengthens His warriors. Joshua 1:9 says "Have I not commanded you? Be strong and courageous. Do not be afraid; do

First trip to watch football after Todd's death

not be discouraged, for the Lord your God will be with you wherever you go."

I had to have faith that He would strengthen me, protect me, and guide me along the way, even as hard as this journey was. I wanted to trust in learning to understand God's purpose for my life, listen to it, and follow it as best I could, regardless of the pain I felt. I knew there would be painful, emotional moments I would encounter on this journey of grief, during this first year especially. But at the same time, I hoped my book of life was filled with good stories in my existence of moving forward from this heartbreak. Stories I could share with Todd when I saw him again in Heaven; at least that is what I wanted to think. I always wanted to keep his memory in my heart.

In the meantime, I knew I needed to walk through the storm I was placed in, not around it, and give myself grace through it all. Todd always told me I was tougher on myself than anyone else, and he was right. He knew me best.

On many days after his passing, I opened my eyes each morning, thankful for this strength God provided within me, and wondered where I would be if I didn't have Him by my side through all of this. With thoughts in my head and a prayer of "God, lead the way," I would step out the door with courage to carry forth to see what life had in store for me.

I PARTICULARLY NEEDED IT ON the day I went to the cemetery to finally purchase my burial plot next to Todd, only a few weeks after he was placed in his own forever resting place. I chose to do this task by myself. And although it wasn't something I thought I would be doing at my age, the current events in my life accelerated the decision to make such an important purchase. To tell someone I bought my burial plot felt so odd to say out loud, and to ask someone to accompany me to this appointment felt even odder. So, I went alone, because I knew it was right next to where I needed to be when that time came for me to graduate to Heaven—to be next to my husband.

I never thought that (1) I would be a widow at 49, (2) that I would be purchasing a joint gravestone, which I had done the previous Friday with my parents in tow for support, and (3) that I would be buying my own burial plot. But these life altering events of the past month would be the cards dealt to me, so here I was. All these statements should have been happening 25 years or more from now, honestly. But, in Todd speak… *it is what it is.*

Even through the overwhelmingness, I found it extremely interesting how much discussion the caretaker and I had on which side I was to be placed next to Todd. Maybe that's just me; I do ask a lot of questions.

Did you know that the husband is typically buried on the left and the wife on the right—as a bride stands to her groom's left during their wedding ceremony? Ironically, this is the same way Todd and I slept in our bed. This is what I wanted. If we slept on opposite sides, which didn't happen often, it just felt weird to us and we joked about it. We would switch back to our proper side, with me acting like a steam roller, rolling over him and laughing to get to my side of the bed.

As the caretaker and I tried to figure out which side I would be on upon my own death, I asked where our feet were in placement of the gravestone. I wanted to make sure I was positively placed on the correct side. "Where are the head and feet in respect to the grave," I asked. I am quite a detailed-in-nature kind of person. I was told the feet are pointed to the east, for the Second Coming of Christ, which would occur from the east. It made sense. Considering this was our final resting place, beside one another, I felt I had every right to be a little OCD about the details, right?

In all honesty, the anxiety rising in my chest before the meeting was mounting, but when it was all said and done, I was glad I took the step. It was just another day of pulling up my bootstraps and tackling all these life changes that have been put forth upon me. Now that it was all taken care of, I didn't have to leave this burden on my children, which gave me peace.

It wasn't easy. Walking in God's strength is hard, and I admit, I faltered a lot. Losing a spouse changes so many parts of who you are and how you go about in this world, on the daily and into the future. And when married to someone as long as I had been married to Todd, losing him changed everything in my life.

ONE THING I HAD TO make sure I did was put my armor on to protect myself from ever falling into a pool of grief so deep that I could not pull myself out of it. I could not have anticipated the major adjustments that would change for me. I realized I had taken my life for granted.

Todd had such a high impact on my life. Everything revolved around being husband and wife; how we raised our children, handled our home, discussed finances, and planning for our future were all intertwined with him.

But now, even a simple trip to the grocery store wasn't the same for me. The first time I walked into our neighborhood store, it triggered so many emotions. Going grocery shopping with Todd was our thing. Although, during the pandemic, Todd mostly did the grocery shopping because I couldn't handle the behavior of our society, with its masks and arrows taped on the floor, forcing people to adhere to rules and restrictions. But before that, he and I would go together, having planned meals for the week, and just having fun getting our weekend errands done together.

As I pushed my cart through the produce aisles for the first time after his death, the pit in my stomach was so pronounced that I felt I would throw up. It was just another reminder of my new life. I didn't even know why I was grocery shopping. I knew I wasn't going to eat the food. It was going to go bad in the refrigerator, which it did, but shopping was a normal rhythm to my former life, and a routine that I felt I needed to carry out.

THE FIRST MONTH AFTER HIS funeral, I was still paralyzed in fear. Mostly, it was the fear of the unknown. Todd and I had done everything right, crossing all the t's and dotting all the i's when it came to living our life within our budget and means, saving for a rainy day, and making sure we set enough money aside for retirement. Or so I thought. Now it was going to be put to the hardest test of all.

With him gone, I didn't feel financially secure anymore. Not only had I lost my husband and best friend, but Todd was also the breadwinner of the family. He was the provider. I only worked part-time, and used my off time to care for our home and the children. How in the world was I going to be able to sustain myself, our family, and keep this house up all on my salary? I was blessed that I was receiving a paycheck during my leave, but Todd's paycheck had stopped upon his death.

I wasn't confident I was going to be able to keep my current work schedule, even with the life insurance policy we had put in place years ago for just this kind of situation. One never thinks it would ever need to be used, but again, here I was, trying to do the math to see how long it could sustain me. My brain was not computing what this altered life would cost without my beloved. *Would I have to work full-time? Would I have to sell the house?* I was thankful my car was paid off, and Todd drove a company truck, which would be picked up by co-workers in a few days. It had been sitting in the driveway since mid-August.

I was also advised that I needed to apply for new health insurance for myself and my children, in my name, before the end of the month. Was it cynical to say that in the world we live in, that I was thankful he didn't die on the last day of the month, because our family's health insurance would have lapsed before he was even buried? At least I had a couple of weeks to tackle that big change. These were the things I was forced to think about.

When I called to add my children as authorized users on my credit card and remove Todd's name from it, I was advised I was not an owner of it, as I had thought, but only Todd. For years we had used the points from our purchases to be applied to the principal of our mortgage, so I mistakenly thought I was a joint owner. The credit card company closed the account immediately, leaving me holding the phone with tears of despair running down my face. It didn't help that I was denied a credit card due to a technicality and had to humbly ask my son, a college student, to add me as an authorized user on his card, which he gladly did, until I could clear up the confusion. It was the brutal reality of our world. It was all too much to take in.

ALL THESE CHANGES AT ONE time can be so overwhelming for a person. There's a good reason why it is suggested not to make big decisions so soon after your loved ones' passing becomes such sound advice, and putting important protections in place before a loss such as this happens.

In those moments, I needed to be reminded that God doesn't give us a spirit of fear; I knew I should fear not, for He is with me. But I was human, and when my emotions of fear wanted to overtake me in this deep valley of grief and new responsibility of being head of our family, God reminded me in Philippians 4:13, "I can do all this through him who gives me strength." And now, as head of my household, I needed to lean on that same strength, trusting that the God who empowers me will also give me provision for every responsibility that was now in my hands. With all strength, I chose to trust that His plan was unfolding as it should, and in quiet surrender, I would rest.

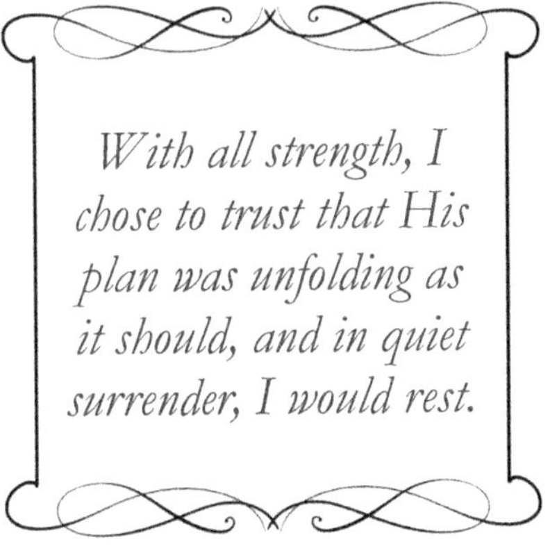

I was thankful that I took care of the accounts and bills in the household, so I knew all the passwords for each account. I was aware of the expenses needed to maintain this home and our life. Our life.

But not this one.

My worries were also considering the hospital bills that were going to be rolling into my mailbox in the coming weeks. Many people advised me that since he signed the paperwork, the bills would be written off; I wasn't so sure, and could not bank on that fact, nor would I even allow myself to be relieved of those expenses. I knew the bills would be high; he was in the main hospital for eight days and in the ICU for eighteen days, with what was supposed to be round the clock care, so I was bracing for a financial downfall of debt coming my way. I would have to figure it out as it came.

Todd and I always had a budget, and each year we would sit down and create a new one based on changes in the household expenses and financial changes, such as raises we received at work. Although looking back, we never adjusted the life insurance to accommodate the increase in salary. But I was so thankful that we were savers, and planned accordingly for some short-term financial hits.

When the pandemic hit, I remember the conversation at the dinner table one night with the kids about money. None of us in the country knew what the stay-at-home order was going to entail, which meant we were not sure we would be working. But we were not worried about being able to pay the bills because we had six months of expenses saved in an account for such an event. We talked to our children that evening about the importance of being prepared.

I just never thought I would be living out my own lesson shortly thereafter. I had savings in the bank to sustain me until the life insurance policy was processed, that I knew. But I wanted to feel financially secure. We had no debt except for a small balance left on the mortgage, for which I was, again, grateful. Todd and I were so excited to know that when both of the kids graduated college, we would be months away from paying off the house and living the life of empty nesters, having the financial freedom to do what we pleased. I was ready to travel, and hoped he could slow his work load so we could take trips together. We would have made it.

We worked hard for this. And now… Todd didn't even get to enjoy the fruits of his labor, at least not down here on earth.

I TRIED TO NOT LET the uncertainty of the future consume me, but I was a natural-born planner. I needed to know what the next day would bring; I would not be settled until I knew the bottom line of my budget and how much I would be able to spend each month.

I needed some kind of control, and at that moment I had none. I can admit, anger set in again at these moments. I was mad at Todd for putting me in this situation, and then immediately regretted my feelings. I knew, with utmost confidence, Todd fought as good of a fight as any to come back home to us.

There was nothing I could do with any accounts or paperwork until I received Todd's death certificate, but I was so overwhelmed with grief that it clouded any clear thoughts I had. I knew I had way too much on my plate; I wanted so badly to hand over the list of things I needed to do after a spouse died, as suggested on a list given to me by the mortuary, off to somebody else to take care of, but it was mine to handle. I was Todd's wife. Update utility accounts. Notify Social Security. Transfer vehicle titles, change the name on the mortgage. Update investment beneficiaries. I felt I was dismantling the infrastructure of our shared life.

I've always been raised to handle my affairs, and I was planning on doing that, but I was feeling this anger bubbling up under my skin each time I tackled a financial obstacle. I didn't ask for this. I kept reminding myself that anger was part of grief, but I wasn't prepared for the rage I felt brewing up inside of me. I was angry at the situation. I was angry at our world for what was placed in front of me. I was angry at how people were treating each other, and how the humanity of everyone had changed during these past two years. I was angry at Todd for not taking care of his health, and I was angry at him for leaving me with all of this even though I knew it wasn't his fault. But I was still mad. I was angry that we had built this life together—one that I now had to carry on alone.

Then I felt selfish, because I knew how many other families had to work full-time and they didn't have a choice in the matter. I did; I just needed the time to sort everything out. I also knew God always provided. I needed to have faith in knowing all of this would be okay, even if I didn't feel it at the moment.

November 12, 2021

Dearest Todd,

I miss you so very much. It has only been 2 months and it feels like forever without you. The house seems so quiet. I took your stuff out of your office last week. It was so hard to do that. I think I am going to give the frames to Jacob for his office when he gets his job in the future. And of course, your Babygirl took your jacket.

You would be so proud of your son and daughter. They have been so strong during this. They call me daily to check on me. Jacob and I are taking a road trip up to see Annie, and Jake's last football game of the season. I wish you were here to join us.

I am trying to figure out life without you by my side. I falter a lot because you are my better half. I am tired of crying—I just can't help it. When I talk about you. I cry. I sit in bed at night and look over at your side to try to picture you looking at me. I miss your touch and your mischievous laugh. I miss all of you. I can't wait to see you again.

Thanksgiving is a week away and I am dreading it. It won't be the same with us not tag teaming it in the kitchen. I missed our date day for Christmas shopping. All of these firsts without you are painful. The pain and anxiety in my chest is not constant at least. I am still in disbelief you are gone but know it's reality. I am taking day by day.

Until we meet again

My love,

Lisa

Chapter Eighteen

BACK TO WORK

Returning to work was another task I had to tackle. I hadn't been back in the office since Todd went into the hospital, but I knew the day was looming ahead of me. And it arrived. I was ready to get back to the rhythm of life and use my work to fill my head with tasks instead of sorrow. I was blessed in knowing my biggest responsibilities at work had been taken care of by mine and Todd's wonderful co-workers, but I knew I had a backlog of work that still needed to be completed.

On the Monday morning after what would have been our wedding anniversary, I pulled into the parking lot full of red company trucks. I looked for Todd's truck, number 83. It wasn't there. I found out later that it had been assigned to a crew working out of town, so I wouldn't have to see it. I began to cry. I did not want to walk into the office. As much as I knew I would be surrounded in love by my co-workers, I couldn't shake the feeling knowing that Todd would not be there.

A toast was made in Todd's honor after the funeral
(photo credit: Sarah Lochmann)

I proceeded to gather all my stuff out of my car, which included my planner, lunch, purse, and a sweet little floral arrangement I brought to lift my spirit. The flowers fell to the ground when I pulled them out from the back seat. As I was picking them up, a prospective vendor was parking his truck next to my car and I was couched down to the ground thinking, *please don't run over my flowers.* He didn't. But he walked around my car, donut box in hand, and asked, "Do you need help?"

I stood up, tears streaming down my face and replied, "No, thank you. I'm okay." *Why do I do that?*

It was quite clear I was not okay, but I didn't have the heart to explain to him why. This was certainly not the way I envisioned this day to start. I felt the strong urge to throw everything into my backseat, get back into the car, and drive home. But I didn't.

The man made his way to the front door, and I made my way to the back door of the office. As I walked in, he was standing at the receptionist's desk, and I realized I was the one that needed to greet him. Thankfully, around the corner came another co-worker I hadn't seen since the funeral, and he walked up to hug me. I started sobbing in his arms. It all happened within five seconds, and this poor vendor witnessed it all.

It was in these moments that the world of a grieving person intersects a normal day for another. I did not have the strength in the moment to hide my emotions.

The vendor just patted the donut box, left his business card, and walked out the door. After I dried my eyes and composed myself, I asked my co-worker and good friend to email this customer to send my apologies and explain the situation. The man's reply was so gracious. I went on with my day, as best I could.

The rest of the morning came with a slew of co-workers stopping by my office to give me hugs of comfort and to welcome me back. I will admit, I don't remember any work getting done that day. The biggest task I had at hand was walking through the door, and I was proud of myself that I at least tackled that. I knew the work would get done somehow, whether in the office or at home, working remotely.

I stayed in my office for most of the day, with a clear view of the steps that led up to Todd's office. It was almost as if I was waiting for him to come down the steps with his lunch box, water cup, and planner in his hand, to head to jobs or meetings for the day. I knew I couldn't bring myself to walk up the steps as I used to, to greet him with a kiss each morning.

By the afternoon, the vendor who came with the box of donuts earlier in the day arrived again at the front door of the office. But this time, he was carrying a bouquet of flowers. They were for me. A handwritten card expressing his condolences was attached, and on it, the statement, "Sometimes things in life just suck." *Yes, they do.*

I realized at that moment that regardless of what the news tells us, with their tales of fear wrapped up in pretty packages of greater goodness, that there was genuine, true goodness in the world.

There are good people. Kind people. It was this kind of love and kindness of others that will get us through. A stranger's kindness and my work family helped me get through that first day back. I am forever indebted.

Working with one's spouse can have its advantages and disadvantages. I loved working with Todd. His office was on the second floor of the house that the company resided in, and mine was on the main floor. Once I was settled in my routine of returning to work, my next task at hand was cleaning out his office. It took me another three weeks to be able to force myself to walk up the steps into his space.

But I knew it was time. I knew it was coming, and I knew I couldn't hide from it. I wanted to hide from a lot of things after he died, to step off the path and take a detour. The journey God had placed me on was one that already had had twists and turns, hills and valleys, and potholes large enough to swallow me. I knew I would remain on the path and carry on however hard it was for me. So, on a Friday afternoon, I made my way up the office steps to his workspace.

It was only the second time I stepped into his office since his passing. For the first few moments, I just stood there and then began to cry. Again, one of my amazing co-workers heard me and stood with me until I could compose myself. Then he left, allowing me to have some privacy in gathering my husband's personal items.

The room I was standing in had been Todd's office since he received his promotion to Vice President over 15 years ago. I remember that day fondly and how proud I was of him. He was so humble about this title, but by golly, he earned it; he did his job so well. Even as I was dealing with countless phone calls, texts, and paperwork over the past two months, I stood there thinking of my husband doing them daily for years, and with such ease. I will always be in awe as to how he was able to do it all.

After Todd passed away, my immediate thought was, "I would like his office." I wanted to move my office up to his space. I felt like everything of his needed to be in my possession. I was reminded of the old Bugs Bunny cartoon where Daffy Duck placed ownership on everything by saying "It's mine, you understand, all mine. Mine. Mine. Mine." Todd loved the old Bugs Bunny cartoons.

With love and care for me, my sweet daughter quietly even made the request to the owner shortly after the funeral. I wanted it as mine. For me, moving to Todd's office was a way of preserving his presence in my daily life.

But, I think God allows time to pass for us to come to the realization that we cannot hold onto everything. Matthew 6:19 says, "Do not store up for yourselves treasures on earth, where moths and vermin destroy, and where thieves break in and steal." I knew I could not keep every item my husband touched, as much as I would have liked to. This included his office.

I had to admit to myself that working in the same space my husband had for so many years would have been too painful for me to bear. As I walked through the weeks and months of changes, I realized I needed that much time to come to this reality. I was so thankful for the patience of my work family to allow me the time to process it all.

But, the day arrived to clean out his office.

I walked over to Todd's chair and sat down. I began to weep. I felt his presence in that office. And the chair I was sitting in seemed too big for me to sit in. I didn't feel right sitting in a chair sat in by such a great man.

I looked around at all his things. His stainless-steel cup, stained with the scent of coffee, sat on the desk with water still sitting in it. Nothing had been moved in two months because my co-workers gave me the ultimate gift of allowing me time to perform this task.

I slowly began to place all his personal belongings in a canvas bag, minus his Cardinal's stadium pictures frames he had on the wall. Frames of photos of our children, their drawings from years ago he had displayed, his mousepad that I custom made of our photos at the lake, his business cards, his granola bars and pepper mix from his snack drawer, the clay finger pots the kids gave him when they were in elementary school that he put paper clips in, and so many other things he collected over the years. It all fit into one bag. I had the privilege of taking the time to take down and pack up his stuff on my own, and not by someone else handing me a box and saying, "Our condolences." I knew I was blessed with not having to imagine one's work life diluted to those two words.

As I walked out of what I could no longer call his office one last time, I turned out the light and made my way down the stairs. I knew who Todd's replacement in the position was going to be, and I wanted to make sure I extended many blessings and success to him in his new endeavor, because I knew it would make Todd proud.

My friend, Jordan, who was also our receptionist, was waiting for me at the bottom of the stairs, ready to give me a hug. As everyone had left the office, she stayed. When I walked into my office to gather my things to leave for the weekend, the song, "Be Alright," by Danny Gokey was playing on my radio. This song became my anthem of sorts. It always seemed to be playing on the radio when I would leave the hospital, or at times I needed to be reminded that God had the whole world in His hands and it is well.

Everything will be alright.

December 12, 2021

Dearest Todd,

Today is 3 months without you by my side. I truly don't know how I am still standing. It's also Sunday, our day. So, I am sitting here drinking my morning coffee while sitting next to the Christmas tree.

Christmas will be here in two weeks, and I truly do not know how the day will go. You would be so proud of our children though. Me and they only want one thing for Christmas. You. 365 days ago, I never thought I would be going into this Christmas without you.

I am still not settled on the paperwork involved since that day. It is so hard to think it's only me now... not we. How the change of one letter in a word changes my world. I don't know if you are near me in spirit as I say my prayers to God every night. I always ask about you and ask that He tells you I said hello and hope you are doing well. I know you are doing well. I want to imagine how heaven is, but just like when I get overwhelmed in imagining the stars and the moon, I cry; that is how I feel about imagining heaven. I guess I'll have to wait and see.

In the meantime, please watch over us. We miss you immensely—your smile, your laugh, your awesome cooking, and for me, your touch. It's hard to go Christmas shopping when I see things that I know you would like.

Until we meet again.

Yours truly,

Margo (it's me)

Chapter Nineteen

THE HOLIDAYS ARE UPON US

I knew this first holiday season would be radically different because of Todd's absence. Alone is ever-present in my day-to-day life, since his passing almost three months ago.

The upcoming holidays had been weighing on me. How would I manage this joyous celebration without him by my side? But as much as sorrow wanted me to hide under the covers and wish it to be January 2, I could not, and I would not. Because in all honesty, I loved the holiday season, and so did Todd. It was our time, our season of generosity and togetherness. Christmas with Todd felt like stepping into a storybook; one we wrote together, year after year, with love tucked into every tradition.

Now, the same songs and scents stirred something different in me. They reminded me of what we had, and what our family lost. But even in the ache, I found comfort. Because I knew Todd's love for the holidays lived on in the traditions we built, in the laughter of our children, and in the quiet moments he and I shared.

All the "firsts" that come with navigating life without a loved one came strong and fast for me. I made it through his birthday and our anniversary, and then I only had a little over a month to mentally prepare myself, the best I could, for the first holiday season without him.

To kick off Thanksgiving week, I received a text from the monument company, telling me that Todd's gravestone had been installed. I'd signed off on the design only a couple weeks ago, so I was not mentally prepared to be ready to see it in person at this moment in time. I was expecting to hear from the monument company around Christmastime. Ironically, this was the same time I was expecting to bring Todd home, based on all the step-downs needed for rehabilitation and healing. All I wanted was for Todd to be home for Christmas. The kids and I could handle the rest of the trials and tribulation, however it was thrown at us. And thrown at us, it had been.

I texted the kids that the gravestone had been placed, and we decided to meet up at the cemetery that afternoon. I felt God orchestrated this moment, as we were able to view the gravestone earlier than expected. The kids were home from college for the extended holiday weekend, so we could be together looking at it for the first time. I was so very thankful for God's little coincidences like these, given to us along this journey. But boy, seeing the headstone with Todd's name and my name on it made it feel so final. After my prayer for strength to get me through the holidays a few weeks back, I settled into planning the Thanksgiving dinner, one that Todd and I had always hosted for his family on the Sunday before Thanksgiving. This was our tradition for years. I would switch my days at work to get all the grocery shopping done, so when Saturday before the big dinner arrived, we would start prepping for it.

Todd loved his smoker and BBQ, and he would fret over the main event—the turkey. He would bring up one of the coolers from the basement, make the brine for the turkeys to marinate in, tie them up in plastic bags, and place them in the coolers. It wasn't uncommon for me to find him looking up brining recipes to up-stage the previous years' turkey preparedness. Todd wanted to make sure his family left the table saying it was the best turkey they had ever had. He just wanted their bellies full and happy.

I oversaw the side dishes. I spent hours making homemade French fried onion rings for the topping of the green bean casserole, along with homemade cream of mushroom soup, sweet potato casserole, stuffing, multiple pies, and homemade whipped cream, rounding out the things being made in the kitchen on the Saturday before our family celebration.

While I was making a mess in the kitchen, Todd would be handling laundry duties and cleaning up the house. We were a team. By the end of Saturday evening, pizza would be ordered. I was not going to make dinner after being in the kitchen all day! Together, Todd and I would set the timeline itinerary for the next day. We were a well-oiled machine when hosting celebrations with family and friends. We loved to entertain.

On this first holiday without him, I wanted to make his family proud. *I can do this,* I thought. I felt it would give me a purpose to be busy, so I would not think about him not being present.

As much as I wanted to tell myself that I would power through it and pull up my bootstraps to face the grief head on, I was only kidding myself. Grief sneaks into the tiniest of crevices.

As I entered the kitchen on Saturday morning to start the Thanksgiving prep, my mind was on Todd. My sous-chef was not there. I had this big task of hosting dinner for his family, and I stood there, staring at the list of things I needed to do.

Okay. I got this.

Jacob, Anna, and Jake making pies for Thanksgiving

But I didn't have it. Shortly into pulling down all the ingredients out of the cabinet, I pulled down one of the baskets and looked in it. There sat the box of turkey bags Todd had purchased on Amazon, preordering them so he knew he would have it on hand to brine the turkey.

I found myself beginning to grip the side of the counter, hanging my head down, and sobbing. Todd should be here helping me. I was mad. *I don't deserve any of this pain.* The to-do list was too much. I was overwhelmed at the thought that I was going to need help, and I didn't want to ask for it. *I was strong. I was resilient. I got this, remember?* That was my mantra.

I tried my best to think fondly of Todd and how he used to fret over turkey prepping because he always wanted to make sure it tasted good and that everyone would love it. He was such an amazing cook. The big tears came when I didn't think I would get it all done and became overwhelmed, which happened often in my world. In all honesty, I got a bit mad that he wasn't in the kitchen with me. But, after I gave myself a moment, I took a deep breath and went back to it.

That is the thing about grief in my world, it hits me hard, and then I must move on. Life doesn't stop.

Mind-tired and emotionally drained, I ended up getting through the day, making all the side dishes as in previous years, with the three children helping me make the pies. We were ready for the next day's feast. I got it done—*we* got it done—and would be ready for tomorrow. And that's all that mattered.

That Thanksgiving Day, the grass was covered with leaves, but that was okay. The house wasn't going to be as spotless as I would have liked, but I decided that was okay, too. So I was delegating some food dishes for others to do. What mattered were the people that were going to be present that day, and being thankful for so many things, like God giving me strength because He knew my pain.

I talked to God a lot. I thanked Him for the love Todd and I shared for so many years. and for all the amazing memories I have with him. I thanked God for our children, family, friends, work family, church and for wise counsel through this process of grief.

And I was thankful for our home, because it was built on a strong foundation of love. Our home would be filled with all the people Todd loved, so Sunday was sprinkled with a lot of big tears, but we got through it together. In spite of my grief, I was still thankful for so many things in my life.

The next day, I decided that although Todd was not here in person, he was here in spirit. The kids and I would continue to bring his spirit alive by continuing in the traditions that we, as a family, have held so dear over the years.

THE DAY AFTER THANKSGIVING HAD always marked the beginning of Christmas in our home; a day of laughter, lights, and the joyful chaos of decorating. This year, it marked something else: the quiet courage of keeping traditions alive without Todd.

With the determination to get the entire house decorated in one day, I jumped out of bed and started a pot of coffee. I was thankful for Jacob and Anna being home from college for the weekend, so I didn't have to do this task alone. I had already decided this year's decorations would remain the same. No big changes. Not having Todd here to celebrate the holidays with us was enough change. I would let the day unfold as it needed to.

I knew I would cry. I had prepared for it. But, I also wanted to keep the day spent in good remembrance of Todd. We had so many happy memories of our family during the holidays, like the annual cookie bakes with the nieces and nephews at our home, hiding the pickle ornament to see who would be the first person to find it, watching *Christmas Vacation* with gift tags for me that read "To Margo, Love Todd." He loved that movie. He loved the holidays. He loved us.

I began hauling up all the decorations from the basement, and the stack of Christmas DVDs from the movie closet. I knew the sound of a movie playing in the family room would lure the kids from their beds. It did. Slowly, they emerged, sleepy-eyed but smiling.

We spent hours assembling the tree, stringing lights, and reminiscing about each ornament as we pulled it out from the storage container. Many of the ornaments were Todd's, gifts I'd picked out each year for his stocking to commemorate that year's gift or achievement. Our stockings hung from metal letters that spelled out N-O-E-L across the fireplace mantel. I took Todd's stocking from the top of the rest of our stockings and gently hung it on the "N." I stood back and looked at it, the weight of reality pressing in. I would no longer have the privilege of buying him Christmas presents. He and I made a competition out of it. We had a budget, and Todd always blew it out of the water. When it came to placing presents for me under the tree, he made sure I was never forgotten, especially in the stocking.

By late afternoon, the house was transformed. The only thing left were the lights being hung outside on the house, and I wasn't sure we'd get to those. The kids were leaving the next day. That was okay. We gave ourselves grace. We didn't have to do it all.

That night, as the lights shone brightly on the tree, I sat back with my cup of hot chocolate in hand, and admired its beauty. It wasn't a tree that showcased a trendy theme or matching baubles. It was a tree built on memories. The many ornaments we placed on the tree were a reminder of Todd. Ornaments of "Our first Christmas," a photo of us in Hawaii on our 25th wedding anniversary, and ones that I meticulously picked out for Todd each year to tuck into his stocking.

As the lights shimmered across the branches, I saw not just a tree, but a testament. Each branch held a story. Each ornament, a moment. To love, to family, to the kind of joy that grief cannot erase. This tree was us. Our family. Our adventures. Our memories. His memory.

December 19, 2021

My Dearest Honey,

We celebrated our first Fulsom Christmas without you present. Honestly, it is not the same. I get overwhelmed with all the stuff I have to do to get ready. Our children are amazing. You would be so proud to know how much they have helped me—especially today. When your parents arrived and the hustle and bustle of getting the food ready, I just went upstairs and sat still, and prayed you would be next to me and hold me up through all of this. I just cried and then had to compose myself before going back downstairs.

It's so hard! The kids and I decided to share your knives with everyone. I wanted them to each have something they could remember you by. Matt was pretty emotional and I think they all appreciated them.

I missed you sitting next to me. It hurt my heart when we took photos and you weren't standing next to me. I miss your touch and your kisses. I miss you. I miss us.

But I did it though. I survived another thing without you. I don't like it, but I have no choice. I hope you are proud of me and the kids.

I love you so much.

You are so missed,

Love, Lisa

Chapter Twenty

THE AIR OF DECEMBER

November merged into December, and the hustle and bustle of the season was upon us. I had tackled so many tasks, physically and mentally, including receiving Todd's medical files from the hospital, totaling 193 pages. The records still sat on the kitchen counter, waiting to be opened. I, at least, had them in my possession as I was hearing more and more stories of other families' loved ones passing away from the identical protocol Todd was given, including one from the same hospital Todd was admitted to. Ironically, one deceased man's son shared with me that his father was buried in the same cemetery as Todd.

When we headed into the month of December, I received word that a close family friend of Jake's family, the wife of his longtime wrestling coach, had died in her sleep. Another family was beginning the walk of loss that our family had started a few months prior. Although I had never met them, not even while attending wrestling matches for Jake, my heart broke for the family.

I knew the pain and despair they were experiencing. The darkness of loss, piercing their hearts.

Jake and Anna returned home from college earlier than the expected Christmas break week to attend her funeral, with Anna making the comment that she would reach out to their youngest daughter, a college student herself, to offer support. I was so proud that she could be a support system to her. I prayed each night that God would give the family as much strength as He was providing me and my children through this grief. I felt like death had surrounded our world on all sides, and there was nowhere to escape.

As the cold winter months continued on, I was learning to walk into the house alone, leave the house alone, go to bed alone, and wake up alone. I continued about my days, waking up and praying for a good day. And I ended each night with my prayers to God starting with, "God, thank you for this day." Some days were good, and others were not so much, but I made it a point to at least make an attempt to bring joy into my children's world and mine, especially around the Christmas season. I knew Christmas Day would be hard for them, so it wasn't an easy feat.

Our world was still recovering from the hangover of all the COVID restrictions, and the news continued to fuel fear into the minds of the public. I personally did not enjoy being out amongst people. I felt out of place, like I didn't belong. Friends and family attempted to invite me to events to get me out of the house, but I declined. I attended a widow's luncheon hosted by a fellow parishioner. And as welcoming as all the ladies were with me feeling gracious for being invited, I still felt I didn't belong. Many women in the congregation had lost their husbands around the same time I lost Todd, and as we all held the same unwelcome title of widow, I was the youngest one in the group. They shared stories of spending almost double the years of marriage Todd and I had shared, and grandchildren their spouses were able to enjoy. As I sat there and listened, grateful that their spouses had these memories, I felt the compounded sadness having the knowledge that my spouse didn't get to be part of any of those moments.

I found I only had enough energy to go to work, church, meetings with financial advisors about my situation, and being with my children.

I certainly did not have the energy to handle anyone in my circle who would take that short supply of it away from me. But the enemy knows when to attack, and he knows my weaknesses. It lies in giving people second and third chances, even after being hurt by them. After the dissolution of a close friendship earlier in the year, after years of discord between us, Todd had asked me to end the friendship for my own mental health.

This friend came back into my life while Todd was in the hospital. I admit, I allowed it because of the grief I was feeling. I lowered my walls and allowed her back into my life, having trust she was well-meaning in reaching out in my time of need. I felt my decision was right while Todd was in the hospital and during the funeral, but it became quite obvious as the weeks wore on in my grief, that I failed in my discernment.

I was placed in direct fire by the enemy through the ways of friendship. During a phone conversation months after Todd died, she felt it was her job to share her opinion and remind me that Todd probably could not hear me while he was intubated. She knew full well I held onto this thread of belief that Todd had heard every word I spoke to him, and how much I held onto the fact that he could hear me tell him "I love you" during his last moments on this earth.

Adding insult to injury to my already shattered heart, she shared how she held a prayer vigil for a co-worker in the parking lot of the same hospital, around the same time Todd was fighting for his life, and her co-worker woke up. We all know Todd did not, as did she. Were her prayers more powerful than my own? I was made to feel it was that way. In her careless words to me, I felt my prayers for Todd's healing weren't strong enough. The enemy was hard at work trying to take me down at all angles!

I was devastated by her statement. After many days of reflection, I wrote her a letter wishing her well, knowing as a Christian I needed to forgive her transgressions against me, but asked her to step out of my life once again and stay there. I had to protect my circle and make sure my armor was securely attached at all times. I was currently in battle. So, when a large, thick manila envelope showed up in my mail from her on the sixth-month anniversary of Todd's death with a multi-paged letter inside addressed to me, I was reminded again to tighten my armor. I handed the envelope over to a good friend to discard it, never to read a single word on any of the pages.

By this time, I was finding that grief had many stages. I was no longer in the stage as I was when Todd first passed away and the couple months after, with the relentless physical pain in my chest as my daily reminder that he was gone. I still cried every day, but I no longer expected him to walk through the door after work. The realization of his death had finally settled in.

For me, grief had become the overwhelmingness that was constantly invading my space. All the little things, like the dropping of my previous day's lunch bag onto the table with it still sitting there the next day, the sink full of dishes I didn't have the energy to wash, the decisions that needed to be made without the person I was used to bouncing ideas off of and make big decisions with, or the medical bills still coming in three months later, to give me another reminder of Todd's experience.

And, I still hadn't read through his medical file. I just wasn't ready for what I feared I would find. And I needed to get through the holidays first.

One night, I found myself laying on our kitchen floor, sobbing because I spilled water from watering the plants, and I didn't have the energy to clean it up.

It was overwhelming wanting to read the grief-related and other books that were graciously given to me that I didn't have the motivation to read, or the Christmas cards so lovingly sent to our family, and seeing it was the first time not seeing Todd's name on it. It was the Christmas gifts needing to be returned because I bought something in the wrong size or color—but still proud of myself for simply walking into the store the first time amongst the Christmas shoppers. Yet, I didn't want to go back.

It was the Christmas cards I bought, where I stood in the aisle quietly weeping in trying to find the most appropriate card to symbolize the year I was walking in; I was determined to keep the status quo and send them out to my loved ones. It was the bag of work stuff that I wanted to tackle on my days off, but ended up taking back to work unfinished, as my planner was filled with dates and appointments to fulfill because I still don't know the word "no."

I felt like I was pouring into others' cups as mine was shattered on the floor. And then immediately, I felt guilty that this thought had even come to my mind. I could not have asked better people circling around me at this moment in my life.

It was the paperwork, always the paperwork. It never seemed to end. It seemed like every piece of paper I had touched regarding Todd's passing had to be touched again… and again… and again. I thought I could cross one of these things off my list, only for it to come back. Let's add to my stack of paperwork to update all of the kids' and my accounts, because there was a state of panic to make sure all was taken care of for myself.

This situation taught me that life changed in an instant. We should all be prepared. None of the paper processes went smoothly. And honestly, it was mentally exhausting. It was a constant reminder that I was now a widow. But I didn't need or welcome this outward reminder. I thought about it every day.

What I did mostly on my days off was tackle paperwork and make phone calls. I was trying to take it all in stride and was told by others that I was handling this part of the process better than most. Most days I didn't feel like I was. I wanted to think once all this paperwork was done, I would feel settled and be able to move forward in healing. At least that's what I kept telling myself. One day, I cried as I backed out of the garage headed to the DMV, thinking *with each swipe of a pen, I was getting really tired of slowly having my husband's name removed from everything, like he didn't exist.* It was such a gut-wrenching feeling.

I reminded myself that Todd did in fact exist for almost 49 years, and I was so blessed to have spent 34 years knowing him and 32 years in love with him.

He will exist forever in my heart. No removal of the name from a piece of paper was ever going to change that.

ALONG WITH THE PAPERWORK, IT was the four hours of sleep I received nightly for the past two months because I laid awake and only thought of one thing: Todd.

I was missing the closeness we had; his touch, and the forehead kisses left by him when he left for work every morning.

It was, well—everything. I still had a widowed brain, and I found myself with thoughts that I couldn't finish. I may have looked put together and even smiled or laughed because I didn't want to make it awkward in the presence of others, but I found myself wanting to be by myself, but not by myself, if that makes any sense at all.

The stress of the situation was all-encompassing, the kind of grief that people feel behind closed doors, safely hidden behind the walls of the home. It's not pretty. It's not put together, and it's the side of grief that we don't want to talk about.

I knew I needed to act in faith during these times when I felt helpless, scared, and uncertain about my life. I felt I was being punished. But for what, I did not know. Had I done something so grievous that God felt I needed to suffer? I knew that was not true, but my thoughts were becoming tabs in my brain that would not close. Things I told myself that were not true. I knew losing Todd was not God's way of punishing me. I also knew that grief was a process, and I needed to give myself grace and patience. One does not simply snap their fingers, and all is well.

I needed to learn to be still and listen to God's words, and lean on Him when the sorrow got too heavy. He would not leave me. He knew my heart and how weary it was. And as my Shepherd, He would carry me if I reached a point of not being able to carry on. All the while, I kept my eyes on Him in the midst of this battle.

When I began to feel this overwhelmingness creep in, I knew it was time for me to step back and take a breath. Losing the love of my life had sucked the air out of my lungs. And grief came in, wanting to finish the job to suffocate me.

I knew what the pool of darkness was, and I knew it wanted me to jump in, swim around, and drown in it. But I wouldn't. Maybe I would have dipped my toe into it, or sat next to it and looked at it, but I knew I would never fully immerse myself into it. And I knew that one day, the plug would be pulled and the pool of darkness would be drained. I had to believe that.

I realized on days such as this, I needed to be still and have an intentional awareness of God's presence. Everything else could wait. One of those days, I told everyone I was okay, but silenced my phone to everyone except my children. I spent the day in prayer. I prayed for strength. The strength that continued to give me the energy to accomplish all the things I had to do, because this world required me to do so. I reflected again on Philippians 4:13, which says, "I can do all things through Christ who strengthens me." And breathe. *Just breathe.*

December 24, 2021

My Honey,

It's Christmas Eve, and I am sitting here next to the tree, drinking coffee and thinking about you. I want to tell you something. I paid off our mortgage. I checked today on the balance and it said "PAID IN FULL." I started to cry. I cried because this act should have been us doing it together. We were so close; this was our dream to get to the finish line of being debt free.

I sit here and think sometimes how life is without you and where I will be. Thank you for providing me with peace of mind with finances as I move forward with this life. Please continue to watch over me and the kids. I will continue to honor you as before and ever more so in providing for us.

I love you immensely… and I miss you.

The love of your life,

Lisa

Chapter Twenty-One

HONORING HIS LEGACY

eeting with financial advisors through our married life was something I was used to, but I was always accompanied by Todd. In early November, the life insurance amount was processed and deposited into my bank account, and I began meeting with a team of financial advisors for guidance. I was now the head of the household, and as I felt savvy in my money knowledge of maintaining a household, I did not want to make a misstep.

The meetings entailed navigating how my future could be laid out in such a way that I could continue to live a life as I had before Todd passed away; the simple and abundant life we had built together. Considering it had been completely altered, I wanted nothing more than to keep some normalcy of my past life intact.

I did not need much in my life—my family, my beautiful home, my gardens, and time spent with each of them. And if I had the choice, I would choose to, in Todd's voice and humor, to "live in a van down by the river" if I knew he would still be by my side. Unfortunately, Todd being here was not one of my options.

As I made my way to one of the appointments with my advisors on a mid-November morning, I sat at the stop light, waiting to make my turn onto the highway and thinking about my future. The song from my playlist, "Strength, Courage, and Wisdom," by India Arie came on. I had about a 20-minute drive to my destination, and all the songs that shuffled on my playlist that day were of that nature, being strong, being a warrior, jumping into a new journey, walking through fire, and becoming God-refined. I felt God became my personal deejay during the ride to my destination that day. The lyrics of the music brought peace to my soul.

I drove down the winding road, with the sun shining down and the leaves on the trees full of color. I felt a calmness come over me; an acknowledgment of the strength I had gained in handling all things that have come my way these past few months. Hard things.

I had always been a "behind the scenes" kind of girl, so in the past, these were things my introverted, quiet self would have avoided, or asked my husband to take care of or help me with, because I felt he could handle it better than me We were a team and supported one another. Now, I had to tell myself to pull up my bootstraps because I was the only one here that had to get it done. I had to give myself a mini pep talk of sorts on the daily.

NAVIGATING FINANCIAL DECISIONS IS QUITE intimidating when you find yourself suddenly alone. After so many years of sharing thoughts and ideas with my spouse, the first month or so after Todd's passing left me with uncertainty of my future. How could I possibly navigate the rest of my life without him? My better half. Walking in this new path God had for me allowed me to understand why it is advised not to make big decisions soon after losing a spouse. A couple months ago, I couldn't see a day, let alone a year or decade ahead of me. I was an utter mess.

In moments like these, it was so important to give myself grace. I reminded myself that I didn't have to see a decade ahead.

I only needed to see my next breath. My life was messy, and I needed to allow time for healing. This mess wasn't a failure, but a season of adjustment. I had to allow myself grace in being able to say to myself, *look at what you've been through. And look at how you are still standing.* Grace meets us in the real, and doesn't flinch at the mess.

I was thankful I was surrounded by knowledgeable people who could guide me in making the right financial decisions. This team of advisors included people I trusted. They sat with me to discuss my goals and future, and I felt at ease as many questions were asked and stories were shared. I know God brings relationships together for His purpose. The owner of the firm commented that our relationship was no coincidence. The plans God has for my life placed these people in it long before that day's meeting.

I had become quite aware of each person and experience that came into my path during this journey, and I knew it was God's doing. He was weaving a tapestry of my life, and in that moment, all I was able to see was the backside of it, with all its interwoven thread and knots. What I saw looked a mess, and God wasn't ready to allow me to flip it over and see the completed tapestry yet. I had to be patient.

In spending many hours with the advisors reviewing my portfolio, one of the discussions surrounded the mortgage on the house. I decided it best to use some of the life insurance money to pay off the remaining balance. Once the mortgage was out of the budget equation, I was able to handle paying all of the monthly bills from my own paycheck, and use the savings for extra expenses, like home maintenance and such. I had forecasted how long it would take to exhaust my savings and was relieved to find that there was no need to touch the rest of the insurance money until many years down the road, unless a big purchase needed to be made or an emergency arose. For the first time since his death, I felt a little bit of peace.

After this particular meeting, I was driving back home, feeling the utmost gratitude in how the meeting went and where I stood financially. I found myself near the cemetery, so I felt the need to stop in for a visit with Todd.

This man was a wonderful provider for his family, and he was still providing. I wanted nothing more than to make my husband proud of me for being able to carry on his legacy on the firm foundation we built together. With that, as I stood near his burial site, I simply told him, "Thank you, my love. I hope you are proud of me."

Life seemed so unsettled for me, and I knew it would feel like that for quite some time. But I knew I had the strength, courage, and wisdom to move forward.

So, WITH MY DAUGHTER ACCOMPANYING me on a cold December day, just a week before Christmas, I walked into the bank, the one where Todd and I had been customers for over 20 years, to pay off our mortgage. I confidently submitted a wire transfer to our lender.

I was thankful that Anna went with me. I was also thankful for living in a small town where people knew me. The employees at the bank knew me, they knew my husband's extended family, so having them walk me through this process helped tremendously.

I acknowledged the weight of my emotions as I signed my name on the paperwork to authorize the transaction. I would have given anything to have shared this moment with Todd. But I didn't get the chance. He worked so hard for his family, and he should have been here, celebrating this goal with me—because this just wasn't my dream. This was our dream.

Over the course of the past few years, we had the goal that the mortgage was to be paid off at the same time as the kids were to graduate from college, and we were making it happen. Little by little, we paid extra on the principal each month for years. We were SO CLOSE. We wanted to go into empty nesting debt-free, so we could live our lives with the peace of mind that we achieved what we set out to do when we were first married at the age of twenty-one.

When I opened my banking app on my phone on Christmas Eve to see I was officially debt free of a mortgage balance, I began to cry. Frankly, it was a lot to take in. I cried because even in death, Todd continued to provide for his family. I wanted to make sure I would be a good steward of it. I vowed to honor every single cent of this money. I did not take any of this lightly.

MANY PEOPLE DO NOT UNDERSTAND the emotional impact intertwined with the financial aspect of our loved ones providing for us after they pass. It gives peace, but it also comes with great responsibility; spending any of it always comes with a question in what purpose will it hold in adding to the life of mine and that of our children. There was a lot of weight on my shoulders in making the right decisions by myself, and I was fully aware of it.

As I turned off my phone and looked at the Christmas lights, sending a disco ball effect up on the ceiling, I thought of the statement, "On my honor, I will try." I was a Girl Scout when I was young, so I said it many times.

I began to think, *what is honor*? How does it manifest in your life? Do you think about it while going about your daily life? Or does it only surface at the sight of a commercial, parade, or a holiday, like today? Honor is defined by high respect, recognition, or esteem. When we honor something, we hold high respect for it.

Do we think of honor in our marriage, in other relationships, in our work, in how we handle our business, and treat others? Are we truly living it? Are we living our lives in such a way in honoring God, and one another above ourselves, to provide such wonderful things in our lives?

I had found myself saying this word a lot, especially when it came to my late husband. One of the things I honored, in everything, was my marriage to him. It was the wife's responsibility to help the husband become all that God wanted him to be, in the same way that God helps us become who He wants us to be. In Ephesians 5:33, the Bible commands wives to respect their husbands. This means revering, admiring and honoring them, just as husbands should honor their wives.

I honored our marriage, and I honored my late husband. I honored him as we built our life together and made goals for it, and I honor him now, as I moved forward in living the mindful life we had planned, for wherever God takes me in this altered life.

January 1, 2022

Happy New Year, my love! I rang in the year 2022 without you by my side. I don't know how that could even be. I miss your kisses.

I guess it's fitting to bring in the year with someone sick. Anna has COVID. She and Jake rang in the new year with me so I wouldn't be alone. And Jacob texted me.

I wish you were here, Love.

I miss you and love you immensely,

Lisa

On this particular day, I found myself writing a second letter to Todd:

I am mad. At first, I was afraid to say this out loud. Everyone tells me how strong I am. I see everyone's smiles as they share their joys about the new year and here I am at a stage of my life that I should be enjoying with you!

But you aren't here…
I am mad that you aren't here
I am mad you put me in this position

I'm mad at you for me being alone and not feeling protected.
I'm mad that I have to take care of this house by myself.
I'm mad Anna got COVID and it took me right back to tending to you and being scared.

I'm mad that I want our children but I can't ask because I don't want to be needy and they have their own lives.

I'm mad.
I want to scream, until I can't, because "I'm strong"
I am mad at you…. I am so lonely for you.

Chapter Twenty-Two

BRINGING IN THE NEW YEAR

In this particular instance on New Year's Day, I wanted to yell and scream, throw a temper tantrum of sorts. But, I wrote another letter instead. I understood that anger is an inherent part of grief, often emerging as a response to the emotional and physical pain one endures. And writing had become a part of therapy for me, even before Todd's passing, but more so now.

I needed to vent to someone or something, but everyone was around me celebrating the new year. I didn't want to let it out to anyone because it wasn't fair of me to be so selfish to do so. Instead, I put pen to paper and released all my anger into Todd's journal. I felt my anger seeping out through my fingers onto the pages. As I began feverishly writing, all of my thoughts and feelings surrounding this anger were rooted in the reality that I now had to deal with life on my own. I felt cheated.

I knew I couldn't still be mad at God, even though people told me He was big enough to handle it. As much as I did not understand why God called Todd home, I knew in my heart there

Spending 2020 New Year's Eve together

was a bigger reason that my little human brain could not understand. I also knew God still had plans for me; plans to prosper me and not harm me. I had to believe and have faith in it. I just didn't know at the moment why I had to journey through this valley of pain. Was I just a casualty of it, or was there something more? I knew my mind dwelled on my thoughts a little too long sometimes, especially then. So, after I spat out my rant of anger onto paper, I closed the journal, went upstairs, took a hot bath, and climbed into bed. The first day of 2022 was not one I wanted to remember.

The next day wasn't any better. Over the course of a couple of months, I felt the house was having its own temper tantrum of sorts in Todd being gone. The toilets in all three bathrooms were running constantly, then little things around the house started breaking, like the track in the kitchen cabinet that held the trash cans coming loose.

But this particular day brought a whole new challenge. As the evening wore on, the house became a bit chillier. The furnace would not kick on. With my stress level hitting an all-time high, I went into panic mode. All I could think about were the dollar signs of repair coming my way. *I just came out of Christmas spending and still have medical bills to pay.*

Jacob and Anna were still home from winter break from college, and Jacob, in his gentle nature, gave me a hug and told me it was going to be okay. He went downstairs with me to see if there was anything he could do to fix it. Jacob was able to get the furnace to kick back on and begin to heat the house, but then it shut off again.

So, what else was I to do? I called my dad. He spoke with his HVAC guy and was told that it was probably something with the computer board electrical system, so most likely it was going to have to be replaced. And, the guy was on vacation and could not help us. Isn't that how it always happens? Thankfully, a good neighbor had reached out and provided another repairman to call instead. She guided me on what to say because my grieving brain couldn't process how to make this call without bawling. It was after hours, so I had to leave a message. What now? There was nothing else to do by the end of the evening except to have all of us bundle up with extra clothes and blankets, attempt to get a good night's sleep, and pray the repairman would retrieve my message and could come in the morning.

I went into work the next day to secure a service call appointment and to gather my things to work from home. Even though I knew Jacob and Anna were fully capable of handling the situation at hand, I didn't want them to have to.

Prior to leaving the office to head back home, I began to share my New Year's Day grief episode and furnace issues with Jordan. I said the words, "Why is God making me so uncomfortable? I don't like this." I was trying my best not only to work through these usual stages of grief, realizing some were friends and some were foes, as my current anger reminded me, but also to walk through them, regardless of how difficult it was. The world was not going to stop on my account, so I knew I needed to trudge forward with as much grace as I could muster. And I didn't seem to have a lot at that moment, if I were completely honest.

My present frustrations, being dealt a nasty hand of furnace issues, had again turned to anger. I was mad because I had to deal with something I wasn't equipped to deal with. Todd handled these things. Life was throwing me monster curveballs, and I didn't like it.

IN THE MIDST OF SHARING this with Jordan, my anger turned to tears of helplessness, and I sank into a puddle of pity, right in front of her. I shared with her that my mind would not stop and rest, and I felt I had to carry all this burden by myself.

In times past and today, I have felt the need to speak my thoughts aloud, letting the words fall to the ground before gathering them up and shaping them into a cohesive concept. In doing so, I have found that many times, I get an AHA moment. They are little moments brought about by God's word and the Holy Spirit working together to get my attention.

So, as I was speaking out into the air of my frustrations, I said, "I can't catch a break. I feel like at every turn God is knocking me to my knees." Bingo! There it was. I instantly stopped crying, looked up at her in disbelief and then smiled through my tears. I think she might have thought I had lost my mind! But grace had seeped through the cracks of frustration, and Psalm 46:1 filled my mind: "God is our refuge and strength, an ever-present help in trouble."

In that moment, I realized that no matter how much I try to control the situation, God reminds me to let go and allow Him to guide me. I needed that reminder. I knew it would all be okay.

In the moments anxiety threatened to rise and anger and tears began to flow, I needed to drop down on my knees and pray, for strength, for guidance, for peace in my soul. God will always provide it. He always has. I just needed to let go.

This was an AHA moment. It was my reminder that I could not do all this on my own. It's not until we lose control that we realize Who is in control. I needed to surrender it to God. Daily, I relied on His help to fight my battles, both now and in the future. He knows my heart. He knows my needs. He knows my journey. He has set my path before me.

I gathered my work paperwork and headed for home to meet the repairman, feeling a little more settled in my soul.

While the furnace situation was at hand, my friend Patrice reached out to me via text to ask if I wanted to accompany her in bringing a meal the following evening to Jake's coach, the one who had lost his wife in the beginning of December.

Patrice was the mother of one of my son's longtime friends. Her son and Jacob were also roommates while attending college, yet oddly enough, she and I had never met until the day of Todd's funeral. She attended the service with her son for moral support. As they went through the receiving line, she introduced herself and asked if she could reach out after the service occasionally to check on me. In the weeks and months after Todd's death, she and I would go out to dinner and talk about writing my book and about walking through grief. She had become a tremendous support to me.

Patrice was a colleague of the coach's family and had signed up for the meal train. I knew she was asking me simply to get me out of the house, but I immediately felt conflicted. I was a widow. I would be walking into the home of a widower. What would he think? What would the family think?

My immediate reaction was that I didn't want to go.

I didn't want anyone to think my intentions were anything other than supporting a family in their grief, and nothing else. I responded to Patrice's text and asked her if I could give her an answer the next day. I simply explained that I wanted to accept her invitation because I understood how important it was to feel supported. I also wanted to show them that, four months after my loss, I was still standing. She told me to just let her know when I decided.

The next morning, Patrice texted me again to tell me she had emailed the family and was given a time to deliver their meal. I knew she wanted an answer from me, and in response to seeing her text, I sighed loudly.

"Mom, what's wrong?" Anna asked from the sunroom.

"Patrice invited me to deliver a meal to Jake's coach's family, and I'm not sure I want to go," I said. I explained my reasoning to her. She looked up from her phone and said, "Mom, you're overthinking it. They are a good family. You should go."

Whether they were a good family or not wasn't the battle I was fighting in my head—I knew they were a great family, especially from the comments shared by mutual people within our circle. So, I had to admit Anna was right. I was overthinking it. I texted Patrice and told her that I would join her for the delivery of the meal.

An hour before she was scheduled to pick me up, she texted me again to confirm her arrival time at my house and let me know she had her friend's two young daughters with her. She was watching them due to a family emergency. Her friend was currently walking the same difficult path with her husband that I had walked with Todd; her husband was currently intubated in the ICU. The difference was that she was much younger than I, expecting their third child, and had just been taken to the hospital due to pre-term labor. I prayed that she would not have to endure the same heartbreak that I, or the family Patrice and I were delivering the meal to, were witnessing. I hoped her husband would make a full recovery.

PATRICE AND I ARRIVED ON time with the two little girls in tow, and made our way into their home. Patrice walked the girls in, while I followed closely behind, carrying the meal. We entered the kitchen, where the husband and one of his daughters were standing.

"Mark, this is Lisa. Lisa, this is Mark and his daughter," Patrice said introducing us.

"Nice to meet you," he said. I noticed that he had the same stature as Todd, his beard flecked with salt and pepper, and an athletic hat that matched his attire. He had just returned home from coaching wrestling at the high school. Since I was holding the casserole dish, he could not shake my hand. He thanked Patrice for the meal, and they began discussing teacher-related topics. She mentioned that we were exploring the idea of co-authoring a book about grief.

While they talked, I placed the casserole dish on the counter next to me, and stood in the doorway between the dining room and kitchen. I felt it was a safe distance to stand, as I didn't want to intrude on anyone's space. I stood quietly and listened to their conversation. Patrice shared with Mark that I had lost my husband a couple months ago. He expressed his condolences, and I offered mine in return. We agreed that we were both walking a path neither of us had ever walked before—nor wanted to.

Mark shared his faith, expressing his certainty that his wife was with the Lord and that he would see her again. As the conversation continued, he spoke about God and his beliefs, while we made small talk about the world.

We began to talk about how, in times like these, people sometimes share unfiltered thoughts while attempting to console a grieving spouse. One thing Mark mentioned was the way some implied there was a reason God took our loved ones, or that, as widows and widowers, we were meant to find someone again. We both felt how incredulous it was to say such a thing so soon after a loved one's passing. Could they not hear the words coming out of their mouths?

He commented that when someone made that statement to him, he had wanted to punch them in the throat, but instead hugged them. I chuckled. He was funny, and I could completely relate to what he was saying.

"Can I ask you… how did your husband die?" Mark asked.

Patrice excused the girls and herself to the living room, shielding them from what I was about to say. Their father was walking through the same nightmare at that very moment, and it was too much for little ears to hear. I waited until they had left.

Mark's daughter had already retreated to the family room after introductions, leaving us alone in the kitchen to talk.

"He died from complications of the COVID hospital protocol," I said, very matter of factly. I felt no need to elaborate, as Mark and I had just met.

"I'm so sorry," he replied.

"And your wife?" I asked, even though I already knew the answer, that she had died in her sleep. Still, I wanted to give him an opportunity to share about her. He told me that she had been sick with a respiratory infection, though not from COVID. Yet, her death certificate stated otherwise, despite there being no autopsy done to confirm the cause.

In that moment, I realized we shared the same consensus of frustration. Families like ours had been forced into an unsettling reality because of the pandemic. My heart went out to him.

Mark went on to say that they had been high school sweethearts and married over 30 years, and were set to retire from their teaching careers in the next couple of years. Just like Todd and me, they had been preparing for the new chapter, rediscovering life as empty-nesters. I felt it was all so unfair. Someone else was enduring the same tragedy that I was—that reality weighed on me.

He added that his wife was buried in a nearby cemetery. Keeping her close to home had been important to him, so that if he or their children wanted to visit her grave, they easily could.

"It is right down the street from the school I teach at, but I'm glad that I don't have to drive past the cemetery on my way to work," he said. "That would be too difficult to handle."

He then shared that he had been teaching at the local elementary school for almost most of his career. Ironically, the school was located on the same street as the company Todd and I worked for. I knew for certain that the school had called the office for assistance on more than one occasion, and I couldn't help but wonder if Todd had answered one of the calls. Had these two men unknowingly crossed paths during that time?

"Your wife is buried in the cemetery down the street? So is my husband," I said. "I pass by your work and the cemetery every time I go to work. They're on the same street."

"Really? Wow," he said, then asked where I worked.

I couldn't help but reflect on how many similarities existed between our lives. What were the odds? But when God was involved, I reminded myself, there were no coincidences.

"I'd like to collaborate with you in the future," he said. "About us walking through grief," he added.

Collaborate? The idea intrigued me. At last, perhaps I had found someone my age who genuinely understood the weight of losing a spouse at such a pivotal moment in life. His perspective on grief as a man could offer meaningful insight in the book.

A few moments later, Patrice and the girls made their way back into the kitchen, signaling it was time for us to leave so the family could have dinner. We had caught them arriving home just minutes before delivering the meal.

Mark walked us to the front door. Patrice said her goodbyes, and she and the girls headed down the walkway toward her SUV.

"It was nice meeting you, and I'm sorry you're walking the same path as me," he said.

I nodded, looking down.

"May I give you a hug?" he asked.

"Yes," I said.

He gave me a quick side hug, and I said my goodbyes before joining Patrice and the girls for the ride home.

By the time we pulled into my driveway, Mark had sent me a friend request on Facebook. He wanted to keep in touch.

I accepted.

SO MUCH HAD HAPPENED OVER the past couple of days. The furnace was finally fixed; my dad had come to my rescue, and the repairman checked everything to ensure it was in working order. In his sweet encouragement, my dad said, "You did everything right, you know. You reached out to someone, called who you needed to call, and let them take care of it for you." He knew how hard that was for me.

And I had made a new friend. A friend who was walking the same path as me. While I was navigating my way into the fourth month of healing, Mark was barely out of his first. He was still trying to catch his breath. I could see the rawness of grief on his face. I knew it well. I remembered those early days, when the unbearable pain of loss felt all-consuming. The pressure in my chest from losing Todd had convinced me that I would die of a broken heart, and, honestly, I was okay if that were to happen. I couldn't imagine my life without him. I didn't want to stop being a wife or any of the other things he had made me.

And here was Mark, experiencing the same loss, but from a husband's perspective.

As I laid my head down on my pillow after returning home from the meal train delivery, I knew God was guiding both Mark's and my separate paths. I prayed for strength and guidance for him and his family, just as I prayed for my own.

January 12, 2022

Hi, Lovey,

I hope you are living as glorious of life as I have imagined you are. I am working on things—on myself. Especially since my last writing. They tell me anger is part of grief—and I have to own it. But I also know I can't sit in it. You wouldn't want me to.

I'm still dealing with bills and trying to make the best financial decisions I can. Anna left for college—she didn't want to go. I think being amongst your things comforted her. Jacob leaves in a couple of days. I think I am acclimated to being in the house alone—I still don't like it though. I would like you here with me. I miss you.

Guess what? I have COVID. Thankfully, it was mild but still stayed home. So did Jacob. We didn't get tested because of too much anxiety if it was a positive result.

I hope you hear my prayers being echoed in the air as I sent them up to God. Thank Him for getting me through this—for the strength, courage, and love He has provided.

So… question. What do you do up there? I'm curious. Seriously curious. If only I could come and visit.

I don't know if you know how purely and truly you are missed by everyone.

I love you more than you know,

Lisa

Chapter Twenty-Three

WHAT IS HEAVEN LIKE?

After I wrote my letter to Todd, I sat back and reflected on the world of grief. I was so thankful God had given family and friends to surround me, so I could lean on them, cry with them, and talk about Todd as I clung to the memories I had of him. God had given me the strength to get out of bed each morning, to take care of my family and myself, and put one foot in front of the other as I walked through this darkness.

He had given strength to my children, who were walking in their own grief but still had lifted me up, wiped my tears, and been by my side this entire time. He had given me humbleness in being grateful for all that He had provided. He had given me the courage to make the phone calls, process the paperwork, and make the decisions needed on this side of my new reality.

I could now make a phone call without sobbing at the mere mention of Todd's name. That was a big accomplishment. God had given me the comfort on my darkest days when I felt alone and in my darkest, most intrusive thoughts. He had given me the grace and mercy that my human spirit needed in gaining knowledge that I could survive such a loss and still be standing. So far, I had made it through Todd's birthday, our anniversary, and the holidays.

This walk had not been easy. But I was still here, standing tall and with God still guiding me.

There were days early on when I found myself lying on the bathroom floor, unable to move. I had accepted the reality of his loss and was now learning to navigate this altered life. I was currently working past the anger at times—anger that he wasn't there, especially when I needed someone to lean on.

On a daily basis, grief still brought a tear or two, where before, I would have been drowning in them. There were days I found joy, only to feel guilty because Todd wasn't there to share it with me. I knew four months post-loss I would still feel that at times. I knew I had to give myself grace.

But, through it all, God had given me an everlasting love; He listened to my cries during my nightly prayers. I knew He was going to dissolve this darkness and bring light to renew my days in moving me forward. I needed to be mindful of my patience in waiting and understanding, knowing that He still had a plan for me. As Jeremiah 29:11 states, "'For I know the plans I have for you,' declares the LORD, 'plans to prosper you and not to harm you, plans to give you hope and a future.'" I held onto this hope.

Grief was still coming in waves, and I was learning that healing and peace did, too.

GRIEF WAS STILL COMING IN waves, and I was learning that healing and peace did, too. I could now admit that my days saw more sunshine than clouds, with far less fog rolling in than before. As a newly-commissioned widow as of last fall, my mind had been clouded, so thick and heavy that I could barely see past my nose. They call it widow's fog, and it was as dense as pea soup.

I was grateful for the light returning into my days, and sounds of laughter filling the air again. I was now finding bits of happiness tucked amongst the overcast clouds of the wintry months.

BACK IN THE EARLY DAYS of loss, not only had my brain been dealing with the trauma of losing Todd, it could also not function properly. It was almost as if I could not compute anything sensible in my head, including the reality of time. Days after Todd's death, I found myself staring intently at the patio chair Todd always sat in, picturing him in full form, sitting there listening to his music and watching his grill. I was wishing he had never left and waiting for him to look over at me and smile. Or, I would lay on the lounge chair in the backyard and just stare at the clouds. The big, white, fluffy clouds that I imagined Heaven was surrounded by. And as my grief brain engaged, I only wished Todd would peek over one of those clouds and look for me; and when he found me, he would smile, and like Forrest Gump seeing Lieutenant Dan, wave, as if to say, "I'm here. I'm okay!"

As I laid there, I found myself holding tightly onto Todd's wedding ring. His gold ring, encrusted with a line of diamonds, was securely attached around my neck for many months. I knew eventually I would take it off, but each time I thought I was ready to attempt to unclasp it from my neck, I found myself bursting into tears. I was not ready yet.

But, on Christmas day, the children gave me the most beautiful gift ever: a custom made, gold pendant that had Todd's fingerprint embedded into it, with our wedding anniversary day imprinted on the other side. It was then that I realized I was ready to take off his ring. I wasn't sure what I wanted to do with it yet, so I placed it in my jewelry drawer for safe keeping.

PEOPLE WHO KNOW ME KNOW that I ask a lot of questions. It helps me find understanding and clarity in my daily goings-on. Since Todd's passing, I thought about Heaven A LOT. I was curious. How could I not be? It's where my beloved now resides and lives in glory. But I wanted to know if he arrived okay, because frankly, he didn't leave this earthly realm very peacefully. I wondered how I would have imagined him in his golden years, bless his heart. He would have been an amazing grandpa.

I think about his first few moments in Heaven and what it had to be like for him. It gave me all the peace I needed.

The necklace the children gave to me with Todd's fingerprint engraved in it

The grief brain is weird, and I don't wish it on anyone, honestly. Including myself. Of course, Todd did none of these things I imagined he would do in the clouds as I laid there, because I knew he now lived in paradise. He was too busy enjoying the magnificent place of Heaven to peek over the clouds at me.

So now, I wondered, what was Heaven like?

To me, it is too awesome of a thought that my emotions overwhelmed me to even be able to imagine it. I remember one night when Todd and I were first married, he and I, and another couple were sitting outside on the patio of our first home and we started talking about the universe, and I got choked up and excused myself. The very thought of the creation of the moon, stars, and galaxy was too awesome for me to feel. That was what Heaven felt like for me. Too awesome to imagine. Ineffable, really.

My thoughts about it, though, filled my head with questions. Especially now with Todd residing there. Was it above us, light years away, or residing beside us, parallel to our earthly realm, with its citizens ready to comfort and send love to those still here on earth? All those who have died before Todd, through thousands of years, are there, so are their levels of age in relation to when they died?

How can one define God's definition of paradise? My idea equated to Hawaiiesque, in nature, but with the most vibrant colors one has ever seen. Now, with the wintery weather coming in our neck of the woods, I began to ponder, was there snow up there? And if so, would he feel cold? I wonder if Todd could have ever imagined last year's snowfall was the last one he would see on earth. I know the answer is no. I hoped it was part of his paradise, although he did refer to it as "white poop," so maybe not.

Some of the weirder questions I had were, did he get to eat? That man LOVED food, especially BBQ. I knew he hungered or thirsted no more, but the tree of life with twelve kinds of fruit was not what he called a meal down here on earth! He needed sustenance! I have read there are feasts though, so… I didn't know. I was sure his belly was full.

See? I had lots of questions. I was curious. And I could kind of get deep in my thoughts, especially as I lay awake at night, unable to sleep. I could hear him say, "Woman, enough with the questions!" Todd was probably elbowing God in the side saying, "I TOLD you to be ready for her when she clasps her hands in prayer."

He knew me so well, as did God. Not only did I have questions about where Todd resided now, hoping all is well and that he was living out his time until the Second Coming, when we would all be reunited. But, I also had more selfish questions, too. I knew others would see him before me, so if I lived my life out as a Betty White wannabe. Would he be there, waiting for me?

One day driving home from church, the song "I Can Only Imagine" by MercyMe came on the radio. I was angry that I most likely would not be the first one in our family to see Todd, because there were others much older than me. I would immediately feel riddled with guilt of thinking of such a selfish thought. Todd's father passed away two years after him, and he joined his baby boy in eternity. I could imagine that the meet up between those men was quite magnificent, I'm sure.

Since I considered I was in my half-life with many more years to go, if the plans God had for me to live out this life involved happiness, abundance, and love, would Todd be cheering me from the sidelines of the clouds? I surely hoped so, because that is how I wanted to live my life, as I did when he was here.

Life is to be lived. And loved. And the hardest question of all was that when I died and arrived in Heaven, would he know me? Would he recognize an old gray-haired lady as the woman he once loved immensely and treated like his queen? That thought alone overwhelmed me and brought tears to my eyes. I knew in Heaven we wouldn't be married, but I wanted to think he would be there with his hand stretched out to escort me to the pearly gates, because here on earth he was my protector. Oh, to hold his hand again and say hello.

So yes, widow brain went into overdrive for me with my thoughts and questions.

IN SHARING MY MIND MUSINGS out loud to a friend in conversation, I received a little bit of clarity, or another one of my AHA moments. It was this: children ask questions. A lot of questions. And many of the questions our children ask us parents seem simple or frivolous in nature. "Why is the sky blue?" comes to mind. Oh, the many questions, I remember being asked by them, when I was a preschool teacher, way back when my children were young. These precious children are only trying to gain knowledge of things they do not understand. And, sometimes, we, as parents, or teachers, or adults in general, don't have the answers to give them at that precise moment.

So, this is how I see it. We are children of God. And being a child of God, these are my child-like questions. Sometimes He gives us the answers, and sometimes God doesn't give us all the answers we want or need. Haven't we all said to our children, "You are going to have to wait and see"?

So, I will just have to be patient and trust. God will reveal them to me when the moment is right and on His time, not mine. In the meantime, I will look to the clouds now, smile, and think of my beloved. In my heart, I know he is doing just fine.

I had to believe that I eventually would be, too.

February 12, 2022

Dear Honey,

I miss you still. It's a couple days before Valentine's Day and although it's just another day, I am not looking forward to it because you always showered me with love and flowers. You knew how much I love flowers! I hope you welcomed Mr. and Mrs. Holmes up in heaven. Scott's son, Camden, was wondering.

Life is not the same without you. I don't feel like living by myself—especially at night. You are missing from it. I finally got the financial stuff almost done. It stresses me out because I don't want to mess it up for what you provided for us.

I dream about you, too—and so thankful that you are in my dreams. I get to hold your hand. If only in real life. Ed came over to fix the toilet. I wanna give you a knuckle sandwich for leaving me to deal with all of this! But I hope you are proud of me.

I am slowly acclimating to life without you. I don't like it and if I had a choice, you would be with me again. I know I need to be patient—because I will see you again. In the meantime, I am fighting to find the truth and pray the doctors cared for you like they should have and not gave up on you. Because I never did, and wanted nothing more than to bring you home. Your flip flops are still sitting by the door.

I miss you so much. Please watch over us. You would be so proud of Jacob and Anna. Jacob has an interview with Boeing for his internship. Please cheer him on and put a word into the Big Guy to make this happen for him. He deserves it.

I love you so much

Your Valentine, Lisa

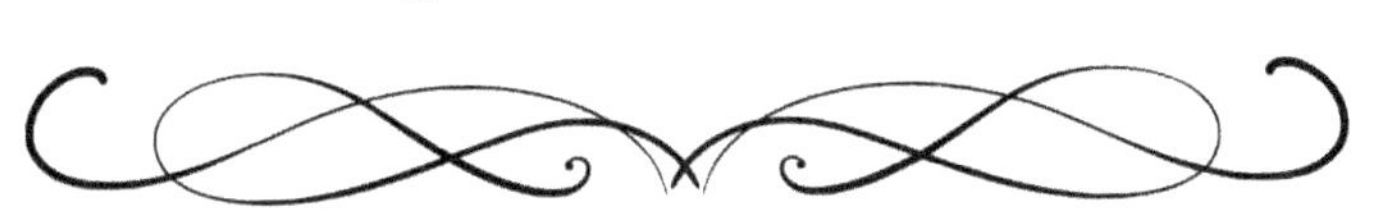

Chapter Twenty-Four

BELONGINGS AND BILLS

January moved into February. The kids returned to school a couple of weeks earlier, and I was in the early stages of sorting through Todd's belongings, deciding what to keep, what to give to the children and other family members, and what to donate. I was also managing medical bills and navigating the emotional triggers that still surfaced, even five months after his passing. I still cried every day.

But I was beginning to see the tiniest glimmer of hope, the freedom to make space for my healing, by slowly clearing out Todd's clothes and shoes from our bedroom. I needed to do this for myself. Many times before, I had stepped into our shared closet, fully prepared to take some of his clothes off the hangers, only to feel a wave of nausea at the mere touch of the fabric. That feeling became my barometer, telling me I wasn't ready. I had to listen to my gut in those moments, walking out of the closet, shutting the door, turning off the light, and reminding myself that today was not the day. I was learning to trust my instincts, letting

them guide me in knowing when I was ready.

On this day, I felt a quiet moment unfold, a space to process this next stage of healing. Seeing his shirts still hanging in the closet was a constant reminder of what I had lost, and I no longer wanted to be reminded in that way. Yet, honoring Todd mattered to me, and I wanted to keep remnants of him through his belongings. But I knew I couldn't keep everything. I did not want to build a sanctuary of sorrow anywhere in my life. Instead, I chose to go into this task, mindful of picking items that would weave a soft spot of remembrance into our lives each time my family and I would see them.

I started with what I felt was the easiest item to go through—his jeans. Many had been ordered online prior to him getting sick and had never been worn, so I had no emotional attachment to them. This step went quickly. I stacked them up and decided to offer them to his brother, Matt.

His collection of t-shirts was different. He loved his t-shirts, many purchased on vacations, and others owned long before we started our family. He had still worn them, and I wanted to preserve that connection. I decided I wanted to make blankets for Jacob and Anna, something they could each have in the future, maybe as a Christmas gift.

Next, I gathered most of his shoes and placed them in a bag that I would donate in the near future. His favorite flip flops still remained by the garage door; I felt it didn't hurt to leave them there for the time being. I emptied his underwear and sock drawer, placing the socks in the donation bag and the underwear in the trashcan. His athletic shorts were folded and placed into the donation bag, as well.

Now on to his shirts. I decided many of his shirts would be donated, but I chose twelve of his button-down work shirts to be used as fabric to create teddy bears for each of his future grandchildren, however many God chooses to bless our family with. I placed these items in the large, clear, container box I designated for things of his I wanted to keep.

I took the rest of his shirts off the hangers and put them on the bed to fold. Finally, I decided to save Todd's hoodies on the top shelf, so that when Jacob and Anna came back into town, they could each choose a couple to take back to college with them, if they wished.

I began the task of folding all of Todd's clothing to be donated, taking meticulous care with each piece. I buttoned every shirt, folded each sleeve toward the center, gently brought both sides together, and then folded the shirt in half-checking for any holes or stains in the fabric. I performed the process almost ceremoniously, knowing these would be my final moments touching these items. He had worn these clothes—to work, at home, throughout our life together—and as I folded them, memories surfaced, one after another. I prayed each piece of clothing I placed in the bag would bring joy to someone in need.

In moving some of his jackets to another closet, I felt something inside the chest pocket and found, of all things, a Taco Bell hot sauce packet. I actually laughed and shook my head. A true "smile moment," indeed. I could only imagine what our conversation would have been if he were here and I handed him the packet. He loved all things spicy.

Sorting through a loved one's belongings is a bittersweet experience, filled with both tears and smiles. That day, I felt both. It was a way to reconnect with our past and find solace in all the cherished memories we shared.

ONCE I HAD COMPLETED THE task of going through Todd's belongings, I knew I needed to shift gears and focus on the mounting medical bills that were arriving in my mailbox. There were dozens of bills from the hospital where he passed and from each doctor who had treated him.

When a person dies, a surviving spouse usually is not responsible for their medical debt, and many people advised me to ignore the bills or call the offices to inform them of Todd's passing. I knew there were some exceptions to the rule, but I didn't want to prolong my grief by ignoring the bills or making minimum payments. It would only be a reminder each time I went to the mailbox that I was living a nightmare.

I reached out to a legal firm and confirmed what I suspected. Under the Doctrine of Necessities, I was indeed obligated to pay these bills. The law holds a spouse liable if the medical treatment was deemed necessary for lifesaving care—a loophole of sorts. They surely did not save his life, but I was bound by this law, and more importantly, by my own integrity and Todd's memory. Regardless of how I felt toward the hospital and staff that treated him, paying his bills was the right thing to do.

Still, I didn't want to pay them blindly. I needed to ensure they had not been sent twice or overlooked by our insurance company for coverage. So, as each one arrived in my mailbox, I placed it in a separate stack, apart from my other mail and bills.

Then one evening, I knew I could not avoid these bills any longer. I logged into our insurance account to review the claims that had been filed. There were pages of them. Each doctor who entered my husband's room had submitted a charge. With a fresh cartridge of ink in my printer, I set out to print every claim submitted to our insurance company, along with the claim list page. A total of seventy-seven claims had been filed in my husband's name, with the largest from the hospital, totaling $256,412.52. The sight of that number made my stomach churn, but I knew I couldn't ignore it.

TODD AND I RARELY VISITED the doctor, only for checkups and emergencies, like Anna's wooden beam incident and Jacob's dog bite. Over the years, I had grown frustrated with rising out-of-pocket deductibles. On this night, I was deeply grateful we had insurance.

I took a deep breath, opened each envelope, and spread the medical bills across the kitchen counter in chronological order. On the claim list page, I numbered each entry and matched each bill to its assigned claim number, ensuring that dates, numbers, and amounts aligned. I stapled the claim to the corresponding bill, marked the claim number in the corner, and checked it off my list.

With a few bills still missing from my claim list, I logged into the various billing department websites and paid each one in full for any portion I was responsible for after insurance coverage. Three hours later, I had paid over $4,000 in medical bills.

Two more tasks completed. Yet one monumental challenge still lay ahead: Todd's medical files.

I wasn't just trying to settle his debt; I wanted to ensure I was in good standing with each doctor as I prepared myself to read through his medical files. I didn't feel ready, but God was making me uncomfortable again. I had enough on my plate, but clearly, this mattered to Him. I'm the kind of person who likes to sit by the water and ease in slowly, but that approach wasn't working here. I felt God pushing me out of the proverbial boat while I clung to its side, crying out, "I'm not ready."

But God knew I was. Why? I still didn't know.

I resolved that I was not ready to go through his medical files, searching for answers after his passing. I knew how painful it would be to see the lab results, the changes in his condition, and the procedures I was neither informed about nor consulted on. I had so many questions—questions I hoped had answers within those reports. I didn't feel as though I had the strength to make the necessary calls, to demand transparency. But God did.

In the past couple of weeks, I realized God had put pieces into place to move me forward. One of them was an ID protection subscription, one that Todd felt we needed and had paid into since 2015. I had intended to cancel it, but I discovered it included a legal counsel-based addendum, with over 300 hours built up for me to use. Hours I could use to seek the answers I needed. God bless my husband. God truly works in ways we don't even realize.

Then, in God's perfect timing, another person from Ohio reached out to me—someone who had lost his father in the same hospital where Todd passed away. He knew of my story through a mutual friend. And yet another connection came from Alabama. It was a widow whose husband had died under similar circumstances. His name was Todd, too, and he passed just one week after my Todd. None of our stories sat right with us. The way our loved ones' lives were taken under these hospitals' protocols weighed heavily on our hearts.

As I wrestled with the decision to review the medical files, I knew I would need to put my armor on once again. That morning, I opened my daily devotion and found this verse: *"Be on your guard; stand firm in the faith; be courageous; be strong,"* from 1 Corinthians 16:13.

As I walked this difficult journey, I prayed that God would continue to strengthen me to help others in their search for answers as I looked for my own, and to stand firm. I prayed I would bring light and truth to the world. I prayed God would grant me stillness as revelations unfolded, and that He would fill me with peace through it all. If I could help others along the way, then that was what I was called to do, courageously, in honor of my husband's legacy.

Time and time again, God had shown me that He would provide. I heard Him, I trusted Him, and so I moved forward.

The following evening, as I sat at my kitchen table, catching up on my sermon notes, I came across a prayer I had written seven weeks after

> *Time and time again, God had shown me that He would provide. I heard Him, I trusted Him, and so I moved forward.*

Todd's passing, when grief enveloped me, and I was constantly calling out to God for the strength to endure. It was the proverbial *writing a note in class*, except this time, it was in church, and I was quietly pouring my prayers onto the page as I sat in the pew.

God,

Give me the strength and grace to wake up each day and walk in trust that the plans you have for me will be fulfilled. I falter each day, and I continue to grieve for missing Todd and I know he is comforted in your arms. I am trying to find strength in knowing this, even as I am alone in this world. Please give me strength each and every day.

In your name, amen.

Healing had been a slow process, but seeing this prayer reminded me how far I had come. Now, five months later, I was intentionally rebuilding joy in my life. There were days when the clouds lingered, but more often than not, they parted, allowing the sun to shine through. And I began to feel its warmth again.

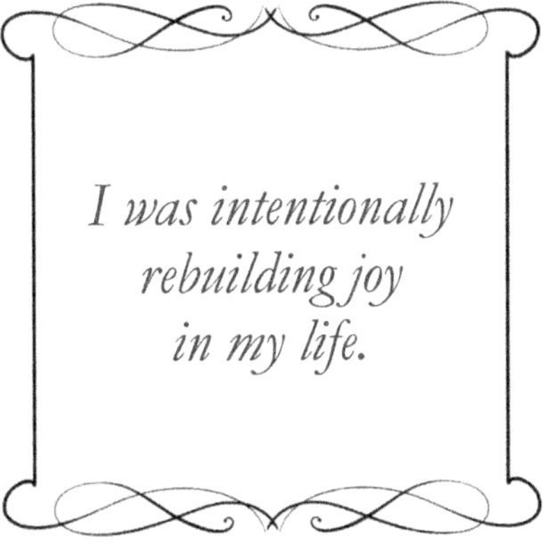

My happiness did not diminish the love I had for Todd, and it took time to release the guilt of realizing that.

March 12, 2022

My Dearest Todd,

It's been 6 months that you have been gone. How can that be? I miss you so very much. I still sometimes can't comprehend this reality. I want you here. I need you here. But I can't. And that hurts. I miss hugs and kisses and holding hands.

You would be so proud of Jacob and Anna. They are so incredible.

I love you so immensely and I struggle with where I should be in moving forward. I know it's God's plan. I hope you have some input into it because just as He knows me, so do you.

I wish you were here. Our world seems to be in chaos right now. Who will protect me? Life is different without you.

I miss you. I love you!

Lisa

Chapter Twenty-Five

THE CLOUDS ARE BREAKING

It seemed like forever ago, but also like yesterday that Todd would come home from work, and walk straight up to me to give me a kiss hello, with his usual "Hey Honeybear!" I missed that. I missed a lot of things. But I was beginning to find my footing in this altered life, as I now called it.

I heard the laughter in my voice again. I saw the smile reappearing when I looked in the mirror. For a long time, I felt guilty for allowing happiness back into my heart because Todd couldn't experience it with me. I had always held peace in my heart, knowing I would see him again. And now I was finding peace in knowing that although I was acclimating to this new path, he would want me to live it fully, and living my life to the fullest would not ever take away the love he and I shared. He was still here, tucked safely into a fold of my heart. The years of love spent together and the memories we created were now healing the broken pieces in it with his passing.

And for our children; Todd would have been so very proud of them. They checked on me regularly through these past months, they checked on each other, and made life stories to share with him when our time here on earth was done. They are the most amazing and precious souls. We were all healing in our own way from the loss we had experienced.

OVER THE PAST MONTH, MY friend, Patrice, felt compelled to start a group for those who had "lost their person." She was surrounded by many people experiencing loss, and received feedback that grief groups often led participants to continuously relive their pain. Wanting to offer a different perspective, she sought to create a space where we could focus on love and remembrance of our lost loved ones.

These were unchartered waters that we, in this newfound grief group, were learning to navigate together. Grief is such a complex emotion, and despite our efforts to find peace, it doesn't always fill the emptiness left in our lives. I began to wonder if that space needed to be filled at all, perhaps it was sacred in its own right.

At the end of February, she added both Mark and me to a grief group chat on Facebook. Aside from his "like" reactions to my Facebook posts about grief and how I was coping with it, he and I had not interacted since our initial introduction back in January, when I accompanied Patrice in delivering a meal. All I knew was that the day following our first meeting, he texted Patrice to thank her for inviting me.

In the group messages, Mark and I shared a couple situations we were both experiencing with people's reactions to healing through this kind of loss, but nothing more.

Then on March 7, I received a personal message from him on Facebook:

> Good morning, Lisa. As I changed my furnace filter this morning, I thought that my wife Amy didn't know how

or when to do that. I hope it won't sound condescending or insulting if I remind you to check yours.

I remember exactly where I was standing when I received his message. I was leaning up against the counter by my coffee maker, waiting for it to finish brewing. My phone pinged, notifying me a new message was received. I smiled as I read it, and I responded:

> Good morning. No, not at all. I have changed it recently and even put a date on it so I know when I changed it last—but better double check that it is not overdue. Thank you for the reminder and have a blessed day.

The next day, I sent him another message thanking him for reminding me because in my forgetfulness with a widow brain, it was three months overdue! I shared with him that it was my turn to offer assistance and mentioned how I handled dealing with the annual personal property tax declaration form we receive in the mail in our state, and how I completed Todd's signature line on the form. Mark responded shortly after, thanking me and explained he guessed on the form—a total "guy move," he commented, and thought these types of situations would be good for the "how-to" guide in dealing with being a widow or widower. I wholeheartedly agreed.

The Midwest weather was warming, filling my soul with energy and motivation to tackle more tasks around the house, including the garage. It had always been Todd's domain; I simply parked my car in it. But now, I needed to start cleaning and organizing, hoping to feel empowered enough to use his tools in case something needed fixing in the house.

As I moved things around, grief overwhelmed me once again. Being surrounded by his belongings still carried a deep emotional weight. I sat on the stoop and cried.

Later that day, I reached out to Mark with a message, sharing my experience.

Good afternoon, Mark. I think you will appreciate this—I had such respect for Todd in all the things he did in maintaining the house, yard, and cars, but boy was it humbling when I attempted to organize the garage yesterday, and seeing everything it took to keep up with it all. Like the string to the weed eater... pfft! Yeah, I never changed that before! I guess that is the journey in trying to figure out on my own now—one step at a time. I hope you are doing well. Have a blessed day.

After I finished my message, I thought about Mark and hoped he was doing well. Walking through widowhood was so painful. I knew the path I was navigating in my own life, and he was just a couple of months behind me in his own journey through grief. Each night, I continued to keep him and his family in my prayers.

Mark responded immediately and said:

Sounds like we have the same garage. My garage would be as intimidating as Amy's holiday decoration workspace. If you ever need someone to pop in for a quick weed eater tutorial it would be a pleasure. And I'd love to get tips on reorganizing our fridge and a tutorial on healthy eating.

I responded that I would definitely reach out and asked him to do the same. Based on his response, I could tell he saw the post I had written about getting my refrigerator back into shape and filling it with foods that brought vibrancy to my health. I kept many of my posts uplifting at this stage of my healing journey, frequently sharing on social media, almost as if to reassure my friends and family that I was okay, even on the days when I wasn't.

I suspect by just this one Facebook post, Mark wouldn't fully grasp yet how important healthy eating was to me, especially in the past month, after the health scare of thinking I was having a heart attack or broken heart syndrome. It was one I hadn't been prepared for. I wasn't ready to share too much about my life with him just yet. But, a few days later, I reached out again with a photo of my breakfast:

> I was making lunch this morning and thought of you and healthy eating. This is your reminder that a person cannot survive on canned soup alone (I tried it and don't recommend it). You are eating, right? And yes, there is yogurt underneath all that fruit. Have a blessed day—off to work I go.

Being in the grief group allowed us to encourage one another, including the need to take care of oneself.

As I MOVED THROUGH THESE months, I realized that healing was so multifaceted. It made me think back to when my children were little, how they would cry out at night because their legs hurt, mainly in the shin area. "Growing pains," I would tell them. I would rub their sore legs, give them Arnica Montana to ease the discomfort, and they would drift back to sleep. Their growth wasn't something I noticed daily, but their bodies knew, hence their pain. It became visible when the seasons changed or when it was time for new school clothes, especially in photos where their height had changed before my eyes. How did they grow up so quickly, I wondered? Because… it was subtle.

That's how healing happens, too. Just like the physical growing pains in our bodies, moving through grief and healing from it brings its own kind of discomfort, an aching of the soul and emotions. Some changes take months, while others take years. And the healing is subtle.

Many times, the pain from our loss becomes physical, too. I had lost a lot of weight in the past year, with the weight starting to fall off when the stress of Todd being in the hospital. It became evident each day that we were in this for the long haul, only in the end for me to walk out of the hospital with merely a bag of his things he came in with. People began to take notice of my change in physique and asked if I had been eating. "Coffee and soup," I would tell them.

One of the lingering side effects of statin therapy I experienced was trouble in swallowing. The stress from grief exacerbated it, therefore I survived on soup for my meals, when I felt like eating, hence why I mentioned to Mark about not recommending it.

Back in February, from most likely surviving on coffee and not taking care of myself, I made a hard call to my doctor for severe heartburn. It felt like a heart attack, and that sent me into an anxiety attack so severe that the nurse called me back and asked me to come into the office immediately. She heard my distressed cry for help even when I couldn't recognize it myself.

My doctor, after running an EKG and advising me that I had the most textbook heart rhythm she has ever seen in her career, advised me that her concern was that I most likely was dealing with something called, "Broken Heart Syndrome." The textbook name of it was called stress cardiomyopathy or Takotsubo cardiomyopathy. It was a real thing, and I wasn't surprised because I felt my heart had shattered into a million pieces when Todd died. I was just now beginning to pick them all up and move forward in my life.

Thankfully, it was confirmed I did not have stress cardiomyopathy, but she encouraged me to take anti-depressants to help with the emotional state during my grieving. I politely declined. Personally, I thought I was doing a good job in handling myself in grieving for the most part. Growing through grief, such as this, is not for the faint of heart; a medical condition can certainly attest to that.

I knew I needed to learn to take care of my health a bit more seriously, just as I had done prior to Todd's death; On the days that I took the time to eat healthy, instead of drinking coffee all day, or taking a long walk now that the winter months were behind me, I found it helped in the physical and mental attributes of grief. And spending my evenings in my bible and leaning into God's word helped me release some of the anxiety I was feeling.

In doing so, I found I was able to handle an emotional trigger, without a full-blown laying on the couch all day with an empty carton of ice cream by my side, finished off by yours truly, when I was taking care of myself.

I still experienced bumps of grief, the nights of laying in the darkness and silence, wondering what life would be like in the future. The mounds of paperwork, bills, and big decisions, wondering when it would all stop. The days of seeing others walking around living life, wondering why I now felt invisible, and why I was dealt this nasty hand in life. The "why me" questions running through my head. My soul had been ripped out of me, and I felt every miniscule of emotion in the early months of grief. Back then, I wondered, in times like these, how would I ever be whole again?

Regardless of my thoughts, I truly believe in order to heal I knew I needed to keep going-one step in front of the other. I was moving from one life journey into the next, trying to still fill my arms with all of the things I wanted to keep, only to realize some things had to be left behind or shifted, so they were easier to carry.

The weight of grief was quite heavy. And it was painful. I learned through this healing process not to make myself invisible in sharing this pain—so that others could understand. I could not resist change, because my life was still to be lived. And, in order to do that I needed to adjust, even when I didn't want to in the early days of this loss. I'll admit, I didn't like change. I still don't, if I were honest.

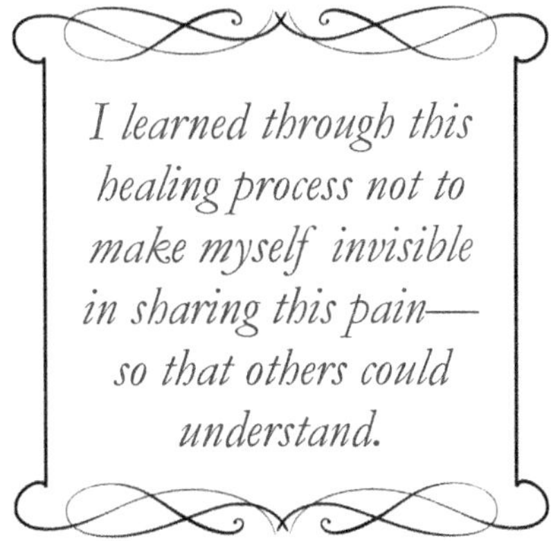

There were still moments when the clouds were as grey as the March skies. But most days, they parted, and the sun shone through. I felt the warmth again. I had come to understand that my happiness did not dilute the love I had for my beloved Todd, and accepting that took time. It took time not to feel guilt for carrying joy alongside my grief.

I TRUSTED THE NEXT CHAPTER, because I knew the author—God. In seeing the clouds part in my grief, I was starting to reflect on writing this story of my life. A memoir of sorts. I was a pen and paper girl, the kind who could spend hours in a stationery store oohing and aahing over the selections of writing utensils. I loved pens, and was picky about how they'd write. If it didn't perform a smooth glide across the paper, it got chucked into the trash. I've always been a bit ruthless about it, actually.

I had this beautiful pen, called my life, writing a story full of years and years and years left of marriage with an amazing man, only for the ink to run out. I had almost 50 chapters in this book of life written, with almost 28 of them with Todd. I didn't want the ink to run out on our story until we were both old. The last couple pages in these past chapters, I was shaking this proverbial pen for it to write, scribbling it across the paper to make the ink run again, but found nothing. I thought, *How could this story continue without one of the main characters in it?*

Todd was the main character in my story. It was then I realized that surrendering my pen was the way. It was hard to believe that my story would continue on into many more chapters, with this past one filled with absolute heartbreak, unbearable pain, and loss.

I thought I had control of what words were placed in my story to build this life, and even wrote about my "Year 48" in my blog, and how wonderful the chapter was going to be, only for the last few pages on it was me holding my husband's hand in the ICU, praying for him to wake up, only to witness him taking his last breath. I thought I was the one in control of my life.

God was reminding me once again who He was, and Who was in control. As I walked through the months of grief, I was humbled to realize that I was only a ghostwriter in this story. I decided to set my proverbial pen down. I had to trust God in continuing writing my story, because He was the author of it. He always had been. Although this chapter of winter began in darkness, light was gradually filling the pages as I stepped into the season of spring.

Grief became a catalyst for redefining myself. He has given me the ability to write, and I'm learning that these gifts aren't meant to be held tightly but offered back to Him. Writing had become the place where I met Him, where I laid down my fears and let Him shape the story, even when the path felt steep and the work asked more of me than I thought I had. Proverbs 31:25 says, "She is clothed with strength and 

dignity, and she laughs without fear of the future." For a long time, I didn't recognize myself in those words. Grief had stripped me bare, of certainty, of identity, of the life I thought I'd be living. But in that unraveling, something unexpected happened. Grief became the very place where God rebuilt me.

I WAS LEARNING NOT TO let the weight of others' spitefulness, strife, opinions, and empty apologies, both while Todd was in the hospital and after, hold me down, preventing me from moving forward. I knew I had to let go of those kinds of friendships for the sake of my well-being.

As I continued on this new path, I was learning not to let the opinions of others dictate how I chose to spend the rest of my earthly life, knowing that God would walk beside me every step of

the way. My life was precious, and I was determined to live it to the fullest. When people asked me what I wanted for my future, I would respond, *"I want whatever God wants for me."*

Grief is neither neat nor wrapped in a shiny package, none of us are perfect, myself included. I was learning to ask for forgiveness in my own dealings with unresolved matters. Through this loss, I discovered the people who were meant to stay in my life; those who stood by me despite the hurt feelings I had caused in the past. They are the family who remained by my side even in my darkest days, offering their unwavering support.

I was learning that it was okay to say no to the things others thought I needed to do to stay busy and cope with my grief. That lesson was a hard one, because I have always been a people-pleaser. I am still working on that.

And now, I was learning to listen to my heart, after such a scare of my own doing, in not taking care of myself after Todd's death. I needed to take care of myself for my children. Anna had already reminded me that I was *not* allowed to get sick. I knew what she meant by that.

I was learning to open my mind to what could become, understanding that moving forward didn't mean forgetting or moving on. I was learning to prioritize the things I wanted in my life, to set new goals, and to make plans without feeling guilty, praying, again, that my plans aligned with God's. I was learning to be patient through it all, leaning on His wisdom. And I was learning to feel excitement as I discovered where I wanted to be, and where God needed me to be.

I would always cherish the memories of Todd. Although I still cried at times, it wasn't daily, as it had been in the first five months after he passed. My heart was now filled with joy, knowing I was privileged to have been such a large part of his life and to have shared it with him.

GOD KNOWS MY PATH; HE is making a way for me. The lightness I was beginning to feel most days was proof of that.

If I could leave anyone with a thought, it would be this: *Just keep going. Just keep growing. You are stronger than you realize, and you will, in fact, get through what you go through—whatever that may be.* I promise.

Regardless of this path of pain and loss, I knew my life was blessed. I was blessed by the life Todd and I lived together, the children we raised, the home we built, and the family and friends who stood by me.

And I was blessed by the new friends who called to check on me, texted me reminders for home maintenance, and shared their own thoughts, which brought me great comfort.

God was placing me in His story because He was holding the pen all along.

April 8, 2022

Dearest Todd,

I miss you. I took a call today at work and they asked for you and my heart stopped. I wish I could have transferred the call. Tears streamed down my face after I hung up the phone. Like how—I'm still asking how. And when I try to move forward, it hits me again that I am in disbelief of you not being here. Like how?

And then… I get scared. Because you aren't here and I know I have to still live life and I want you to be looking down on me cheering me on. Because I get so discombobulated with the thought that someone may come into my life that I'll care about. I even talked to Sheila about it and I cried because my reality is nothing that I even imagined it would be spent without you. And, I prayed to God that if He had plans for another man to come into my life, that you would be part of helping to send him. It is all so overwhelming. I struggle looking at your medical files and wonder if I'm strong enough. I know God will guide me. I pray for you.

I know you are doing well.

I love you,

Lisa

Chapter Twenty-Six

LISA, PARTY OF ONE

I thrive in warm weather and sunny skies, and I felt that my grieving season was traveling alongside the four seasons of the year, with winter being the roughest for me. With spring's arrival, I decided I was ready to start reviewing Todd's medical files.

In the previous months, a friend connected me to another family whose father had passed away in the same hospital as Todd. In our discussions, I shared with the son that I needed to go through Todd's file, which included 193 pages. He told me the hospital did not provide me access to Todd's entire file. He added, if Todd had been hospitalized for a month, the file would have been extensive. His own family had experienced the same situation, and their father's file had amounted to thousands of pages. Something was definitely missing.

He encouraged me to place another request with the records department at the hospital. I knew I needed the records to ensure none of them were altered, and I hadn't yet decided what I would do if I found medical errors in his file. Errors that might have contributed to his death.

My mind went back to wondering about the whistling issue in his tracheotomy tube, and the replacement of the ventilator machine on the day that he died. I submitted my request for his files online and waited.

IN THE MEANTIME, I HAD reached out to Mark one particular Sunday with thoughts from one widow to another about "saying their name." I shared with him that as the months went by, I started to experience less people surrounding me, less mail arriving with words of condolences, less meals being dropped off, and less people talking about Todd or saying his name. It seemed that only myself, Jacob, and Anna spoke about him.

The natural progression of life going on for people had started, and I didn't fault anyone for this. It was merely an observation. I found myself not wanting to bring Todd's name up in casual conversation for fear people would assume I was seeking sympathy. This hesitation stemmed from a comment shortly after his death where someone had expressed frustration that another widow, whose husband had passed a year earlier, still spoke of him at every opportunity. I didn't want to be that person.

But now, many months later, I witnessed something beautiful happening: people were approaching me to share their memories of Todd or their thoughts of missing him, too. So, in the text to Mark, I shared my hope that people were still showing up for him and his family, and that they were still speaking his wife's name. And if they weren't, I wanted to remind him that the pendulum would swing back again, and people would say her name into the air and fill it with beautiful colors of her memory. I ended the message about how the weather was uplifting my soul and how I was going to spend the day working in the backyard after coming home from church.

Mark responded shortly after, and thanked me for reaching out. He shared his own experience of working through the disbelief of widowhood, but that it helped that his kids were around and the people he worked with were checking on him a lot. He thanked me again and expressed how helpful it was to talk with people who understood the situation.

Later in the day, Mark sent me another message asking about peppermint plant starts. He mentioned that if I had any to spare, he would love to plant some in his yard. I found myself beginning to enjoy and look forward to our conversations, even though they were only in electronic form. I responded back to his message that I would check on my plants and get back with him.

And although I felt this newfound giddiness about our correspondence, I was also weighed down by guilt. How was it that only seven months after Todd's passing that my thoughts were wandering between my husband and another man? It seemed like a double-edged sword.

I knew I eventually wanted to be loved again, but realizing it only two months after losing Todd was terrifying to me. I was lonely. Lonely in a way that I missed all that went with having a connection with another person, going on dates together, going out to eat, taking hikes in the woods, planning weekend trips, having long talks, or laughing at the inside jokes that only we knew about. I was quite confident I did not want to live this life by my-self, but I knew I was not ready to date, especially just seven months after my loss.

I was still overwhelmed with grief. I lost my spouse to death, not divorce. The difference for a widow or widower is that the love for their spouse remains. It never fades. I knew that was where the confusion and guilt began to set in.

As a surviving spouse, I wanted to be able to open my heart to a man who was going to love me the way I needed to be loved. I was blessed to be in a long marriage with a man who loved me unconditionally. I was spoiled in that department, so now I felt like I was being washed back out to sea amongst the rest of the people looking for love, but barely treading above water because I was not prepared for this path I had been placed on.

I just knew that when the time came for me to choose to date again, I was not going to settle for any less than what I deserved, because frankly, Todd had treated me like a queen. But I also knew that I needed time to heal first.

ABOUT A MONTH PRIOR TO this realization, and just a couple of weeks after Todd's passing, my friend Sheila had warned me that men would pay no mind to my situation and begin moving in wanting my attention. I had to be prepared for it. I was attractive, she said. They noticed, she reminded me.

In all honesty, I was shocked at her statement. *I am grieving my husband. I now have to deal with this, too?* I still wore my wedding ring. This thought only made me not want to go out into public. She knew from experience was all she said, so be ready, she warned.

It was all so incredulous.

Dating was such a foreign concept to me. The thought of even stepping out into the dating world again, as a mature woman and not a young, teenage girl, was not something that I wanted to do. I knew I didn't have the skills to play this dating game. Todd and I used to joke with one another, saying we were glad we were married to each other because neither of us could imagine having to deal with that world.

I did not sign up for this, but here I was: *Lisa, party of one.*

Our boss, Tom, lost his wife, Lisa, in a car accident, and was preparing to marry Sheila, my friend, who herself had lost her husband to a health issue. The week before attending their wedding, Todd and I were sitting on the patio talking about life, and the subject of marriage timelines for widows came up.

Todd and I talked about how we didn't understand how one could marry shortly after a loss, but we both acknowledged that it was not something we had ever experienced, therefore we had no place to judge. We were not in their shoes, and had no idea of the pain they had walked through that led them back to the altar. It was simply none of our business. We just wanted nothing but happiness for them after the tragedies they have both been dealt.

But then, Todd made an off-handed comment that caught me off guard. One that will be forever etched in my memory.

"If you died before me, I would never remarry," he said.

"Really?" I asked.

"No," he said. "It will only ever be you. Why?" He looked at me. "Would you?" he questioned.

"Well, I don't know," I replied, laughing off his question. I was being honest. I didn't like being put on the spot, nor imagining living my life in love with another man. Todd was the love of my life.

It was such an awkward conversation for him and I to have, I thought. Todd and I were young, so why were we even discussing this? I had always been someone who never wanted to hurt another person's feelings, and now my husband was sitting beside me on our patio, asking if I would ever remarry if he died. How in the world would I have ever conceived he would be gone just a year later?

That conversation is part of the guilt I carried as his late wife. Was I somehow less, as his spouse, for not wanting to follow in his footsteps in remaining forever true to me, even beyond death? He was the only man I ever loved, so the realization that I wanted to love again, if such a tragedy struck us, felt like a betrayal.

Along with that, I felt immense guilt for wanting to be loved again so soon after Todd's death. Shame crept in at the thought of voicing my feelings, but I chose to entrust my innermost thoughts to my friend Patrice, knowing she would keep our conversations private. One night at dinner with her a couple of months after Todd's passing, I blurted out my feelings on the subject, and then began to cry.

"Lisa, think of it this way. When you found out you were pregnant with Anna, did your love for Jacob lessen?"

I shook my head.

"So, there is enough room in your heart to love again. Your love for Todd will never fade, and the man that chooses to love you should understand that. And if he doesn't, then he is not the man for you."

"I know," I said, with my head bowed low. "I never thought of it that way," I replied.

Her perspective gave me a little bit of reprieve in the war going on in my head, but I still did not feel settled.

One sleepless night after our conversation, I lay there, a woman who was very comfortable living life as Todd's wife, and pondered Patrice's explanation of expanding my heart to be able to love again. But, now, I had to navigate life without the "Honeybears," the gentle morning kisses on my forehead, the goodnight kisses in the evening, the way he instinctively reached for my hand while crossing a parking lot. And all the quiet, unspoken gestures of love he had given me freely, without prompting, for almost three decades. I didn't know how to go on without them. Todd had always known how to care for me.

I felt lost without the daily touch of hand-holding and embraces, an essential part of my love language. Yet, admitting aloud that I didn't want to walk this life alone felt like an invitation for judgment, and not in the most favorable way. Like it or not, widowhood had placed me in a fishbowl, with every step scrutinized. Whether out of care or curiosity, people watched, and often judged in silence.

Nor did I want any man to exploit the delicate state I was in. I hadn't been in the presence of another man's attention since I was 16, and so much had changed—dating sites, texting, situationships, and countless other things, including my own body. As I approached 50, I found little enthusiasm for the chapter God had placed before me.

As I lay in bed, trying not to glance at the pillows I had still carefully stacked to block out Todd's empty side, loneliness wrapped itself around me in the darkness once again.

In that moment, I surrendered. I didn't know what else to do but to lift it up and give it to God, trusting Him to carry the weight of my grief. The guilt of acknowledging my reality pressed heavily on me—Todd was not coming back, no matter how much I longed for him. And yet, I couldn't ignore the truth: I didn't want to spend the rest of my life alone.

God and I have had our many conversations, mainly for strength, courage, and peace, but this particular prayer was different. There were specific things that I prayed for that night only God knew I wanted. And, God knows me. He knew me before I was formed in the womb. He knows the number of hairs on my head. He knows what I need. I could not write a better love story than God himself, so I clasped my hands and began to pray.

"God, thank you for this day. I'm lonely, and I know I am in this season of grief and waiting. So God, if you see fit that I need a man in my life to fulfill Your purpose, you are going to have to drop him in my lap, because I am NOT going on a dating site."

I was not too eloquent in my prayers that night. Again, way too early to share these thoughts with others, so I proceeded in my prayer to share with God what I needed. Like He didn't already know!

As you can see, I still had issues with wanting to steal the pen back!

"First and foremost, God, he needs to be a Christian man, a Godly man, not a lukewarm one. You know what I mean by this— a true man of God. A man who isn't afraid to say out loud that he loves you, Lord, who isn't embarrassed to share your Word whenever it is needed, and admit he is overcome with emotion during a sermon. A man who reads his Bible; one who would lead me in prayer and to church, one who fiercely guides and protects his family, and loves his community, all while having the character of integrity and honor, and with a strong moral compass. Lord, along with that, a man who will love me fully and out loud."

It was a big order, I knew. And I didn't stop there because, frankly, when I married Todd, I expected to live my life out with him, not this reality of considering a second chapter. But here I was. Go big or go home, I thought.

So, I continued, "And God, I know this sounds weird, but I have raised my children, and I just got to the finish line. I know you have a sense of humor, but please don't send me someone who has middle schoolers. I can't deal with the chaos that adolescence brings again. And one who doesn't drink. I don't need to say any more about that. And finally, one who didn't just get a new puppy. God, I have never lived a life without a pet, and I need the freedom to do so."

I know, it's not the grandest of prayers said by yours truly, but one of pure truth. I was sure God was planning on adding to the list of things He knew I also needed that I hadn't said out loud.

"Amen," I said and patted the pillows beside me, closing my eyes for another night alone. Being a widow is quite the lonely road.

I was not prepared for God to place a man of that caliber in my path so soon after I prayed for companionship. But He had, and I simply did not recognize it yet, nor was I quite ready for it. What felt unexpected to me had already been arranged by Him, quietly unfolding long before I understood what was happening.

Fast forward to the day after Mark and I had the discussion of peppermint plants. I arrived at work to see my friend, Sheila, in the office. She was visiting Tom before she ran her errands. She walked into my office and asked how I was doing.

I blurted out, "I think I have feelings for a man," and began to cry.

"Why are you crying?" she asked. handing me a Kleenex and giving me a hug.

I explained my extreme guilt in having emotions for someone else other than Todd so soon after his death. I was shocked by my own behavior. It had only been seven months since his passing.

She patted my hand and smiled.

"Lisa, there is nothing wrong with what you are feeling," she said. "You fulfilled your marriage covenant with Todd. Til death do you part. That is what God asked you to do. It's okay. As hard as it is to realize, it is no longer. You are free to find love again," she reassured me

She reminded me of the Bible verse Isaiah 43:18–19, that says, "Forget the former things; do not dwell on the past. See I am doing a new thing! Now it springs up; do you not perceive it? I am making a way in the wilderness, and streams in the wasteland."

She continued and said, "It's longer for us than for them, but I know that God wants the best for you. How much more does our Father in Heaven want for you? It's okay… cry… then wipe your tears, get up… laugh… and keep going until you cry again, and again, and again. But keep moving forward; you are not alone."

She then said, "Todd would really want you to enjoy life. He's in glory! He's having fun. And he just glanced at his watch in Heaven and said, 'Lisa will be here in a second' for a day with the Lord is as a thousand years!" she exclaimed.

Her affirmation was what I needed to release this guilt weighing on me. Love is eternal, and grace covers my heart's longing. I wanted to embrace the path set before me, knowing I was guided by love and faith. I was allowed to seek joy again.

My time without Todd will stretch from weeks to months, to years, to decades. I could choose to cherish our love, honoring and celebrating the life we built together, or I could live in fear of what the future held. I knew he would want the former, for me to find joy, not suffering.

Time feels longer here on earth than it does in Heaven, but it brought me peace to know that he wouldn't be waiting as long for me as I was for him. In the meantime, I knew I must embrace this altered life, collecting stories to share with him when we met again.

Sheila reminded me that even though I may not see it now, God was making a way—for me, for all of us. As much as I loved my former life, married to an incredible man, and would turn back time in a heartbeat to have it again, I couldn't. This was the path I was now traveling. And she urged me to hold on tight because it would be more than I could ever imagine.

"God will restore to you double," she said.

I looked up at her and nodded. She always knew what to say to calm my heart, and I needed someone to give me permission that it was okay. As a widow herself, Sheila understood.

"Now, tell me about this man who has captured your eye," she said, smiling.

Dearest Todd,

How am I still standing? This has been the hardest walk in life I have ever experienced and the person I need to lean on is gone. I miss you! I miss your morning forehead kisses, our hand holding, our cuddling on the couch, our closeness. This is what I am craving. This is what makes me sad. You are no longer in my presence—your things are, but you aren't. And how do I convey to people how raw and painful it is?

I have this gaping wound that scabs over from time to time, and then the scab gets scratched and it's bleeding again—this is how I have felt these past couple of days in the realization that you aren't here. I so struggled last night and cried harder than I had in a while.

Life is harder and I made myself open the patio door to breathe in fresh air and remind myself I am here for a purpose, even when for a couple of seconds, I wanted to join you. That is hard to say out loud—even harder to explain to people—I think they think I should be over the grief, and this is just not true! I lost one of my favorite people. You were my person. And I feel so alone in this big world now… No one comes around anymore to check on me. I don't know where I fit any more. Another thing that is hard to say out loud.

I pray today turns out to be a nice day—I need sun, I need the garden, I need to be in the dirt. I need life. I need you.

I pray to God nightly for strength and clarity and grace—so much grace.

I wonder if you can hear them as I say them too. Please keep watch over me, and our children. We miss you so much.

I love you always and still,

Lisa

Chapter Twenty-Seven

MEDICAL FILE NIGHTMARE

The night I wrote Todd's letter, I stood outside in the cold spring air, feeling utterly broken. Earlier that week, a large box had arrived in the mail. It was Todd's medical records. All 2,759 pages of them. I was stunned by how quickly they had arrived, especially after spending two months navigating bureaucratic hurdles just to receive what the hospital deemed necessary, which was only 193 pages of an "abstract" medical file.

I was grateful that God had placed another family in my path, one that had, unfortunately, endured the same experience at the hospital. Without their guidance, I would have never known to pursue the full file.

The families I had met going through this journey had all felt something didn't sit well with our loved one's care. I agreed. I felt it strongly in the week leading up to Todd's passing, and even more intensely the night before, leading into the day of his cardiac arrest. If the files revealed anything, perhaps it could offer me the peace my heart so desperately needed.

I stood, staring at the box sitting on the table for the longest time. It held the records of the last twenty-seven days of my husband's life; a life I felt was cut short by a system driven by greed and control. Some chose to believe there was only one way to treat this virus, shutting their eyes to alternative measures, nutritional support, and requests from Todd while admitted. My own pleas for a simple blood test early in his care, one that I believed could have altered the trajectory of his healing, were ignored, even as they injected him with six bottles of the anti-viral drug called Remdesivir. But I would never know unless I opened the box before me.

As I pulled the packing tape off the cardboard box, tears began to flow down my face. I thought, "Lisa, be careful what you wish for, because once you open this "Pandora's box" of files, you won't be able to shut it."

It's heavy when you finally sit down and take it all in. It took me six months to find the strength to read the abstract file, and the details within it were gut-wrenching. What shook me most was the glaring bias in the records: "PATIENT IS UNVACCINATED" written over and over, a harsh judgment rather than a neutral fact. Those words turned my stomach. The doctors had pledged to "first do no harm," yet the prejudice was undeniable.

My purpose in requesting the full medical records, this humongous box now sitting before me, was more to settle my soul in ensuring Todd had received the utmost care while he was there without me. I needed to know that their opinions hadn't overshadowed the level of treatment he was given.

"Please God, give me strength," I prayed.

God knew what I could handle. I knew I was strong, but I still prayed for added strength to get through these pages and the courage to ask the hard questions for the answers I needed. I felt I owed that to Todd. He protected me and our children in life, stood up for our family, provided for us, and loved us with his whole heart. He deserved for me to seek the truth in his passing.

If I wasn't willing to protect my family and others from what was going on in this world or stand for what was right and just, then what was I doing? I couldn't let Todd become another casualty, nor allow the fallen others to be dismissed, only for health officials to later clear their conscience by saying, "We just followed the protocol."

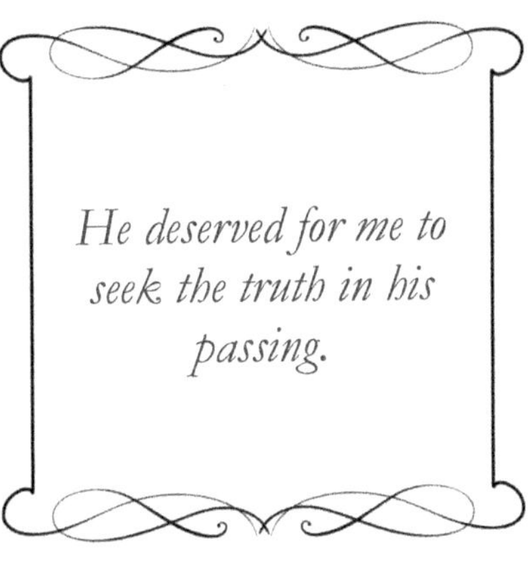

I felt God had put me on this path for a reason. I did not know why yet. Whether it was to give me peace in my knowledge of the situation and then let go and let Him handle the rest, or to stand up in advocating for future care of others, but I was sure God would reveal the reason once I dove headfirst into reviewing the pages in the file. With a deep breath, I proceeded to gingerly pull the file out of the box.

After creating a set of five, three-inch wide binders to house all of the pages, I went about trying to psych myself up for actually reading the paperwork, because I truly did not want to do it. I just didn't. It felt like ripping off a bandage from a wound that was just beginning to heal. I knew the emotional toll it would take, reading page after page of data, seeing the biased comments from doctors in the notes, and coming across my husband's signature on a consent form, knowing now that it was the last time he ever wrote his name.

It was going to be *hard*.

THIS IS WHERE I LEANED on God. We are called to do difficult things for God's purpose, things we may not want to face, but must. Whether this task was meant to make me an advocate for holistic health practices, to help others through this process, or simply to find the answers I needed, its purpose would reveal itself as I walked through it.

I prayed over these binders. I asked God for the strength to relive the most painful moments and read what was recorded with a sound mind. I prayed for the courage to uncover truths I wasn't sure I was ready to know, for clarity in documenting what I saw, and for discernment, so that when I came across certain notations in his file, I wouldn't mistake a piece of hay for a needle in a haystack, but instead see the full picture of his care. Care that, above all, I hoped had been given to him with the utmost compassion, regardless of his vaccination status.

The day I received the file started quietly, only to turn loud when I answered the phone at work, with a person on the other end asking for Todd about a bid. I had to explain why he wasn't available, forcing me to say the words again. "He passed away." It shook me. So, I asked myself, *Was I really ready to look at his files tonight?* I tried to talk myself out of it. But deep down, I knew it was time.

I opened my laptop to an empty spreadsheet and reached for the first binder. I spent the evening creating a spreadsheet with all of Todd's medical stats during his hospital stay, hoping to trace the patterns in his care. I wanted to see the full picture, as clearly as my knowledge allowed me to. Throughout the night, I combed through Todd's files, confirming that the ventilator in question had not been recalled, meaning I would never know if it had malfunctioned. I uncovered countless heartbreaking details about his stay, starting with the gradual decline in record-keeping.

There were gaps in his lab readings, days when certain tests were neither recorded nor, as far as I could tell, even run. To prevent bedsores, Todd had been repositioned three to four times a day, but that care abruptly stopped on September 10th, just two days before he died. They didn't know he was going to die, so why did they stop? His oral care ceased as well, on September 8, four days before his passing. Why? With a tracheotomy tube in his throat instead of his mouth, they could have still cleaned his mouth.

And then, the hardest blow of all stared back at me from the pages. At two o'clock in the morning on the day of his death, Todd suffered a possible inferior infarction, a lack of blood flow to the inferior side of his heart. A heart attack.

And no one from the hospital called me about it.

I sat at the kitchen table and sobbed upon realizing it was quite clear his care was inadequate during the last days of his life, especially for a patient in an ICU. But, how could they not call me on something as significant as a heart attack? I knew there was nothing I could do, but at least I could have been by his side!

They should have given me the decency of being by his side. I SHOULD HAVE BEEN BY HIS SIDE!

After the ECG, or electrocardiogram, reported the infarction, I read further into his reports that the doctors on staff had attempted to perform a CRRT, Continuous Renal Replacement Therapy, which was a different kind of dialysis than what Todd was currently receiving. I thought again, why had I not been notified? And why did they choose to do this therapy in the middle of the night? I had received paperwork to sign for administration of the first type, so why did they not need my permission for this type? It wasn't an emergency-related procedure.

And that day, Todd's kidneys began showing signs of waking up, evidenced by the urine output in the bag. It wasn't enough to remove him from dialysis completely, but we celebrated the small victory. Still, I was so confused.

As I read through more of the files, I came across the timeline of the day Todd passed, including all the cardiac tape readings. I had to mentally prepare myself to face them. I continued reading.

At 6:50 a.m., his readings showed a "flutter." At that exact moment, I was just getting out of bed to start my day. At 8:59:34 a.m., the first code blue was called. I was walking out of church, ready to head his way and spend the day with him, completely unaware of what I was about to walk into at the hospital.

His second and third code blue calls were not fully documented in his medical file. But at that point, it didn't matter. I had witnessed them myself.

I wanted so badly to stop reading the pages before me, each one revealing the progression of his death. But, I couldn't. I kept going, even as the weight of it began to take its toll. Sitting at the kitchen table, I felt the onset of an anxiety attack overtake me.

My mind raced, struggling to process the information set before me. My vision blurred with tears, and a wave of nausea hit me. I couldn't seem to get air into my lungs, so I pushed myself up from the table and stepped outside onto the patio, hoping to catch my breath. I stood there, looking up at the stars.

At that moment, I asked the question, *"God, why?"*

Not only the general, blanket statement of why, but why wasn't I there? Any other day, I would have been in his hospital room at the same time he coded the first time.

I knew I shouldn't have asked this question; I knew God wouldn't answer, especially not in the way I expected Him to. I still didn't understand why Todd was called home.

Was God protecting him from something more devastating than this in the future, or was it the pain he endured in the hospital that I could have not imagined? I did not know. I would never know. Only God knew. What I did know was that anger rose up in me, knowing I could not bring my husband back. Nothing could.

Todd was in Heaven and at peace, and I was trying my best, standing under the stars, to give all of this pain of emotion to God to carry for me, because frankly, it was so heavy.

And if I could bring Todd back, in these times, he would probably say, "Nah, I'm good up here."

I stood there, drawing deep breaths to steady my mind and soul. As painful as it was to read the files before me, I knew I couldn't sit in resentment or hate. I reminded myself that God is not a God of hurt, but of hope. Though I may never fully understand why things happened the way they did, I found comfort in knowing that He understands the pain we carry, and He would never lead us astray.

I had to have faith in that.

I WENT BACK INTO THE house and sat down at the table to continue my research, feeling a bit calmer. As I was going through the pile of all the papers and notes I had jotted down sitting next to the binders, I came across a notebook. It was a notebook that I took to the hospital every day to make notes in. The notes that I would then transcribe to send out to friends and family to keep them updated on Todd's daily condition. As I was flipping through the pages prior to my daily notations, I realized this was our previous "catch-all" family notebook, kind of like a junk drawer for house happenings in written form.

I must have just grabbed it off the counter on the first day he was in the ICU, when I was finally able to be by his side. I needed something to write in. Running on only two hours of sleep the night before, I knew I was on autopilot. One thing the notebook included were weeks after weeks of built-up grocery lists and weekly menus that Todd had written. I recognized his handwriting immediately. I envisioned him writing the lists out as I shouted out the ingredients across the kitchen, as I was looking in the fridge and pantry, for what we needed on it. It was something we did every week.

But on one particular page, something caught my eye; Todd had started writing a list to run to the store for me, and I must have passed by it and decided to leave him a little note of gratitude. I had simply written, "I love you." Seeing that memory brought a smile to my face. So many of the mundane things we had done as a married couple were done together, and followed by little actions of love to lift one another up, or to show care for each other in the most simplistic of ways. No fanfare, but showing how love is a verb in action. The mundane was at times taken for granted, but those were the ones I truly missed. All the memories of our little "love winks" had now become so precious to me.

I continued turning pages of this catch-all notebook; it also held notes of a sermon that I had listened to online, talking about the Book of Ecclesiastes, with Solomon and his wisdom for living well. There were notes about finding the path of happiness and contentment, making the choice to enjoy life, even in the moments of uncertainty, which was most certainly true on this path I was walking, living a life wise through the eyes of God, and stepping out of one's comfort zone to be bold in speech and action, that reminded me again to step out in faith.

These little jot-downs were just one of five pages of cliff notes of the sermon; there were so many more wisdom points within the scripture. And then words I had written on the last page were, "God gives you a purpose; I need to be wise not to waste this gift."

I sat back in my chair and sighed. Once again, I was reminded that we must not let the pages of our life story pull us into despair, that is not what God wants for us.

Reading through these medical notes was painful, yet I was profoundly blessed to have shared over thirty years with this incredible man. In the many days and weeks after Todd's passing, grief consumed me so completely that I often wondered how I had made it to another day. But now, I was becoming aware that joy and grief could coexist, that even as I faced this Goliath truth laid out before me on the kitchen table, I could hold both sorrow and gratitude in unison.

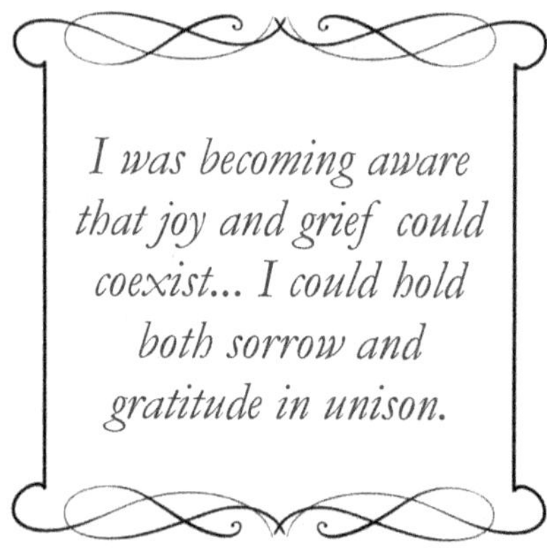

I wanted to acknowledge that I was beginning to see glimmers, small bursts of joy sprinkled throughout my days. Maybe not today, sitting in front of medical files, but they were there. The simple act of sitting in the backyard was becoming a sanctuary again, as the new season arrived with vibrant colors in my garden.

I looked forward to mornings in the sunroom, sipping coffee with the windows open, listening to the rustling of the trees, the birds singing, and the wind chimes composing their own melody, all while waiting for the sun to rise. I was grateful for the friends who listened to my sorrows and, in the next breath, filled my world with laughter when I needed it most. In these moments, I was finding joy. I had so much to be thankful for.

It was the assurance that God is in control, bringing a quiet confidence that everything would be alright; a calming hope.

Yes, we all have pages in our book of life filled with pain and darkness that cut us to the core. But I was becoming aware that, tucked within each chapter were countless blessings, the sweet memories, family, good friends, community, and the gift of living in peace, hope, and love. It was our choice to see these blessings and embrace each day God had given us. I was striving to reach that blissfulness daily.

WITH RENEWED STRENGTH, I WENT back to Todd's files, looking for anything related to the ventilator malfunctioning. I continued to read the last documentation of the final hours of his life, when I turned the page to see the words:

> Family presently at bedside. Coded 3 different times this morning starting at 0900. Went into PEA. CPR started immediately. Got pulse back twice. On the third code, wife was here and we were not able to get a pulse back.

And there it was. The reason why I needed his medical files. It was the moment I felt God lift my burden of guilt I had been carrying over these past seven months since Todd's death.

All this time, I felt the decision I had made to give the doctor permission to turn off his ventilator sealed Todd's fate in dying. I felt it was my fault. I didn't want him in any more pain; Todd had endured enough. And at the doctor's urging, I complied.

I had been carrying what I know now as exaggerated guilt on my shoulders, by myself, without anyone else's knowledge all this time.

And, God freed me of it in one sentence.

I sat back in my chair and cried for Todd. I loved that man to the depths of the earth, and though I still didn't know what I would do with these files in the future, I knew one thing for certain, this was the reason God had led me to retrieve them. To give myself grace in the hardest decision I had ever made.

I got up from the table and stepped away, retreating to the sunroom to let my tears fall.

AFTER I SPENT THE REST of the evening pouring over the volume of information in Todd's binders, I collapsed onto the sofa with a spoon in one hand and a carton of Breyer's vanilla ice cream in the other. I was going to eat my sorrows away, because my mind was exhausted and my world was still loud with grief, especially on this day.

As I was eating my ice cream, I posted on Facebook about the reality of managing grief, or the lack thereof. Within a few moments of hitting "post," I received a message from Mark, saying he just read my recent post. And after a long conversation with his children that evening, he polished off half a pint of Edy's Chocolate Cobblestone ice cream. He commented how good it was and asked "Why do they even make this kind of stuff!"

I giggled to myself as I read his message, then immediately responded, thanking him for making me smile, because I truly needed it. My fingers had started typing before my brain even caught up with what I was saying. He had no idea what kind of day I had, but somehow, he made me smile.

Curious, I asked him what kind of ice cream he was talking about. As a self-proclaimed ice cream connoisseur myself, I had never heard of it. Meanwhile, I was over here with plain vanilla, pretty boring, I thought. I told him I was glad someone understood—*really* understood grief, and then I hit "send."

And that's when it hit me. I was flirting. I gasped out loud, staring at my message. But it was too late. It was sent. Mortified and confused by my own actions, especially after the evening I had just endured, I sat frozen. *Who are you?* I wasn't used to acting this way with anyone other than Todd. Panic set in, and I slowly closed my laptop and walked upstairs to my bedroom. It was unsettling how quickly grief and joy intertwined, how they could catch me off guard like that. I felt blindsided and confused. Deciding it was best to just sleep it off, I climbed into bed.

The next morning, I messaged Mark back about getting good sleep, exercise, and a healthy breakfast after an ice cream binge. I gave him my cell phone number, asking him to call me. I felt I needed to set the record straight. He messaged me back saying he would call me after his wrestling tournament.

I kept myself busy cleaning the house, awaiting his call and rehearsing in my head how I would explain my behavior from the evening before. A few hours later the phone rang. It was Mark.

"Hi," I said. It was the first time I had spoken to him since our first meeting back in January, over three months ago. I thanked him for taking the time out of his busy schedule to call me.

"I need to share something with you," I continued. "I write better than I speak, and it's clear I speak better than I text, because I feel what I messaged to you last night was a bit of an overstep and flirty in nature."

I was grieving and he was grieving, too. I didn't want to make our interactions in the future awkward, even if I admitted to myself that he had caught my eye. He appreciated my requesting him to call me and said he did not take any offense to my forwardness. *Thank goodness,* I thought, and he began to talk to me about my writing.

"Lisa, I have read all of your Facebook posts. Many of the things you write about are emotions that I feel but cannot put into words myself. You write beautifully," he said.

"Writing has become my therapy," I confided to him. "There are many times that I open my laptop and let my emotions pour out onto the screen, and within a few minutes, a post is written. Sometimes though, I feel I share too much of my grief," I admitted.

"Please don't stop writing," he said. "I look forward to your posts. It helps me with my grief in not feeling alone in it, and it will help others, too. So, please, don't stop writing."

By this time, I had settled myself into my chair in the sunroom to talk to him on the phone. Our conversation continued into talking about his current wrestling season, how spring makes us both feel energized, and about our late spouses. Mark shared a couple of things about himself, as to when he started his teaching career. I realized he was a bit older than me, by four years.

Mark spoke again about his strength in his faith, and how he was looking forward to morel mushroom hunting later in the day. I had heard of it, but did not know what went into hunting these little mushrooms. I listened as he spoke excitedly about his hopes in finding some.

He shared with me a couple of things about Amy, such as her teaching career, as I shared some things about Todd. Our conversation flowed effortlessly. When we finally said our goodbyes and expressed appreciation for finding another person to share this pain with who truly understood, I ended the call, realizing we had spent an hour talking on the phone to one another.

The next day I messaged him telling him how much I enjoyed talking with him. It was comforting to be able to talk to someone who wasn't afraid to share grief and the depths of God's love for us as He comforts and strengthens us through this walk. I knew God had a plan and purpose for this all, even on the days we didn't see it. I ended the message saying I hope he was successful in his morel hunt and wished him a blessed Palm Sunday.

He responded shortly after admitting this "club" of widowhood we were in was not one he'd ever thought he'd be in, but that it was comforting, refreshing, and encouraging to not be in it alone. He told me he had no luck in finding morels but wasn't a quitter, so he was going to try some of his secret spots that day and returned my Palm Sunday blessing back to me.

A WEEK LATER, I MESSAGED him again, sharing my thoughts on grief and how it felt like an enigma. I told him that after our phone call, when he encouraged me not to stop writing, it reminded me to step forward, unafraid, and finally begin the book I had envisioned for over a decade.

I admitted that I wasn't meant to write it back then because, over time, it had transformed in my mind into something far more beautiful, woven with God's Word, just as it was intended to be.

I went on to explain my "procrastinating perfectionist" tendencies, how fear sometimes kept me from stepping into joy on this new path, and how I hesitated to begin writing. But I realized the blessing of my part-time work schedule; it would give me the time I needed to write. I thanked him for his encouragement, which was both needed and deeply appreciated. His words gave me the confidence to step out of my comfort zone, take a risk, and finally put pen to paper.

Since Easter weekend was approaching, I shared my thoughts and prayers with him and his family as they celebrated the holiday. We were both facing the "firsts" of holidays without our spouses; days that carried a unique weight of grief.

He responded, saying my writing uplifted him and that he would love to see me turn it into a book. He said he'd be first in line for an autographed copy. He admitted he loved the noise in his house and spent the day with extended family, frying mushrooms and coloring Easter eggs. He felt blessed beyond what he deserved and told me he appreciated me as a friend.

FROM THAT POINT ON, MARK and I began exchanging regular messages, small words of encouragement as we walked our separate paths through grief. Running on caffeine seemed to be a shared vice, and we both wanted to get back on track with healthy eating now that summer was approaching. He admitted that ice cream was his kryptonite. That made me smile. It was mine, too. More often than not, our conversations revolved around food.

Another week had passed when, one evening, I heard my iPad ping, a message on Facebook. I opened the cover to see it was from Mark. He asked if I had any experience with ferns. He was looking for some to hang in baskets on his porch, admitting that it was his "big project" for the weekend. I understood all too well how even the smallest tasks in grief could feel monumental, even something as simple as buying three ferns.

He could have easily gone to Home Depot and picked them up without asking me, but instead, he reached out. I was tickled by it. He knew, from my Facebook posts, that I was an avid gardener. And that made me smile, something I found I was doing a lot of recently.

I admitted that I was a bit impatient when it came to waiting for plants to fill out, so I encouraged him to go "big" and referred him to a local produce stand that sold plants.

He commented that he would definitely check out the selection the next day, since it had already closed for the evening. I asked him to let me know what other flowers they had, as I needed to start planning my gardens for spring and summer. I was eager to get outside, to sink my hands into the dirt. Gardening had become another form of therapy for me.

"I sure will. Let me know if there's anything in particular you're looking for," his message said.

I responded that I was looking for an elderberry bush and hibiscus plant, and noted that I was kind of a kid in a candy shop when it came to going to a plant nursery. I definitely could get myself in trouble overbuying plants!

As we were messaging back and forth about gardening, the subject turned to pests in the yard, mainly deer. We had a big deer problem in our area, and I sent him a photo of my decimated Hosta plants planted along the outside back wall of my sunroom.

I was threatening to hunt the deer down for revenge for ruining my garden, jokingly of course.

I shared a story about the escapades of my resident chipmunk, who lived beneath the rain barrels. His morning routine of scurrying across the patio had once been endearing, but his status was quickly elevated to "jerk" when I woke up to find he had taste-tested all the cantaloupes in my garden. That led to a conversation about Mark's pest control business. He offered to come over and take care of the problem, only if I wanted him to.

The chipmunk was cool, I explained, so I needed no assistance with it, but I asked if he had any suggestions for moles. He suggested stomping down their paths, sitting there waiting for it to move, and then using a shovel to "take care of the problem." Mark also had one in his yard and messaged, "Its days are numbered." I laughed out loud at picturing this scene unfolding.

I really enjoyed our banter back and forth. It was refreshing to feel comfortable joking and talking about topics other than grief and pain. I finished the conversation telling Mark how he made me laugh at his mole comment, and I asked him to let me know how fern shopping went.

THE NEXT DAY WAS SATURDAY, and I started the day off with a long walk. My walks, along with my writing, had become another therapy for me. I would set off with a playlist of gospel music playing in my ears to ground me, letting God set the tone for the day. Jeremy Camp was becoming one of my favorite Christian artists to listen to, especially knowing he had walked the same path of widowhood. I understand the pain and hope in the lyrics he sang.

I loved these walks. They allowed me time to listen to my music, enjoy the warmth of the springtime weather, contemplate my life, and step forward into it, all the while. also keeping Todd in my thoughts. This morning, I had Mark on my mind, too.

I realized I enjoyed talking to Mark and looked forward to our next conversation. It never felt forced. In the weeks after being freed from the heavy guilt I had carried for so long, I felt lighter in my soul. My mood shifted in ways I hadn't experienced in a long time, even before Todd became ill.

During my walk, I mentally ran down the list of things I needed to get done that day. One of the tasks involved fertilizing the yard. Todd had always done this task. But I didn't know what kind of fertilizer was needed. I had found a half-filled bag in the garage, but I wasn't sure how to adjust the settings on the contraption he used, the one hanging on the wall next to where I parked my car. The garage was his domain, not mine. So, I messaged Mark and asked, "Is it too soon to apply lawn fertilizer? I found some in the garage. And are there settings I need to know about?"

I didn't always want to rely on my dad to help me, so I felt comfortable reaching out to Mark with this type of question, while also trying to portray myself as a pretty independent woman. I did not want to be seen as a damsel in distress! He responded immediately, advising me it was fine to put fertilizer down now.

Then he asked if I had a drop spreader or rotary spreader. Dude! I had to look up the name of this rolling contraption hanging in the garage to even ask the question to him. I surely did not know what type I had! I replied, "A rotary, I think," though honestly, I wasn't sure. I just hoped my guess was right.

"I'm out bug spraying two houses today. I'd be happy to stop by and look at what you have." Mark texted back.

What?! He was offering to come to my house? I was not prepared for this response, I thought. I felt this feeling of nervousness and excitement overcome me. It felt strange and welcoming, all jumbled up together. We were becoming fast friends in our communication, so why did the idea of seeing him in person again feel so intense? But, if I were to be honest, deep down, I knew why.

"That would be great! What time are you thinking?" I asked.

"11:00-ish. If that works." He answered.

"See you then." I texted back. "You probably need my address."

I looked at the time on my phone. *Oh, my goodness!* I realized I had been walking for over an hour and was a mile from my house, near the local park, and he was going to arrive within the next hour!

He couldn't see me like this! My hair was shoved up into a hat, I had no makeup on, and I was sweaty from my walk, and probably not smelling the freshest, either. I needed to get home, shower, and had no time wasting in strolling back home. Without hesitation, I sprinted down the sidewalk, racing toward my house as fast as I could. Despite the rush, excitement bubbled within me. I had to admit to myself that I was excited to see him again.

When I got to the house, I kicked off my running shoes and ran up the stairs to my bathroom, turned on the shower, and mentally timed how long it would take for me to finish getting ready with enough time built in case he arrived a few minutes early. After my shower, and doing my hair and makeup, I put on a T-shirt and shorts. I looked at myself in the mirror. *Nope, that doesn't look right.* I took it off and tried on a dress. *Nope, again!* He knows I am fertilizing the lawn today, so I couldn't look too dressed up.

Back in the closet, the dress went. I grabbed a tank top and a pair of running shorts and put them on. I looked at myself in the mirror and decided that was the outfit I'd wear. Not too dressy or too messy. Just right. I put my flip flops on and went downstairs. I had about fifteen minutes to spare before he arrived.

Around 11:00, my doorbell rang. My heart skipped a beat. I opened the door. He looked good, wearing a t-shirt and khaki shorts. I hadn't seen him since our original meeting, and I had to play it cool. I noticed that he had shaved off his beard. I liked his new look, and commented on it. He explained that beards and shorts don't belong together, so he shaves it once the weather gets nice. I didn't know what he was feeling as he was talking to me, but I felt a nervous wreck!

I went to step outside, and my flip flop caught the threshold of the door and I tripped out onto the front porch, stumbling a bit. *Lisa, you are such a goof,* I thought to myself. I laughed it off. There goes any way of me trying to be nonchalant. I recovered, looked at him with a smile and said, "Thank you for coming to the house to help me with this."

"My pleasure," he said.

After adjusting the dial setting on the spreader for the fertilizer, he poured the contents of the bag I had found into the hopper and rolled it across the lawn to make sure the granules were dispersing evenly. I told him I would finish the job later and invited him to the backyard to show him the expansiveness of the square footage of the yard I had to figure out fertilizing. I admitted I was new to all of this and Todd took care of the majority of the outside chores. It was a bit overwhelming having to keep up with it, I shared.

The midday sun was beginning to heat up, so we found some shade as we stood talking about household chores and such.

Then, Mark looked at me and asked, "How are you doing?" I knew what he meant with this question. I felt I couldn't get too deep in my answer because I didn't want to cry in front of him.

"I'm doing okay. Most days are better than they used to be. The warm weather helps," I answered.

Mark proceeded to share with me about Amy and how great of a mother she was. He said she always made sure she made it home so her kids didn't have to come home to an empty house. I could totally relate to that because I did the same for my family. I shared with him that my nieces attended the elementary school where she had taught, so there were more connections with our circle that we were beginning to realize.

"Do you find it hard for people around you to see you happy and living in joy, knowing that your spouse is in Heaven? I mean, I know Amy is up in Heaven and I will see her again, so I have peace in that," he said.

"Yes, I feel the same way. It's hard for us left down here on earth, but I know Todd is in Heaven waiting for me." He admitted that it was rare that widows, such as us, had such a strong confidence still trying to find joy amongst the heartache of loss.

We began to talk about the pandemic and I shared that I had requested Todd's medical files, but wasn't sure if I wanted to proceed in any legal action for medical malpractice. I knew that would be the only way to find restitution for Todd's memory. I felt comfortable in sharing this information with Mark, and I continued by explaining my fear of dragging my children and myself through the heartache of reliving Todd's death during a drawn-out trial and concern of depleting the money Todd had left to support us to pay lawyer fees.

Mark acknowledged that was a hard decision to make and commented that sometimes healing starts with letting things go if they aren't fruitful, and if my kids and I were at peace, would it be worth walking through a trial? I had to agree. I wasn't worried about money, nor getting any kind of restitution from the hospital. It was more on bringing awareness to pandemic protocol.

Now that I had met with my financial advisors, and Todd's medical bills had all been paid, my soul was settled in being able to make a life with what Todd and I built. I was blessed with the legacy Todd had left and I did not want to waste it on fighting a conglomerate, like a hospital. I decided I would let Mark's words of advice simmer in my brain for a bit.

Mark stayed and visited with me for about an hour, and I let him know that I had to get ready to leave for my nephew's birthday party.

"It was good seeing you," he said, gave me a side hug, and climbed into his truck.

I watched as he backed it out of my driveway. I wondered what he was thinking in seeing me in person, and when I would see him again. I liked him. He was a nice gentleman and a family man. And, he was clearly a man of God. He spoke about God a lot during our visit. I liked that, as well, and it gave me comfort. And then I wondered—did he have the same excitement in wanting to see me, or was he merely helping a newfound friend in her time of need? Only time would tell. One thing I knew for sure was that I was so thankful he was my friend. I waved as he drove off, and I started to push the spreader to finish my now added job of fertilizing the yard before leaving for the birthday party.

Later in the day, I messaged Mark, asking if he ever went to the produce stand to look at the ferns. He told me that he got caught up in yard work and was hoping to get there soon. I had some errands to run near the stand, so I offered to give him an update on the inventory. After taking a quick trip to the produce stand, I sent Mark a message, letting him know they still had a large selection of plants for him to choose from.

"I enjoyed talking with you today," he messaged me.

"I did, as well. Anytime." I responded.

May 12, 2022

Dearest Todd,

My love, my love, my love,

Oh, how I miss you. So many photos come up on my memories of you, of us, and the kids that I smile but my heart still breaks with the knowledge of you not here. I hope you are watching over us and see all the amazing things J and A are doing.

I am headed out to Rolla tonight to celebrate Jacob's finished semester. Their birthdays are next week and how I wish you were here to celebrate with them—Anna wanted so badly to bring in her 21st with you.

8 months—how? 8 months since I had your touch, and your kisses. I truly miss you and struggle to find my footing with it on some days. Tuesday was one of those days where I wanted nothing more than to be with you because you were my protector, and our world has gone mad. I feel so much weight on my shoulders being here and taking care of everything—I need you to lean on.

The kids made my Mother's Day so special! You would be so proud. We started your grill—it felt weird—that was your place and when Jake sat down in your chair, unknowingly, it just brought back so many thoughts of you.

As I talked to Jake's mom today, I said you are in my heart always, that special place I will always hold for you. You were to be my rocking chair on the porch buddy! So many of us are hurting. We are trying to live in a world without the loves of our lives.

I love you to the moon and back and then some more...

Lisa

Chapter Twenty-Eight

DO HARD THINGS

We need to have some rain to see the flowers. March comes in like a lion and goes out like a lamb. April showers bring May flowers. We have all heard these expressions; the well-meaning sayings of life. And with these sayings comes the talk of change. The change to bring in renewal after a hardship.

In life, sometimes changes are ones we didn't want. They're placed in our lives without our consent, but still made for us to walk through. Change that upends everything we ever knew. So many of us walk through the grief of losing our "beloved ones," as I now referred to them. In the Bible, the term "beloved" means being highly esteemed, cherished, and dearly loved. For me, that was Todd. He is my beloved.

Change can be dark. It can be scary. It can be fraught with such anxiety, wondering what tomorrow would bring. Sometimes, those of us who find ourselves in this unimaginable scenario find ourselves lying on the bathroom floor, unable to move. It can drive us to our knees.

I'd been there. I was still there on some days, but much less now than before. It wasn't easy. Some days I wasn't sure I was strong enough to make it to the next. But eight months after Todd's death, I was still standing, and I knew others like me would be, too.

When I went to bed each night, I prayed that God still had things for me to do when I woke up in the morning. Faith that tomorrow would bring a new day of courage. I hoped that the darkness would soon bring new light. Faith in healing from sorrow and moving forward in remembering our loved ones in fondness and joy, knowing that we would be reunited with them in Heaven.

In the meantime, I knew God was not done with me. I knew I would continue walking the path He had laid before me, even if it meant not seeing what was around the bend.

I was beginning to feel joy and happiness fill my days.

I NOW UNDERSTOOD THAT LEARNING to live again after such a loss doesn't take away from all the wonderful memories experienced with our loved ones. Because of all the love we held for our loved ones, grief is the path we were made to walk. This feeling of grief was one that I knew would continue to show up numerous times down my path of life, for many years to come.

But as the ivy of grief's tendrils attempts to pull us into the darkness of the forest, the flowers of hope and healing line the path to help us keep our eyes steady. My hope may have been shaken over these many past months, but it is still strong—and my faith, even stronger.

> *But as the ivy of grief's tendrils attempts to pull us into the darkness of the forest, the flowers of hope and healing line the path to help us keep our eyes steady.*

One morning as I sat in the sunroom, I saw a post on social media about welcoming the month of May with peace, love, and joy. And then I looked up into the gardens in my backyard to see one flower. The only iris to bloom in my garden as of yet. An iris symbolizes wisdom, courage, hope and faith. Looking at this one iris, standing firmly on its own, reminded me of my own strength.

Day by day, step by step, what was meant for me on this path would find its way. I was confident that finding joy again wouldn't dilute my husband's memory. I felt finding joy would enrich it, bringing life and sharing it with him when I saw him again in Heaven. I truly believed, and still do, that although there is a scar on my heart, that God was still working things out for my good. And I knew it would be amazing.

With the springtime months upon us, it brought two more grief "firsts" in holidays, Easter and Mother's Day. Todd and I had hosted Easter at our home since the children were young, and it was convenient for the rest of the family to convene at our home afterwards, considering our church was located up the street. Todd and I would tag team the food duties for brunch, and make sure it was ready to eat within a short time after arriving back home from Easter services.

The night before the brunch, I arranged the dining tablescape to include cherished items of our loved ones. I felt with this first Easter without Todd, I wanted it to be especially meaningful to his and our family. I desired to honor those still here and those who had graduated to Heaven. Surprisingly, I found myself more relaxed in preparing for this holiday than Thanksgiving, which was proof that healing was happening in my heart.

The dishes, wine glasses, and cutlery were wedding gifts to Todd and me, almost 30 years ago. We used them every Easter, because the soft, floral, pastel pattern on our Noritake China went perfectly with the colors of this day. I lined the center of the dining table with blue Ball canning jars that were passed down to Todd and me from his grandparents, who used them for canning for many years. The tablecloth runner was sewn by my mother-in-law, a staple placement piece at the dining table every year. I was so thankful she was in town to celebrate with us this year.

The cake plate that held the centerpiece of a beautiful cage belonged to my Maw Maw. Inside the bird cage centerpiece, I quietly placed a keepsake of Todd's so he would be part of this day. I didn't want to make a big deal about the items I used on the table, and I only told a couple family members that Todd's piece, his inscribed gold money clip, was there. I felt he needed to be represented in such a joyous celebration of our Lord. And of course, the table's center was lined with flowers… always flowers. That Easter was spent enjoying family and fond memories of Todd.

And for Mother's Day, the children came home from college for the weekend. Since one of them had finals the following week, we celebrated early at a restaurant the night before. We decided to go to dinner after the attempt to fire up Todd's grill, Bessie, failed. That was another thing I would have to add to my list of things to figure out now that he wasn't here: how to clean and start the grill, because it had always been Todd's job.

I was finding my list of new duties as a sole homeowner of this house were beginning to mount up. But, on this day of celebration, I didn't want to worry about it. I knew how truly blessed I was in this life, regardless of the trials bestowed upon me in the past year. Mother's Day was pretty uneventful and calm, which was something I needed. I didn't want any materialistic items as gifts on this day; I only needed to be surrounded by my children. And they lovingly obliged.

By now, with it being eight months since Todd's passing, most days started off on the right side of the bed, which was the side I preferred to be on—metaphorically and physically. On my days off, I would usually walk a stretch of five miles around my neighborhood. And with my garden starting to show signs of life, with its sprouts starting to peek out of the soil for me to use, I also found myself wanting to focus more energy on eating a much healthier diet.

I had the new task of learning how to use the sprinkler system in our yard, so one afternoon, I reached out to Mark to see if he had one himself and asked if he could give me guidance on it. He responded that he had his system disconnected years ago because he never really used it since his yard was so small.

Then, Mark texted me a photo of his front porch, showcasing the ferns he had purchased, and thanked me for recommending where to buy them. In response, I sent him a picture of peppermint seedlings, just beginning to show tiny green sprouts above the soil. It was my small way of letting him know I hadn't forgotten his request from weeks prior. He was beginning to learn of my love for gardening through our conversations, so I appreciated his asking for my assistance in this yard project of his. I told him I'd keep him posted on their growth and let him know when they were ready. In the meantime, I ended my text complimenting him on his beautiful front porch and wishing him well.

Later, I shared with Mark an excerpt of a book that I was reading about hope. It explained that although we could not predict or control the outcome of our life's circumstances, we could know with great certainty that we will be okay because God is victorious. I confided that I did still struggle in walking the path of excitement in living life and finding joy in it, while still wearing the backpack of guilt of not having Todd by my side. I admitted that I needed to give myself grace in working through this emotion. I then extended Mark well wishes for the summer vacation ahead that he was heading into as a teacher.

He responded that he, too, was a reader, and shared some of his struggles in closing out the school year, since both he and his late wife were teachers. He was excited about the upcoming vacation that he and his children were taking out west.

I shared the struggles of sorrow and joy intertwined; a call from my mother-in-law, telling me that my father-in-law's cancer was in remission on the same day they were celebrating their 55th wedding anniversary, was an example. I was a ball of happiness and sadness all rolled together within this tight ball of grief.

In talking to her about the news and wishing them a happy anniversary, my thoughts went to *Wow, 55 years! I will never have the privilege of meeting that milestone now.* But at the same time, I felt so grateful for the 28 years of marriage Todd and I did get to have. It was crazy how these thoughts of grief were experienced within seconds of one another.

I shared with Mark how I experienced joy and sorrow while attending a movie event with a friend and her husband later that evening, after the phone call with my mother-in-law. I explained to Mark how overwhelming it was to witness so many couples walking in and out of the premiere holding hands. I went home and cried while sitting in my bathtub. I admitted that in the future, I needed to drive separately from others, in case I needed an opportunity to leave before the triggers of grief grew too strong. Mark understood. An exit plan for grievers, of sorts.

BUT EVEN EIGHT MONTHS LATER, grief had a way of creeping in when least expected, and some days, I found myself spiraling downward, unable to accomplish anything I set my mind to. Widow brain would take hold, and everything I started, I abandoned, as if caught mid-stride before the finish. Calls that needed to be made went unanswered, tasks remained incomplete, and even well-meaning reminders from others only reinforced that I was now a party of one. I had to navigate this alone, carrying the weight of our family's matters entirely on my shoulders. In those moments, I questioned whether I was doing it right.

On this particular spring day, I sat on the front porch watching the busyness of the neighborhood. Moms were pushing strollers, children were riding their bikes, and I waved as my neighbor and her husband rode by on his motorcycle. After I waved, I immediately felt melancholy. The world was alive and active, and I still sometimes felt on the outside of it.

I was constantly told I was strong, but if sitting on my front porch with tears streaming down my face, almost a year into this journey, wondering what my life would be like was considered strength, then I guess I was Superwoman. And this Superwoman didn't want to burden others with her struggles. So, I kept to myself, even though the very people I longed to reach out to shouldn't have to carry my burdens.

Very quietly, Mark became one of those people. He and I didn't talk a lot, maybe once every couple of weeks, but we were texting regularly at this point. Our communications were a check-in of sorts. With us both voluntarily having left the large widows' grief group thread that had started months prior, we decided we enjoyed one another's company and took comfort in how naturally we had connected. I was surely thankful he was a friend that I had added to my circle, and he shared with me that he felt the same.

If there is one thing to know about me, it is that I am a bit of an introvert, so reaching out is NOT in my wheelhouse. Even if it were, discussing the raw, painful realities of widowhood, the deep conversations that no one could truly understand unless they had walked through it, felt nearly impossible to share even in the grief groups, I found.

There were things I wanted to do, but I felt the weight of doubt pressing in, as if Satan himself whispered that I wasn't worthy. That I didn't have what it took to live life fully after such heartache, dragging me down even further in these moments. The guilt was real, the selfishness of still needing certain things, like the ones I confided to Todd in his monthly letters. And then came the added burden of knowing I had to turn the page of my own story to make those things happen.

At times, I asked myself why this heavy burden had been thrust upon me. Did I deserve it? Or was I merely an innocent bystander, just another casualty of life's cruel turns? The weight of grief on this particular day was overwhelming, and in that moment, I even felt imperfect in my own suffering.

In my heartache, I always clung to hope. The hope that rested in God. Some days, like this one, the only thing left to do was surrender to exhaustion. I would climb into bed, weary, with the emotions of mad and sad draining my soul. And I would pray, asking God, "Why did life have to be so hard?"

Yet, despite everything, I knew I would pull up my bootstraps and carry on.

THE NEXT DAY AT WORK, after throwing all my woes into the air, my co-worker, Ed, and I began talking about an unrelated topic that gave me another AHA moment, and it made us both stop in our tracks and start laughing. It was a discussion that came up about finding some younger adults not having the guidance in self-motivation nor having a solid work ethic. We weren't judging, simply trying to figure out how to be an example in guiding these youths, especially in the work force.

I mentioned to him the book *Do Hard Things* by Alex and Brett Harris. It was suggested to me many years ago by a Tom's late wife, Lisa, when I shared with her that Jacob's upcoming confirmation ceremony included the verse he chose to share with the congregation, which was 1 Timothy 4:12, which says, "Don't let anyone look down on you because you are young, but set an example for the believers in speech, in conduct, in love, in faith and in purity." After reading it, I decided to buy the book and give it to Jacob, as part of his gift of becoming a confirmand.

In our conversation about this book, Ed and I discussed how it challenges society's low expectations for youth, encouraging them to stand firm in their faith and "do hard things" for the glory of God. Believe me, there are incredible young people in our world stepping up and doing just that, often unnoticed. He and I both agreed. I shared with Ed the part of my testimony on my journey to baptism that included one of these types of incredible young people. It was Jake, my daughter's boyfriend.

Then, out of nowhere, the words tumbled from my mouth: "God gives us hard things to do that we may not understand." BOOM! I stopped, looked at Ed, his mouth agape, and we both burst into laughter. That precise moment felt like a humbling nudge from God, like He had figuratively smacked me across the face, not that He would, of course because He is a gentle and loving God, but it was as if He were saying, *"Woman, have I not been telling you to trust Me?"*

I absolutely love moments like this, when I am surrounded by people who lift me up during my struggles, reminding me to give myself grace and to trust that God still has a plan, even when the thief of self-pity tries to steal it. I cherished my work family for being my anchor on days when I felt like I was drifting out to this proverbial sea of grief, with their words of faith weaved seamlessly into our conversation, holding me still. It was a powerful reminder that God is always by my side, even on the days when I wrestle to find the strength to move forward in this new chapter of life.

As I am sharing my story, I find myself humbled in knowing He has given me this ability to write. It is a testimony of His glory. 1 Corinthians 12:4–6 says, "There are different kinds of gifts, but the same Spirit distributes them. There are different kinds of service, but the same Lord. There are different kinds of working, but in all of them and in everyone it is the same God at work." When God calls us to bring Him glory, He plants us where we are in life for that purpose. We may not know why, and I'm learning that these gifts aren't meant to be held tightly but offered back to Him. Writing has become the place where I met Him, in my healing, where I laid down my fears and let Him shape the story, even when the path still felt steep and the work asked more of me than I thought I had. So, to do hard things? Yes! It is an opportunity to do the Lord's work, even when the road is difficult.

June 12, 2022

Hey Babe,

How's heaven? I bet it's magnificent! Not like here. I feel like our world is a mess. You would be quite mad at what is going on with our country right now. I keep reminding myself that this too shall pass and I know God is in control. I just wish you were here to protect me; ya know? I'm sure you feel the same.

It's hard to believe that I have not held your hand in 9 months; 10 months in you kissing me. I still miss you. I miss all the little things. You made me feel so loved and so special. I miss that. I miss cuddling on the couch with you. And your laugh. You had the best laugh. I hope you are cracking jokes up there and making everyone laugh. You are "ashume." I am starting to accept this altered path—people say "new normal." I hate that.

None of this is normal, but I am finding joy in my days. The garden helps. The kids being home helps, and so does summer. I think of you often when I sit on the patio or when we fire up the grill. I am going to try to use your smoker to make jalapeños next weekend after we get back from the lake—Jacob and I are going to see your parents.

Your dad's cancer is in remission. I am so thankful for that. I don't know how your mom would have coped if she lost both of you in one year, so we will spend Father's Day with him.

Anna moved into her new apartment and Jacob got his first paycheck from Boeing which made him super happy. They are doing well and missing you! I hope you are looking down on us and feel proud. Your memory is always with us—you are the first person I think of when I open my eyes and the last person I think of when I close them at night. Until we meet again.

I love you immensely, Mr. Fulshom!

Love Always,

Mrs. Fulshom

P.S. I found your Father's Day card I gave you last year; it made me laugh.

Chapter Twenty-Nine

CROOKED ROADS

The warmth of early summer mornings allowed me to sit outside on the patio, sipping coffee and soaking in the peaceful stillness of the world. As I listened to the birds chirping and watched the delicate swirls of steam rising from my cup, I finished my letter to Todd.

I sat there, thinking—*nine months. How could this be?* Yet, I felt my heart slowly mending, stitched back together with the thread of sweet memories from our life.

On this particular morning, I felt calm. I strived to find the stillness to be able to heal from this tragedy, and I realized that I was finding more joy in my daily life. I never thought it would ever fully return. I felt settled in the acceptance of it all.

I truly never thought I would get to this place, but here I was. And I was so very grateful for it.

As I was trusting God in the whole process of this journey, I continued to praise Him in this storm of grief, knowing this bro-

kenness didn't get the final word. God did. I knew He would make it right in the end.

I sat and thought of my own progress of grieving, and how it was changing. Grief was never far from my mind. I felt like I was sitting in a quiet zone mode, but at the same time hoping it was not any of the "calm before the storm" kind of stillness. Frankly, I felt like I had been on high alert for far too long, with waves of uncertainty crashing down on me, barely keeping afloat at times.

This high alert feeling, in the only way I could describe it, was this feeling of stagnancy, but not unpleasant. Although my situation did stink, so maybe that word was fitting for how I was feeling. I still experienced moments of sadness and frustration, mainly because I found through this process that I was quite an impatient person. I was a Pollyanna, a moving forward kind of gal, a brush herself off and get along gal. Yet I felt I needed to be sitting still right now in this grief because it was part of the healing. But if I were to be honest, I didn't want to.

I realized that, no matter how desperately I wished otherwise, I couldn't change what had happened. Over the past nine months, everything in my life had shifted so rapidly with Todd's passing, finances evolving, the dynamics of my home changing as I became the head of household, accounts needing adjusting, budgets having to be reworked that every aspect of my world felt in flux.

Through it all, I realized I had been rushing, with this constant movement in making hard decisions on my own and trying to keep up with the relentless demands. I was mentally exhausted. And yet, in this quiet morning, for the first time, I felt stillness. So much so, it felt almost uncomfortable.

Stagnant.

I WANTED MY LIFE TO flow again, for it to move in the direction I needed it to, or perhaps in the way I simply wanted it to. I just didn't know how yet.

During this time, I began reading a memoir in which the author described an emergency medical crisis that caused her intense pain and suffering. She lay in wait, praying desperately for relief, crying out to God to take the pain away. But, He didn't. At least, not in the way she had hoped. Instead, He performed a miracle. A miracle, because she survived something that most do not, allowing her to continue living her life.

I felt the words hit me at my core.

There had been so many nights right after Todd's passing that I cried out to God to do the same for me. *God, please just take this pain away!* I needed my heart to be repaired and be put back together. I didn't know how, because Todd wasn't there, as he would have been sitting next to me on the patio as I was now, but I needed it done. NOW. Remember, my impatience? The pain felt too great at times when some of the triggers hit; and they hit hard in early stages of grief.

"Just fix it God," I would say, knowing full well my demands were not going to be filled anytime soon. He didn't take the raw pain away, at least not immediately, nor very subtly, as I had wanted.

Why would I think all my pain would be taken away when I knew all wounds took time to heal? And this wound was a MASSIVE one.

But, ever so slowly, the pain was subsiding. And as I sat on the patio in stillness, I knew God was listening.

NOW, MY MORNINGS STILL BEGAN with a thought of Todd, but they were no longer with the sharp, stabbing pain that had gripped me in the months after he passed. Instead, the ache had softened into fleeting twinges, some more difficult than others, but manageable.

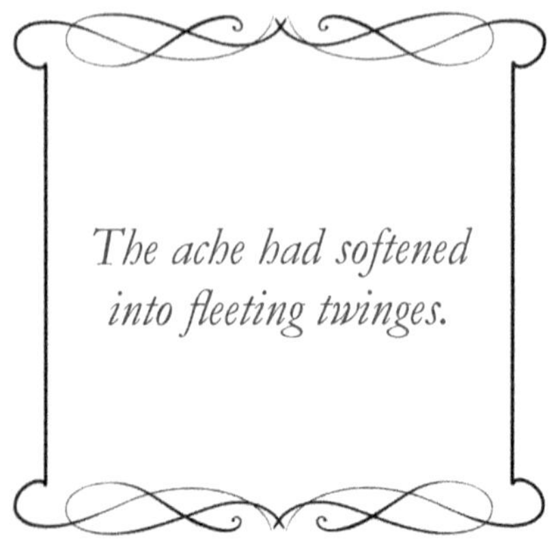

I began to understand that healing from this kind of grief took time.

The day before, a dear friend's husband had delivered a sermon at the inaugural service of their new church. His message spoke to the way seemingly crooked roads are often straight in God's plan, that His timing governs the unfolding of our lives; it's not our own timing.

God is not in a rush, but we are.

The pastor used the life of young Joseph in the Book of Genesis as an example, showing how lengthy and winding the path was before God placed him before Pharaoh to interpret his dream.

I realized that I was in rush mode, a subset of survival mode. A lot of us are, honestly, because life is hard. I don't think anyone comes through their life unscathed by hardship.

We often perceive our path as crooked, or, in my case, as strewn with obstacles, especially for me with stones I kept stumbling over as I navigated the uncertainties of life. *Did I handle this well? Did I make the right decision? Am I worthy? Will I forever walk this life alone?* These are the heavy stones of doubt and healing that littered my seemingly crooked path.

Many times, I stopped on the path, not wanting to go any further, trying to catch my breath. Sometimes, I wanted to fold into myself. At times, I felt like a child not getting her way in any of this, but still knowing I needed to carry on. I realized that carrying on was my hope, kicking into full gear!

I knew I wanted to see the end of the path God had placed before me, to understand what was ahead. But at this moment, I couldn't. My vision faltered, clouded by the crookedness I perceived, even in the stillness and stagnancy. But God has a calling for each of us, a purpose that is uniquely ours. It may feel unclear to us, but never to Him. I was not meant to see the full path yet.

Hello, again, impatience. Nice to see you.

EXCITEMENT FOR WHAT GOD HAD planned stirred within me, yet the weight of grief and guilt still clung to my shoulders. I felt like I was stumbling through this journey, tripping over my own feet more often than not.

These were the moments I had to remind myself to give grace, to accept that healing and clarity take time. As Todd used to say, "You are harder on yourself than anyone I know."

And to that, I'd reply, *"I haven't changed, honey."*

As I sat that morning, looking out at my gardens and sipping my coffee, I thought back to when we first moved into this home. There was hardly a stitch of vegetation, just grass and a few baby Bradford pear trees planted neatly across the yard. Those once-tiny trees now stood tall, shading me from the heat as I cut the grass. The gardens we built over the years had transformed into a beautiful landscape, providing both a picturesque view from the patio and fresh, delicious additions to my family's meals. The patio itself had become a place of gathering, where time was spent with friends and family alike. It took time to create all of this. Time spent planning, patiently shaping our vision without rushing, because we didn't yet know how it would come together. A crooked path, in a way. But as I looked at it now, I thought, *it is now so beautiful.*

That is why I have faith. I believe that God *is* working things out for my good, and this season of stillness was part of His plan. I knew He hadn't forgotten me.

God's loving hands were healing my heart, and I was

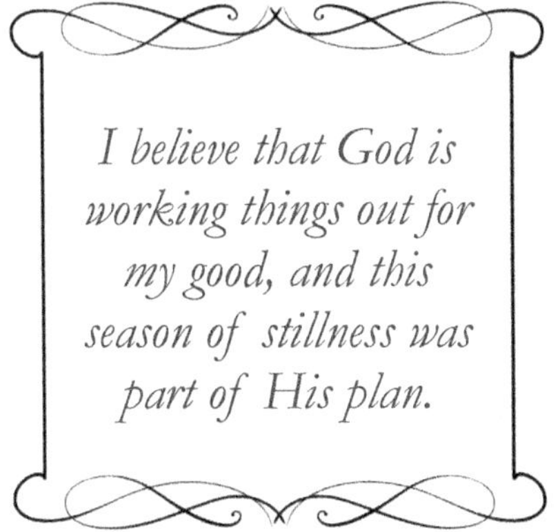

confident that His path for me would be completely renewed in His way.

He was preparing me, and His timing was perfect.

I just need to be patient in the waiting.

July 12, 2022

Babe,

Sometimes I just sit here in the early morning with coffee in hand and think about you. This week has been rough—I don't know why. It just is. I think partly it is because I am lonely. I miss us. I miss all the things we did, even down to you holding my hand as we would cross a parking lot. Our mornings in the sunroom drinking coffee. Your kisses. I miss it all. I miss your presence and your loving touch and wonder if I will ever have that again. And then I feel guilt for wanting it. I hate this and I wish I could snap my fingers and life would be back the way it was.

I feel like I am losing my patience because life is so overwhelming. The house—there is so many things to do to keep up with it and not the energy to do it. The dogs! Hair is everywhere. I am so over it and sometimes wonder if putting up a for sale sign would just be better. But then, I sit here, outside with my coffee, listening to the birds and see all that we have built. This is all truly heartbreaking. I know you are looking down on us and all I want to do is make you proud.

Jacob and I went to the cemetery on Saturday. I felt I needed to go even though only your body is there. I don't like thinking of it 6 feet under from where I was standing. Still in disbelief and it is said that the 2nd year is harder than the first. I surely hope not—I don't know if I will survive it. 10 months has been hard enough.

Love,

Lisa

And a few days later…

July 18, 2022

I am tired. I am mad. I feel alone. I don't feel I will ever love again. No one wants to hear about my grief anymore. I'll just be quiet. I am angry at you…

Chapter Thirty

WARM WEATHER FEELS LIKE HOPE

I felt like I had become quite the connoisseur of grief's many faces. Most days, I felt I was handling life well, but again, some days, like the one when I sat down to write Todd's letter in his journal, it just didn't happen. And I was finally okay with that.

Our family made it through two more "firsts" in holidays: Father's Day and the Fourth of July. In years past, Todd would start Father's Day by making a big breakfast, and then we'd all pile into Jacob's Chevelle, with Todd riding up front with him, on our way to the movie theater to watch a film of his choice.

This year was different. Jacob and I traveled to Table Rock Lake to spend the weekend with Todd's parents and celebrate my father-in-law. As I lay in bed at the lake house on a day to celebrate fathers, I thought about how one of the greatest callings God can bestow upon a man is the call to fatherhood. And Todd embraced it so well. I knew how proud he would have been of these two incredible children God had given us to raise. They were truly amazing.

I texted Mark to wish him a well-deserved day, knowing he was busy preparing for his daughter's upcoming wedding. Over the past month, we had corresponded frequently about a variety of topics, like gardening, exercising, and food. We seemed to have much in common.

I was learning about the foods he enjoyed and would often share my own, sometimes sending a photo of a meal I had prepared. Cooking for one was still an adjustment.

In his text, Mark mentioned he was looking forward to a busy summer, with plenty to do, not just his daughter's wedding, but also his son's wedding in September. I couldn't imagine the emotional weight of planning two weddings within the first year of losing a spouse. My heart went out to him, knowing how deeply layered the emotions must be during such momentous celebrations.

So, whenever I could, I sent Mark a note of encouragement.

Many times, the encouragement would come through a podcast or a writing in the margins of my Bible. I wanted to remind Mark that I still had days of unsettledness, but was confident that God was still writing my story, his story, and all the others who have lost a loved one. I knew too well the pain and healing that would be used for His glory.

After Father's Day, I sent Mark a text along with a photo of a pot full of thriving peppermint starts.

"Are you still wanting peppermint starts? The ones I put outside are growing like gangbusters!" I wrote.

"Yes, ma'am, I am!" he responded.

He told me he'd be out and about the next day and could stop by my house with his truck, saving me the trouble of transporting the plants and keeping the dirt out of my car. We planned to meet at my house after I returned from work, and I assured him I would call once I got home.

On his way over, Mark sent a text to let me know his estimated time of arrival. I appreciated that small gesture. Todd used to do the same, anytime he would be heading for the "homestead," as he called it.

It had been a few months since I had last seen Mark in person. With summer in full swing, my children were back at home. As Anna and Jake sat in the family room watching TV, I gave them a heads-up that Mark would be stopping by and why.

I wasn't concerned about them questioning his visit, but I wanted to be respectful by preparing them for his arrival. They knew him personally, and Anna was aware that he and I had been communicating for a while.

When Mark arrived, I invited him inside and let him know the kids were there. He stepped into the family room to say hello to them before we made our way to the backyard through the patio door. I led him to the potted peppermint, and he carried the pot to the front of the house to load it into the back of his truck, with me following behind. After securing it, he stepped to the side of his truck, lingering for a short visit.

Mark mentioned he was headed to his Bible study group but had a little time before he needed to leave. He expressed how grateful he was to have that additional support in his life.

"How was your trip?" I asked him.

He shared how wonderful his family's trip out west had been, and how he did not plan any of it prior to leaving, not even a hotel room reservation. *Now, that's an adventure*, I thought. Me, being the planner I am, could never. He laughed, and said his youngest daughter was a planner, too. He and his children had taken his wife's van at the request of his children to take one last vacation in her vehicle.

Switching topics in our conversation, Mark asked, "Do you notice that every movie has some storyline in it about someone dying? It's like every movie we choose to watch had it; we couldn't get away from it. After a while, we start to guess 'who would it be?'" he said, meaning which character would succumb to loss and grief.

Ah, the dark humor we sometimes lean on to navigate life's challenges. I definitely had it, too. And my daughter? She had buckets of it!

I chuckled, and said, "Yeah, I noticed that too. And don't watch a Hallmark movie then. There is usually a widow in it."

I laughed again and admitted that I had watched quite a few of them last Christmas. It was comforting to know that I wasn't alone in this journey. After all, if movies were made where a widow played an important role in the plot, it meant that others had walked this path, too.

Earlier in the month, Mark and I had exchanged more photos, mine of the kids and me at Elephant Rocks State Park, and his from a wrestling tournament. As we talked, the conversation drifted to his oldest daughter's recent wedding, his son's upcoming wedding in September, and his youngest daughter preparing to return to college.

He mentioned that he was about to experience life on his own, and having them leave in stages felt like God was giving him a *soft release.*

"God knows me well," Mark said.

"He knows what we need before we even ask," I replied.

"I love my kids, but I'm also ready to try life on my own," he admitted.

We talked about his preparations for the weddings and how his late wife, Amy, would have had everything planned out perfectly. I was learning a lot about his love for his late wife. He shared how grateful he was to be surrounded by the women in his family, who were helping guide him through the process.

Mark mentioned that he was one of six children—three brothers and two sisters—and how deeply connected he was to his family.

We stood by his truck, chatting back and forth for about an hour, him sharing memories of his life with Amy, and me reminiscing about my time with Todd. Our conversation flowed naturally, touching on our love languages and the foundation of our marriages. I felt comfortable opening up to him. He felt safe.

"I loved being loved," I admitted, and shared how blessed of a marriage I experienced with Todd.

He nodded.

He began reminiscing about Amy and her fierce love for their children. "She always made sure she was home, so none of us ever had to walk into an empty house," he said. I told him I could relate to that level of motherhood.

After a few more minutes of talking about Todd and Amy, he looked at his watch, and he said that he best be on his way. He thanked me for the plants and excused himself to head toward his Bible study meeting.

Shortly after Mark left, Anna, Jake, and I headed to the new sushi place in town for dinner.

"I didn't think you guys would ever stop talking outside! I was starving!" Anna said. It was her way of acknowledging that she had noticed Mark and I spending time together.

I had to admit, it was nice to see Mark again in person instead of just connecting through texts.

The day after our visit, I texted him to say how much I had enjoyed our conversation, and invited him for a walk. I usually headed to the paved trails in the next town to get in a few miles, and I told him he was always welcome to join me, especially if he needed to talk to someone who understands.

Navigating widowhood is complicated, and sometimes it helps to have a "walk and talk." Anna and I had done many of them when she was working through the challenges of her teenage years and needing guidance. There's something about looking ahead while talking out loud that makes difficult conversations feel more natural, easier than sitting across from someone and trying to speak openly, especially when the words are hard and vulnerable.

I ended the message by thanking him for sharing his thoughts and memories of Amy with me.

"The appreciation and enjoyment are mutual. I may take you up on one of those walks. I've got a wedding suit to fit into and a bunch of sympathy food weight to walk off," he responded.

I texted back, "You have a personal cheerleader in me, especially when it comes to wellness and health!"

Health was important to me, though I knew grief could sometimes push it to the backseat; it had for me these past few months. But I wanted to live a full life, one where I could keep up with my children and, someday, my future grandchildren.

With summer's warmth finally settling in, I felt a renewed energy stir within me.

I felt happy and alive again. Anna noticed the lightness in my steps, too. A couple of weeks later, she looked at me, wrapped me in a hug, and said, "You know, Mom, I know how much you loved Dad, and I'm okay with you finding love again. Just… not now."

I looked at her and immediately felt tears well up in my eyes. In her own sweet way, she was giving me her blessing, but with a little stipulation of her own. I understood completely. We were all healing in our own way.

"I know, Babygirl," I said softly. "I'm so thankful you understand, and I want you to know that I would never forget your father. I loved him to my core, and I hate that we even have to talk about this."

I wiped my tears and pulled her into a hug. As I held her close, she whispered into my ear, "It's Mr. Gentry, isn't it?"

I pulled back and looked at her. A smile slowly spread across my face, and I asked her, "How did you know?"

"Mom, it's so obvious," she said.

August 12, 2022

My dearest Todd,

Oh, how I miss you! This is the last time I can say months. It will now be years since I last touched you or held your hand. Sometimes, I can't wrap my head around the fact that you aren't here with us physically. Anna had me listen to a video with your voice in it and it took me back to expecting you to come home so I could hear your sweet voice. I miss it, and your smile, and your kisses, and you.

I think so much of heaven and wonder what you are doing. I know you are resting—there are no worries. I sit here in the backyard amongst everything we created and the beauty of it all, and think of you (and as I finished writing this sentence, I looked up and a hummingbird flew up to the feeder) Was that from you?

Jacob finished his internship at Boeing today and left with an offer for employment to be sent to him in the coming weeks. You would be so proud of him. He has worked so hard and is turning into an amazing young man. And Anna—your Babygirl girl is finding her way too. She is back at Truman with Buds the dog, living by herself in her apartment. They are doing well. Jacob goes back to Rolla tomorrow, so by myself I am again.

Jacob and I are planning on going up to Kirksville to see Jake play in the first game of the season on Labor Day weekend. My birthday. I am excited to be turning 50 but a bit mad that you aren't here with me. I feel people will forget my birthday; you know how much I love that day.

I am going into this next month with so much trepidation. Last week I parted with some of your clothes and donated them to charity. I felt ready until I started placing them on the porch and backed out of the driveway knowing they would be gone when I got back. All this is so hard.

The emotions of knowing you won't be back on this earth, trying to force the memories of your last day out of my mind, and have the strength to move forward is so hard.

I have come to the realization that I want to be loved again, which adds so much weight and guilt onto me, because you were supposed to be my one and only, and now you are gone. I pray for blessing in this and hope you have a little say into it as God is making His plan for me.

I want to be happy.

I love you with all my heart,

Lisa

Chapter Thirty-One

NO MORE SAYING "MONTHS"

I headed into the month of August with trepidation. After this month, I would now say "years" when referring to Todd being gone. I was closing down on a full year of grieving and sharing my healing journey with my writing on social media for all to see. I wasn't sure I was going to continue sharing after this next month. I didn't feel a need for it to be part of my healing anymore.

Although I was so thankful that God had given me the gift of writing to share my journey through grief, I wanted to put it to use in a bigger format than a social media post. I wanted to write a book about my experience. So, I resolved that after the first anniversary of Todd's death, I would shed the black garment of grief as best I could and prepare to embrace something new. In order to fit the new garments, so to speak, I needed to surrender the old ones.

It was no disrespect to Todd whatsoever.

I STILL DIDN'T KNOW WHAT I wanted to do with his medical files just yet. Were these findings worth reaching out to a lawyer to pursue? Was there enough evidence to prove medical malpractice? Would a lawyer touch a case such as this, involving COVID protocol? I wasn't sure. What I was sure of was that I still had time to think about it. I had a total of two years from the date of an alleged malpractice to file a lawsuit under the statute of limitations in my state, and I had all of his files in my possession for safe keeping, if I needed to use them. I would trust God in providing me wisdom in how I needed to proceed, so I quietly pushed the task to the back of my brain.

In the meantime, I found myself taking frequent walks, both to occupy my time and to process my thoughts and grief. As the upcoming month approached, I felt a deep trepidation, my mind reliving each day of the past year leading up to the first anniversary of Todd's passing. I had survived all the "firsts" so far. This would be the last of them, and I felt the need to batten down the hatches, bracing myself for the wave of emotion that awaited me on that day.

On one of my walks, I was listening to my playlist when a song I've cherished for years came through my AirPods, the song "Beautiful" by India Arie. I love how we can hear or see something in our world a hundred times, as I've heard this song, and then God uses it for us to see or hear it differently. On this day, it was this song. It's a powerful anthem about breaking free and finding solace in a higher state of existence.

In many ways, I felt like it was my grief song because over the past few days, I had been overwhelmed with anxiety, feeling like a caged animal, desperate to escape myself. The weight of widowhood, the restlessness for the future, and the struggle to endure it all had fused into a single, unrelenting ball of stress beneath my skin. My mind felt like it had too many tabs open at once, and I was hitting a wall of uncertainty. There were moments when thoughts of Heaven, vast and indescribable, overwhelmed me with emotion. Now, even more so, knowing that Todd was there.

I felt feral inside. I was restless and trapped all at once, like I was being pressed against the bars of my own thoughts. Adding to this was the lingering to-do list of grief, the necessary tasks that come with losing a loved one. I still felt each one was erasing Todd's presence from the world, yet I knew that if these things weren't completed, I wouldn't be able to move forward.

The week had started with the task of a seemingly mundane act of donating clothes feeling like a quiet heartbreak. To those outside my circle, it may have seemed like an easy task. But for me, it chipped away at the corner of my heart. They were Todd's clothes, the ones I had folded up ceremoniously months ago, and I knew that when I backed out of the driveway to go to work that morning, it would be the last time I would ever see them again. I still wore the armor of strength, shielding what lay behind it, using it to hide on days like this. And yet, carrying that armor was exhausting.

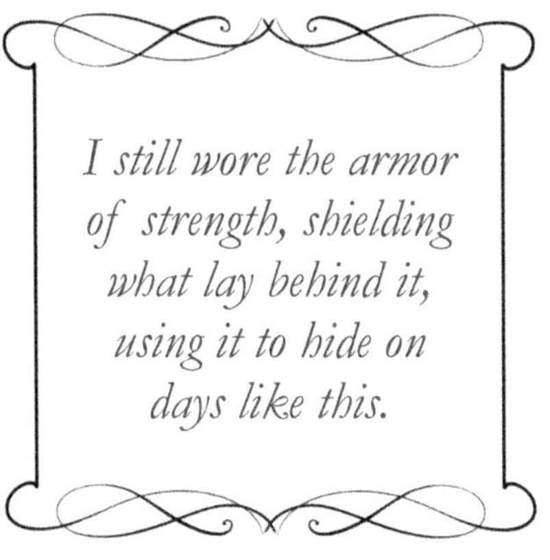

And as much as I attempted to unload my backpack of these emotions at the feet of God, I found I left some crumbs of despair at the bottom that had remained, and they stuck to me, like sand after leaving the beach.

This feeling of anxiousness moved through my Friday into my Saturday. Maybe it was the realization that my children were preparing to go back to school, and the house would be quiet once again. Yet, it was also knowing I needed this time to myself to begin feeling excited about life while not having the weight of guilt of judgment pressing down on my shoulders. Or, perhaps it was the awareness that I was entering into a month of overflowing memories filling my mind. It would be forcing me to transition from "months" to now acknowledging and saying aloud "years."

I was embracing the change while grappling with the loneliness of widowhood; the ache of having no one to share the weight of the hardships of life with. What I missed most were deep conversations, the intimate exchanges that once filled the quiet spaces of my days.

Determined to fill my day with things that brought me joy, I headed up to a nearby walking trail to exercise and clear my head. As India Aire's song, "Beautiful" played through the speakers, it perfectly captured everything I had been feeling. For me, the song explained grief. The knowledge of love everlasting and the quiet pursuit of hope in the future. It was the constant balancing act of breathing out the sadness and loneliness while deliberately inhaling hope. Both must coexist to navigate the journey of grief. And all I wanted to do was live inside the glow.

It again reminded me that I had to stay the course in healing, while also understanding that it would not always be linear. This was a journey with no map, and only faith kept me moving.

Meanwhile, Mark was preparing for the new school year as a teacher, but he still made time to stop by and help me replace the string on my dilapidated weed eater. Over the course of a couple of weeks, we texted back and forth congratulatory messages of my being 50 and being welcomed to the "club," since he was a few years older than I, and my well wishes of blessings for him and his family on his son's nuptials the following day. I texted well wishes and thoughts of him as he stepped into a new school year, knowing it was going to feel different.

I thought of him often during the first week of school and sent him a message, encouraging him to find hope in the support of his family and colleagues. Coming from a family of teachers, I knew that many traditions surrounded the first day back to school, adding another layer to his grief. I prayed that the smiling faces of his students would bring him joy and comfort.

During the Labor Day weekend, he sent me a photo of all of the mums he purchased, telling me it was time to focus on the homefront. I had invited him to go to the produce stand with me a couple of weeks prior, but he was out of town. Still, he said he would have gone with me, for sure. I chuckled when he told me how many mums he had planted in his front yard, and he joked back to me that he thought it was a competition after hearing how many I had planted in my yard. I told him that he clearly won this competition with 16 mums! He mentioned that once he got his front yard in shape, he might need me to come over and pick my brain about his backyard, as it posed some terrain challenges. I gladly obliged and mentioned that I'd love to get his opinion on landscaping for my front yard, because unlike my backyard, which has undergone numerous changes over the years, my front yard had seen none.

After our conversation about landscaping, it got me thinking again about how God allows us to see things with new eyes. There's a view from one of my kitchen windows, where I stand while prepping food, baking cookies at Christmastime, or chatting with my children on FaceTime. It's my spot in the kitchen.

About 15 years ago, Todd built the first two top tiers on half of the slope in our backyard after I nearly tipped the lawn mower trying to cut the steep hill. Four years after that, we expanded the kitchen, transforming what was once the dining room and creating the window above the counter. Then, about nine years ago, the bottom tier was added, giving us a flat space for yard games as the rest of the backyard underwent its transformation. We also built a patio for the fire pit, completing the space that now holds so many memories.

Now, when I look out this window, I see a beautiful section of the backyard. In the summer, it bursts with color, the three bushes on the top level covered in hundreds of pink blooms. It almost feels like we planned this view, but we didn't. For me, this beautiful view wasn't something we purposefully planned. Instead, it slowly revealed itself, through steps taken over time and in the patience of waiting. Though I couldn't see it all yet, and it may look different than I imagined—one thing I know for certain was that I had faith it would be beautiful once again

This was how I saw God working in my life. I thought about it a lot as I took my walks and on this particular day. There was nothing random or spontaneous about God or His works. Often, the things God builds in our lives remain unseen at first, because His plan was written long before we were born. Though He does not wish sorrow upon us, life inevitably comes with grief, loss, and sadness. Such is life.

In losing Todd, I will never know the reason why, but I trusted that God still had a plan and purpose in all of it. He is purposeful in all things. I was becoming confident He had set aside a future of hope for me and Todd and for our children. I trusted that God was continuing to build upon my view, working in harmony, always connected to what has been and what lies ahead because both were necessary.

What has helped shape the woman I am today, with the grief, the healing, the courage to begin again, was the very thing preparing me to create the life waiting on the other side of this chapter. It became the foundation of the life that lay ahead, because regardless of the circumstance, there is always hope.

In the meantime, there was no need to rush what God was taking time to prepare. As Jeremiah 29:11 says: "'For I know the plans I have for you,' declares the Lord, 'plans to prosper you and not to harm you, plans to give you hope and a future.'" In His divine planning, God orchestrates the right timing and provides the necessary resources to bring His plans to fruition. Sometimes, that includes sending the right person in His timing. And when He places people in our paths, will we be willing and open our hearts to receive them? I was learning that when we allow God the space to work, He will bring the one who truly fits.

Which brought my thoughts back to Mark. I was thankful that God had brought him into my life. Someone to share the journey of grief with, to understand its multifaceted pain, and I was grateful to feel safe in beginning to open my heart to sharing more of my thoughts with him.

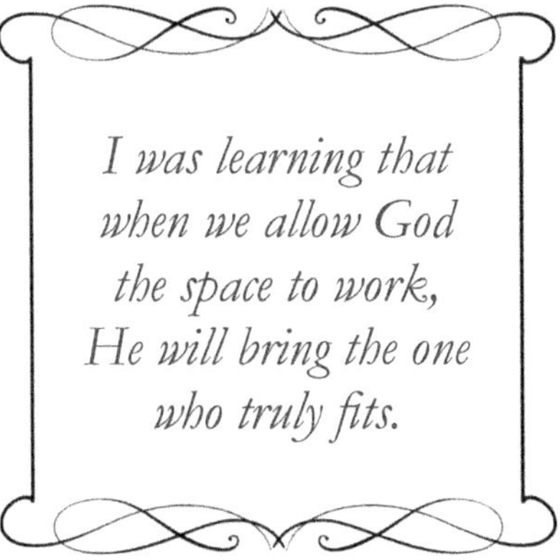

September 12, 2022

Babe,

How has it been a year already? More than a year of your hugs, kisses, and snuggles. I miss having those kinds of things in my life. I miss being the center of someone's universe to be honest. I miss you terribly. Life is not the same. I am moving forward in finding my happiness as you always told me to do and I am working on it.

I haven't had to make any big decisions lately—that scares me in having to do that by myself when those times come. Oh, how I wish you are here. I know you are cheering us on from heaven.

So many things are happening that I so wish you were part of. You deserved to be part of. Continue to look down on us and watch over us. We are having Whities for dinner in your honor. Matt and the boys are coming over and your dad put his order in. You sir, are still so loved. Just wish I could put my arms around you to show you.

I love you forever,

Lisa

Chapter Thirty-Two

REMEMBRANCE DAY HAS COME

A couple of weeks before this day last year, my husband reached for my hand and spoke his final words to me. I had no sense of what was coming. I hoped I said all the right words to him to calm his soul. I hoped that, in the pure fear I was feeling, that it didn't show. I hoped he knew how much he was loved and prayed for, and how we were all rooting for him to come home in a couple of weeks. He and I had hopes and dreams, and we talked about them that night. I hoped that what had transpired within the walls of that hospital during the pandemic eventually would come to light. A year had passed, but at times it still felt like yesterday.

My letter to Todd this month marked the final culmination of what was to come on that fateful day. Although I hadn't realized it at the time, I began to wonder if God protects us in ways that we don't understand until much later. Was He preparing me for this journey of loss, knowing how difficult it would be? Shielding me from witnessing certain situations as best He could? We may not

Honoring Todd on his 1st Remembrance Day with the family

understand it. We may fight, kick, scream, and wrestle with anger. We may question why. I tried not to, but faltered in asking that question many times in this journey.

But one thing I do know now, God was placing me exactly where He needed me to be. Sometimes, He lets us peek at the reasons later, again in His time, and after some healing has taken place. A year later, I was grateful to see how, through timing, He protected me that day.

For many months after Todd's death, I struggled with the thought: *I should have been there.* He died on a Sunday. On any other day, I would have been up at the hospital promptly at 8 a.m., the start of visiting hours. But Sunday was my day to go to church and put my worries at the feet of God and pray.

For so long, I was mad at myself for not being there by his side as he endured such pain during those cardiac events.

Now, I understood.

God was preparing to call him home, and not in the best of circumstances. I believe God was protecting me while doing so. He shielded me from what I wasn't meant to witness, for my own good. I can say that statement with full certainty now. Because what I witnessed in the month leading up to his death and in the following hour before Todd graduated to Heaven was enough for my heart to carry that horrible day. God knew I couldn't carry more. For that I am deeply grateful. This blessing of protection wasn't one I understood at first, but through many months of healing and prayer, I finally saw it.

THROUGH THESE MICROBURSTS OF HEALING, hope had emerged. My hope now? It's still here. It's the promise from God that He will fill my days with joy and peace as I trust in Him. My journey was not one that was planned, at least not in my mind. This past year, I had felt so lost, and learning to navigate life as a widow has been one of the hardest parts of it.

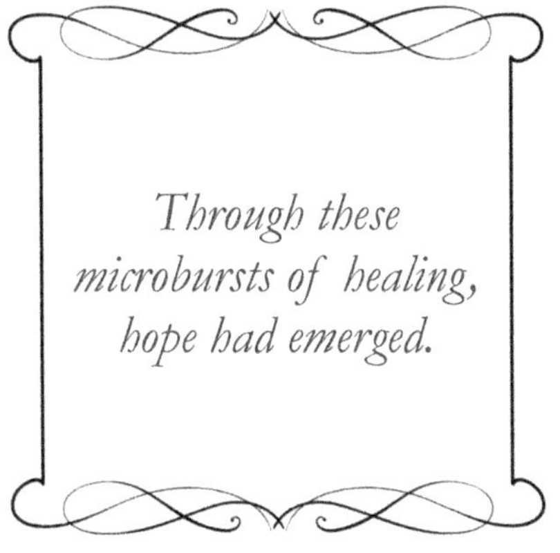

But, I am still here. I am still standing. I am still trying, still putting one foot in front of the other, because I have faith in the future. As Isaiah 43:19 says, "Behold, I am doing a new thing; now it springs forth, do you not perceive it? I will make a way in the wilderness and rivers in the desert."

I hold onto the faith that all things will be made new again, however God chooses to do it. I needed to be reminded that I was not forging the path blindly, but one that God had already ordered my steps. So, in moving onward in this new beginning, as I now called it, and upward in faith, my hope remained in knowing that God was able to give us more than we could ever imagine. And that hope still endures.

I knew Todd was cheering for me and the kids from Heaven the entire way, as we created new memories; ones we would share with him when we saw him again.

ON THE ANNIVERSARY OF TODD'S passing, I made a Facebook post honoring him and reflecting on what a remarkable man he was. Within a minute of hitting "post," I received a private message from Mark. It said:

> What an amazing picture of Todd walking the path. Your words add incredible context. It's an amazing testimony of a Godly marriage for your children to emulate. I'll be praying for you, especially today. I'm thankful for your gift of written expression. And I know it's good medicine to your children's hearts. I am thankful to call you friend. May peace and grace surround and comfort you.

I appreciated Mark's kind words. He was a thoughtful man, expressive in the way he spoke. I replied that I had woken up with a prayer for peace and admitted that, while I might shed a tear or two today, I held onto Todd's words from years ago, when all the kids were leaving for college and I was struggling with the concept of being an empty nester. He had told me, "I need for you to find your own happiness." Todd was such a good man.

I THANKED MARK FOR ALLOWING me to share my thoughts with him and let him know how much I appreciated him.

Later that morning, Anna shared with me that Mark's youngest daughter had reached out to her via text, and how much she appreciated it. I felt the same. These young women were walking similar paths, offering each other support and encouragement, just as

Todd walking the path

Mark and I had this past year. Both girls had such sweet souls. I mentioned their interaction to Mark, and he responded that his youngest daughter also appreciated Anna's effort to connect.

Mark and I continued texting, checking in on each other more frequently. I often asked him about maintenance-related things, like figuring out my new electric weed eater, and he always offered to stop by and help in between his bug spray rounds. He never hesitated to tell me to holler if I needed anything.

This most recent time, I managed to figure out the weed eater myself, not wanting to seem too much like a damsel in distress. Still, I looked forward to seeing him in person and genuinely enjoyed his company. So much so that I invited him for another walk. He admitted he was dealing with an upcoming knee surgery and said he'd take a raincheck once he had his new knee.

As the weeks passed, our communication was increasing, and I felt a new sense of calm after surviving the first year and passing Todd's anniversary. Honestly, I was not prepared for how difficult his day of remembrance would be. But I knew I could no longer sit in my sorrow and simply stare at it. I found I was beginning to allow myself the freedom to move forward again because I still had life to live. And in walking through the past couple of months, I found the ability to begin sharing it with someone else while still honoring Todd's memory and legacy.

I was growing fonder of Mark as our conversations continued, discovering how compatible we were in so many ways. We talked about mums, empty nesting, chipmunks wreaking havoc in our yards, stocking a fridge and pantry for one, new ice cream spots we both wanted to try, since ice cream was our shared kryptonite, cauliflower pizza crust, his love of bluegrass music, and his dream of having property with a greenhouse or at least a large garden with high fences to keep forest varmints out. What he didn't know, or maybe he did from my many posts about my gardens throughout the summer, was that it was a dream of mine, too. He and I shared so many of the same interests and values. We both shared our excitement for autumn. I expressed that it was my favorite season, especially with the joy of sitting by the firepit and indulging in comfort food, which made it even more special.

Toward the end of September, our messages bounced back and forth like ping pong balls, about upcoming fall activities, always keeping the conversation light. Feeling confident, I added a playful touch, sharing my excitement about mastering my new weed eater and jokingly suggesting that if he needed any yard work done, I knew someone. He responded with a teasing warning, he never said no to offers of help, so I should be careful in asking.

THE LAST WEEKS OF SEPTEMBER flew by in a flash, and through the first week of October, we continued texting on a regular basis. One evening, I invited him to stop by my house to pick up a small gift, a token of appreciation for all the help he had given me over the summer as I struggled to figure out the weed eater and its many quirks. The gift was tea. Over time, through our conversations, we had learned a lot about each other, likes, dislikes, and small details that made us who we were. One of those details was his love for peppermint tea.

He said he could stop by that evening and would be home any time after 4:30 p.m., when he left work. As planned, he arrived, and we spent the next few hours talking about life. I enjoyed his company and hoped he felt the same. We spoke openly about our grief and our hopes for the future, for ourselves, our families, and the paths we were now walking. We reflected on our marriages to our beloveds and on raising our children in a Godly way. Both of us were navigating a new journey, trying our best to move forward with grace and understanding.

As we stood up from the kitchen table, I handed him a package of peppermint tea from a local shop, a small gesture of gratitude. I then led him into the sunroom to show him how the backyard had transformed, bursting with autumnal colors. I pointed to a large mum just outside the window, its rich rust-colored blooms vibrant against the fading greens of the season.

He looked at me, brushed the sleeve of my blouse, and remarked on how perfectly the color matched the mum. I felt butterflies in my stomach. That was the moment I knew: this fondness was deepening.

We wrapped up our conversation, and as the evening grew late, I walked him to the door. He hugged me before leaving, and as I went upstairs to get ready for bed, a quiet smile played across my lips. I wondered when I would see him again.

Two days later, he sent me a photo of himself making hot tea with the peppermint tea I had given him. I noticed his fall décor in the background and mentioned it. He told me his youngest daughter was coming home from college for the weekend, and he had wanted her to see everything in place because that was how Amy always did it. He then described how she kept photos of where everything belonged, so he knew where to place the decorations. I admired Amy's organizational skills!

I shared with him that I had started my book and had written the first 2,500 words. He responded with certainty: "That book is going to bless many lives."

I surely hoped so.

November 9, 2022

Dearest Todd,

Throughout the journey of losing you and the months of healing, I have developed a friendship. A friendship that now has turned into a fondness.

He is such a good man, and I want to think you and God had a hand in this.

There have been many months that I wondered how he felt for me, and on November 4, Mark shared that he was fond of me also. He lost his wife too, and we bonded through our grief.

I am happy, Todd. It's been a while since I have been able to say that.

Love,

Lisa

Chapter Thirty-Three

A FONDNESS

October 2, 2022 would have been Todd's and my 29th wedding anniversary. In the past, I would have acknowledged the special day on social media. Instead, I spent the day quietly remembering what this day meant to me. Only those who have shared your life's intimate moments would remember you and your spouse's anniversary date without a reminder on social media, so I wasn't too surprised when no texts or calls came through to bring attention on a random Sunday. Honestly, I hadn't expected anyone to. Only my children recognized it, and I was okay with that.

As I got ready for bed, I thought about how different this day was compared to decades past. I had spent it alone, since Jacob and Anna were away at school, so when I climbed into bed that night, I was thankful the day was coming to an end.

That was when my phone pinged that a text came through. It was from Mark.

We texted back and forth for an hour, talking about me taking my first solo drive three hours away to visit Anna, and the autumn colors that I would see along my drive. We both agreed that we loved this season. He told me to be careful, explaining that the deer were really moving due to archery season bringing hunters into the woods. He immediately apologized for the "dad" speak, but I wasn't concerned. We had to watch out for one another, and I found it quite endearing honestly. He sent me a photo from his hunting spot a few years back, and then another. The woods looked picturesque, almost like something out of a painting. I told him that walking through the woods in the snow, surrounded by silence, was an unmatched experience. I recalled bundling up last winter, taking my sidekick, my camera, out to capture it all. It was a break for me in the grief I was dealing with back then.

He shared how his dad called the woods his "cathedral" and how his parents fostered a love of the outdoors in all their children. With him being one of six children in his family, he joked that his parents probably needed them outside from time to time. I smiled at the thought. I am sure having to parent in a large family must have required some moments of peace and quiet! I agreed that our world could use more "cathedral" time in nature. I also shared that I had three brothers and had been a total tomboy in my younger years, so I loved the outdoors.

After an hour of texting back and forth to another, he said he had to get up early for a workout and bid me good night, telling me to sleep tight. I wished him the same.

I turned out my bedside lamp and thanked God for the day. I lay there feeling grateful for this remembrance day of marriage, for the life Todd and I built, for the love we shared, and for our children, who would carry his legacy forward. We knew we had set the example of what a marriage should be: filled with love, faith, laughter, honor, respect, selflessness, and commitment. I kept this day in my heart, knowing I would carry these memories forever. As I moved forward into life, I wanted to live fully and joyfully, and I knew Todd would always be tucked into a fold in my heart. I was loved well.

And Mark, not even knowing how profound the day was for me, had reached out to say hello. I appreciated him for that.

That night, I slept soundly for the first time in months.

THE FOLLOWING WEEK, MARK REACHED out again to tell me how thankful he was for me being his friend and acknowledged the recent social media post I made on God's provisions of worry. I had written about being paralyzed in fear for my future after Todd's passing, but that I was learning that each day came with the faith that God was providing all that I needed, and that He was preparing the way. It was all in His timing.

Honestly, it was sometimes easier said than done, not worrying that is, especially this past year for me. When the future I expected to walk through, with the person I expected to walk with was taken from me, I felt this crippling terror that I would not survive this tragedy. But through faith, I was learning that each day came with the reliance that God was providing all that I needed; I had been shown this time and time again through this journey during this past year.

While I was allowing for God's plan in my life to unfold, I was slowly emptying my proverbial backpack of the rocks of guilt, anger, sadness, pain, fear, and loneliness to pave the path of yesterday. I admit that I felt lighter walking into this next year, with my backpack now full of feathers; ones of hope, joyful remembrance, and happiness. My backpack of rocks had been so heavy that I carried it all day, every day, often dragging it behind me, until I finally decided it was okay to let it go. And, you know what? That release made me feel stronger, empowering me to carry on and trust God with my tomorrows.

This year hadn't been easy, but I knew I needed to be intentional in healing from this grief. Frankly, no one was going to do it for me.

I felt that Mark and I crossed paths for a reason. Although the way we each lost our spouse was different, the grief was the same. I was thankful for him, too. In him, for sharing this walk that no one chooses to embark on during the journey of healing, and for God, who places people in our lives to make the path less lonely.

Mark and I didn't see each other in person often, mostly texting back and forth, with the occasional stop at my house when he helped with a maintenance project. But on this particular Friday afternoon in mid-October, I unexpectedly saw him twice within ten minutes.

Once I arrived home and settled into my comfy chair in the sunroom, I texted him, joking that I wasn't stalking him, but asked if he did bus duty at his school. I had spotted him there while driving by after work, and then, just minutes later, I saw him again passing by as I sat at the stoplight, waiting to turn left toward home after delivering work-related mail to the post office.

"Glad I wasn't picking my nose," he responded.

I laughed at his response. I found I enjoyed his one-liner type humor. He was pretty quick on the draw with them. Me? Not so much. He confirmed that it was indeed him working bus duty and how much he enjoyed interacting with the kids and their parents.

"Tonight, and tomorrow, there is a conference at the church I used to attend. That's my big plan for the weekend," he texted.

He then sent me a photo of the conference flyer showing what it was about and the times set for the conference. I was intrigued, and also wondering what his intention was in sending it to me. Did he want me to join him?

"That sounds like a pretty good conference to me," I texted back and mentioned that he'd have to fill me in later. He responded and said that his Bible study had been in the Book of Revelation for the past year, and this conference was kind of a cap for it.

"It's free and open to the public," he then texted back.

I sat there in my chair, immediately recognizing what was happening. It was a hint, and my first thought was, *Dude, just ask me!*

Wanting to keep the conversation going, I texted back. "Isn't that the church Jake's family attends?"

"Yes," he texted back.

He explained in his text that his family had been part of that church for a long time when all the kids were young. I knew where the church was located and shared with Mark that I had been there once before. Jake's family had invited me on Sundays, knowing I was attending church services alone.

"I'm sure there will be room for last minute people to show up. I'm gonna head over there in a little bit," he responded back.

Come on! Just ask me to join you already!

I knew I had started to develop feelings for him, but I wasn't sure if he felt the same, especially when he would respond by expressing his appreciation for our friendship. Was I misreading everything?

I wasn't sure how to maneuver through this conversation because I wanted to attend this conference with him, but did not want to invite myself. I was a bit old-fashioned when it came to dating, and I felt it was un-lady-like for me to show up uninvited, even to public events. But I also knew there are moments when you need to take the bull by the horns. And to my surprise, I did just that.

"Did you want a tag along? If not, I totally understand," I typed. I hit send. I clenched my hands into fists, pulling them to my mouth. Nerves surged through me as I anxiously awaited the response, because there was no turning back now.

"Sure. It should be fascinating," he immediately responded.

Sure? Fascinating? That was not the response I was expecting, but at least it wasn't a no. Navigating this back-and-forth of newfound feelings was something I wasn't prepared for. I felt so awkward, like a middle schooler waiting for a crush to ask me to dance at the spring formal! How had I even found myself in this place in life?

How do I respond now?

Keep it cool, Lisa. I steered the conversation back to naps since he had mentioned he was taking one after work. Finally, I responded with a roundabout "I'll be there," adding a joke about how this conference better be worth it, considering I had to drive on a winding road with my "old lady night blindness." He responded with a laughing emoji.

The meetup was set, arranged as awkwardly as he and I could manage, I suppose. I ran upstairs to freshen up before heading to the conference. I was excited to see him again; it had been a couple of weeks.

I texted him when I arrived and found a seat in a row a few back from the main stage. He replied that he would be in shortly and look for me. A few moments later, I felt someone approach from behind my chair. It was him. He looked at me, said hi, and sat down next to me.

He and I had met up many times over the summer, but always at my house. This time, it was out in public. I felt both elated and nervous, especially since it was obvious we were together, sitting side by side as the only two in our row.

My first thought was, *How would I respond if I ran into someone I knew?* Only a couple of people were aware of my newfound friendship with Mark, and of the romantic feelings that had started to stir within me. I knew this was something I would have to learn to navigate just like many of the other changes to my life. And for the most part, I felt I had adapted well. I was determined to keep moving forward while granting myself grace when I stumbled along the way. And tonight? I just hoped I wouldn't fall. The nerves were real.

The conference began, and the Master of Ceremonies walked out onto the stage. Her name was Kimberle. She was a family friend of Jake's and the wife of Mark's Bible study host family. *Oh, my goodness!* I had heard so many wonderful things about her. Though I had been to her home once, when Anna dog sat for their family and asked me to accompany her one afternoon, I had never met her personally.

I also knew how close her family was to Mark's. He had shared with me how much she and her husband had stepped in to help after his wife passed away.

Deep breaths, Lisa. I closed my eyes and reminded myself that I had every right to feel the way I felt in being excited to be sitting next to Mark and permission to move forward with my life. Over the past few months of our conversations, many of the things that I prayed to God for, in the prayer I made months after Todd passed away and before meeting Mark, were coming to fruition. One of those blessings was to be in the presence of a man who loved God, and here I was standing next to him, as he sang aloud during one of the worship songs. I stood there in awe, and quietly thanked God.

As the evening wore on, I caught glimpses of him looking at me and smiling, which helped ease me into a calmness as I settled into taking notes while the speaker discussed the end times. When the conference ended, Mark thanked me for joining him and mentioned he wanted to take a moment to go speak to his friend, Kimberle. That was my cue to take my leave, and expressed how much I enjoyed attending the conference with him. He was attending the next day and asked me to join him, but I couldn't because I was attending a funeral for Todd's cousin, so he promised he would send me notes. He gave me a hug, and I walked up the aisle and out the church doors to my car. I knew it was a good night, and I felt truly happy.

The next day, I texted him to remind him to take notes for day two of the conference and admitted it might be best for me not to attend if they discussed COVID, a topic very sensitive to me. He understood. By mid-afternoon, Mark sent me photos of the slides along with links for additional information. I thanked him for remembering and asked for his thoughts on the material, but I received no response.

A FEW DAYS LATER, I texted him again to check in, offer words of encouragement about the upcoming wrestling season, and mention that I needed the house sprayed for spiders, a topic we had discussed a couple of weeks earlier. Finally, he responded, saying he was good and that he would add me to his schedule, ending his message with *"my friend."*

There it was again, "my friend." Did I read that right? I truly didn't know how to navigate the game of showing interest in someone, and felt I may have messed it up during the conference. We texted back and forth about the bug-spraying schedule, wrestling season, and the beautiful autumn weather that was heading toward the Midwest that weekend.

Then, communication between us went quiet for another week.

I knew he was busy, perhaps busier than I was, so I let go of the thought that it was merely the timing. Or maybe he only wanted to be friends and nothing more. We had both been through a lot over the past year, and perhaps he wasn't ready to step into something more. I truly believed I was ready, yet even I felt the tremor of doubt rising in me. I didn't want to force anything that wasn't meant to be.

I received a text from him asking about the sermon I'd mentioned earlier, and what it was about. I had shared my thoughts on God's purpose and how He has given each of us a gift to carry out His will, along with the AHA moment I experienced when I realized I hadn't written my first book because I wasn't ready. I wasn't ready mainly because its focus wasn't on our Lord and Savior, but on the world. But the book I was now writing, this book, showed my readiness.

Writing this book on grief became my testimony to how His strength and love carried me through the pain. By writing it amidst my struggle, I surrendered and allowed His words to flow from my pen, sharing His love for me during my journey through loss and offering hope to others on the same path. I went on to explain to Mark that God certainly doesn't make it comfortable when He wants us to step out and we think we're not ready or good enough to leave the boat. I admitted that over the past year, I had felt as though I had been pushed out of the boat and into a raging sea!

I shared with him that the sermon text came from 2 Timothy, preached by Pastor Dar, the one who married Todd and me. Though retired now, he preached a couple of times a year, and I always enjoyed listening to him. I told Mark that the sermon focused on the importance of passing down faith within families and standing firm in our belief, even if we find ourselves standing alone.

The message posed two thought-provoking questions: *If you died tonight, are you confident you would go to Heaven?* and *When you stand before God, what would you say to Him?*

I also shared that we had discussed John 6:47 that says, "Very truly I tell you, the one who believes has eternal life." In a world where universalism suggests that everyone is bound for Heaven, the sermon emphasized that there is only one way, through Jesus Christ our Lord. As disciples, it is our responsibility to share that truth lovingly and genuinely with those who have yet to know Him. That was why I wrote my book.

By now, I felt comfortable sharing my faith with Mark, and his openness gave me the confidence to do so. He loved my message by sending me a response, and I bid him good night.

ANOTHER WEEK PASSED, BRINGING HALLOWEEN. When the kids were little, our neighborhood was *the* place to be on Halloween night. But now, with most of them grown and the rise of trunk-or-treat events, the number of trick-or-treaters had dwindled, from over 400 children to fewer than 100.

This was my second official Halloween without Todd, and with the house silent, Jacob and Anna away at college, I spent the evening with the porch light off, watching *It's The Great Pumpkin, Charlie Brown.* Maybe next year I'd find the gumption to hand out candy again.

October faded into November, and I received a text from Mark. He apologized for forgetting to schedule the pest control treatment and asked if the upcoming Friday worked for me. He offered a time but said that if it didn't work, he could schedule it for the following week. *Oh, I was definitely not waiting until next week!* I quickly replied that Friday, the very next day, would work. Since he had refused to take any payment for the service, I asked if I could make him dinner instead.

"Dinner… now that's an offer I won't refuse. We'll call it the barter system," he responded.

"See you tomorrow," I texted.

"Perfect," he responded.

The meeting was set, and now the pressure was on with the question of what was I going to make for dinner? I worked that day, so I needed something quick. I decided on potato soup, a dish I could prepare in under half an hour while still leaving me time to get myself ready before he arrived.

With just a few moments to spare, the butterflies in my stomach began to stir again. I was excited to see him and could only hope he felt the same. Then, it hit me. He was going to spray my entire house! He'd be walking into *every* room! He would see all my things! Was my house clean enough? Would he judge me for it, if not? That realization made me pause for a moment. And then the question, was I just another customer to him, and if so, did he do this with every spraying job, bartering with a meal? But, somehow, that made this feel different. My head was spinning.

I took a breath and reminded myself that I couldn't dwell on those thoughts and not read too much into it. Thankfully, my house was always clean and organized, given that I lived alone. And I was a pretty good cook. I needed to let my confidence in myself take the lead instead of my fear.

Friday arrived, and he texted that he was on his way, and a few minutes later, there was a knock at the door.

He was here.

Stay calm, Lisa. Stay calm.

I OPENED THE DOOR TO his warm smile. He greeted me, then mentioned he would start by spraying the outer foundation before coming inside. I left him to his work, returning to the kitchen to stir the potato soup I had prepared and set the table. Occasionally, I peeked out the window, catching glimpses of him as he passed by, and each time, my butterflies fluttered all over again.

Once he finished and washed his hands, we sat down at the kitchen table, bowls of warm soup in front of us. He looked at me and asked if he could say a prayer before dinner. I smiled and nodded.

After eating, I placed the bowls in the sink and sat back down across from him. We began talking about life, the upcoming holidays, and how different they felt now, his children, my children, and grief. We *always* talked about grief. But not in a sorrowful way, instead, we discussed how both of us were navigating through it. Over nearly a year of friendship, we had grown comfortable sharing the difficult parts of grief while also offering each other guidance, identifying what helped and what didn't.

Mark was easy to talk to. And many times, through him visiting my home to help me with a maintenance task or to visit, we would spend hours talking. There were no uncomfortable pauses in between our many discussions. Our conversations flowed seamlessly. I enjoyed that, and I enjoyed being in his company.

As the evening wore on, there was a pause in our conversation. I felt it. I stopped talking, waiting for him to continue, but he just looked at me and smiled.

Tilting my head, I asked, "What?" *Did I have a piece of green onion stuck between my teeth from dinner?*

"Can I tell you something?" he said.

"Yes," I replied, suddenly nervous about what he was about to say.

"Through these months of seeing you, I have become quite fond of you."

I felt myself melt into my seat at his words.

"Really?" I said through a smile. "I'm quite fond of you, too. I wasn't entirely sure how you felt about me, but that makes me so happy!"

I couldn't contain my excitement, and he smiled, with the quiet happiness that lit up his face. I jumped up from my chair, ran around the table, and wrapped my arms around him in a hug.

He looked down at me and smiled—the kind of smile that quietly said he was exactly where his heart wanted to be.

At that moment, I didn't know where this path would lead us, but everything felt right and beautiful. I was confident that the next chapters would be filled with courage, strength, hope, and happiness, woven together with the fruits of the Spirit. And I firmly believed that the beauty of it would continue to unfold.

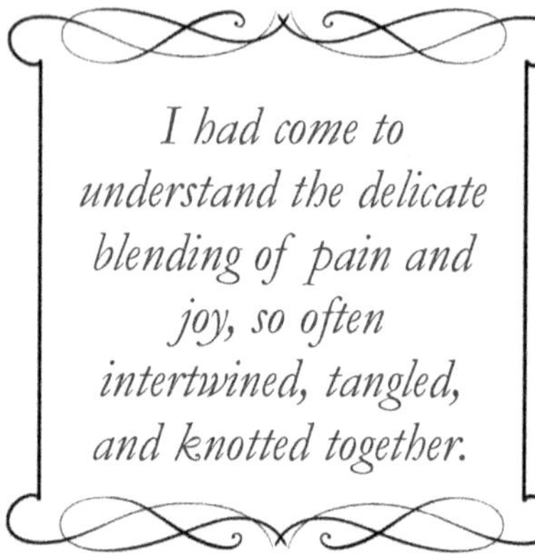

I wasn't sure if the pain on this journey was part of the best of both worlds, but I had come to understand the delicate blending of pain and joy, so often intertwined, tangled, and knotted together.

Yet, love was always present. It's quietly tucked away in our hearts for the loved ones who have gone before us and remain steadfast for those who walk beside us.

Through it all, God had given me His everlasting love. He had listened to my cries in the quiet of my nightly prayers. I trusted that He would dissolve the darkness and bring light to renew my days, guiding me forward to where He wants me to be.

I've come to know this with a deep settled assurance.

Life doesn't pause; it keeps moving forward. This journey is a bittersweet, beautiful mess; a delicate weaving of joy and pain, bound together by the steady, unbreakable love of God. So, as we travel down the road of it, I hope we pave the ones of pain with beautiful memories of our loved ones.

I was now ready to let go and see where the path God placed before me would take me. It was my bittersweet surrender.

To be continued…